Lean Library Management

Eleven Strategies for Reducing Costs and Improving Customer Services

John J. Huber

Neal-Schuman Publishers, Inc.

New York   London

Published by Neal-Schuman Publishers, Inc.
100 William St., Suite 2004
New York, NY 10038

Copyright © 2011 Neal-Schuman Publishers, Inc.

Printed and bound in the United States of America.

The paper used in this publication meets the minimum requirements of American National Standard for Information Sciences—Permanence of Paper for Printed Library Materials, ANSI Z39.48-1992.

Library of Congress Cataloging-in-Publication Data

Huber, John J., 1958-
  Lean library management : eleven strategies for reducing costs and improving customer services / John J. Huber.
      p. cm.
  Includes bibliographical references and index.
  ISBN 978-1-55570-732-3 (alk. paper)
  1. Library administration. 2. Libraries—Cost control. 3. Public services (Libraries) 4. Organizational change. 5. Organizational effectiveness. I. Title.

Z678.H84 2011
025.1—dc22

                                                            2010050755

Contents

List of Figures and Tables … v

Foreword … ix

Preface … xiii

Acknowledgments … xvii

Introduction … xix

Prologue: The Power of a Lean Transformation … 1

Strategy One: Recognize That Service Performance Is the Key to Customer Retention … 7

Strategy Two: Transform Your Change-Resistant Culture … 11

Strategy Three: Understand How Delivery Service Chains Drive Your Library's Performance … 33

Strategy Four: Align Your Performance Metrics with Your Delivery Service Chains … 41

Strategy Five: Transform Your New Book Delivery Service Chain … 69

Strategy Six: Transform Your Customer Holds/Reserves Delivery Service Chain … 101

Strategy Seven: Transform Your Cost Control Philosophy to a Lean Service Improvement Philosophy … 121

Strategy Eight: Transform Your Overall Library Service Performance Metrics … 129

Strategy Nine: Transform Your Digital Research Delivery Service Chain … 139

Strategy Ten: Transform Your Delivery Service Chain from a "Push" to a "Pull" Philosophy … 149

Strategy Eleven: Think Lean Before the Concrete Is Poured   159

Afterword: Lean Continuous Improvement   169

Appendix: More Lean Tools   173

Index   191

About the Author   197

List of Figures and Tables

FIGURES

Figure 2-1	Lean Project Organization Chart	24
Figure 3-1	New Book Delivery Service Chain	37
Figure 3-2	Customer Reserve/Hold Delivery Service Chain	38
Figure 4-1	Holds Delivery Service Chain Flowchart	48
Figure 4-2	Balloon Diagram Sample	49
Figure 4-3	Delivery Service Balloon Diagram	49
Figure 4-4	Customer Delivery Service Balloon Diagram	50
Figure 4-5	Service Log Label	56
Figure 4-6	Service Performance Chart	58
Figure 4-7	In-Transit Aging Report	59
Figure 4-8	Audit Results	61
Figure 4-9	Circulation Desk Checkout Time Study	63
Figure 4-10	Circulation Desk Time Chart	65
Figure 5-1	Technical Services Delivery Balloon Diagram	72
Figure 5-2	Staging Area Carts in Process	74
Figure 5-3	Preprocessed Technical Services Flow	77
Figure 5-4	Tech Services—All Flows	77
Figure 5-5	U Flow	79
Figure 5-6	Technical Services Staging Areas	80
Figure 5-7	Large Batch Impact Diagram	82
Figure 5-8	Small Batch Impact Diagram	83
Figure 5-9	Peak Load Impact Diagram—Copies Ordered	87
Figure 5-10	Peak Load Impact Diagram—Copies Received	87
Figure 5-11	Technical Services U Flow Layout—After	94
Figure 5-12	Receiving Station—Before	96
Figure 5-13	Receiving Station—After	97
Figure 6-1	PLYMC Customer Balloon Diagram	105

Figure 6-2	PLYMC Customer Balloon Diagram—Performance Metrics	105
Figure 6-3	Customer Reserve/Hold Delivery Chain	106
Figure 6-4	Balloon Delivery Gap Analysis	108
Figure 6-5	Customer Reserve/Hold Delivery Service Chain	109
Figure 6-6	Hold Shelf—Before	109
Figure 6-7	Holds Sticky Label—Six Up	111
Figure 6-8	Holds Sticky Label Layout	111
Figure 6-9	Sorting Flow Diagram	113
Figure 6-10	Sorting Flow Diagram—Short-Term Solution	114
Figure 6-11	Book Truck in Box Truck	115
Figure 6-12	TCCL Sorting Area	116
Figure 6-13	Customer Holds/Reserves Delivery Service Chain—Project Benefits	118
Figure 9-1	Research Delivery Gap Analysis	141
Figure 9-2	Customer Discovery to Delivery Service Chain	142
Figure 9-3	Traditional OPAC Search Results	143
Figure 11-1	Circulation Desk Performance Issues	161
Figure 11-2	Incoming/Outgoing Traffic Flow	162
Figure 11-3	Second Book Drop	163
Figure 11-4	Compressed Space for Checkout Stations	164
Figure 11-5	Relocated Terminal for Book Drop	164
Figure 11-6	Hold Shelf Service Issues	165
Figure 11-7	Reorganized Hold Shelf/Public Terminals	166
Figure 11-8	Relocated Public Access Terminals	166
Figure A-1	Acquisitions CD Receipt Process—Before	175
Figure A-2	Acquisitions CD Receipt Process—After	176
Figure A-3	Workplace Reach Diagram	184

TABLES

Table 5-1	Cart Backlog Analysis	74
Table 5-2	Unpacked Boxes	75
Table 6-1	Performance Gap Analysis	107
Table 6-2	Holds Service Chain Project Results	119
Table 7-1	Technical Services Delivery Service Chain—Transactional Cost–Benefit Analysis	125
Table 7-2	Gifts—Transaction Cost Analysis	127
Table 8-1	Perfect World Service Turns	131
Table 8-2	Adjusted Perfect World Service Turns	131
Table 8-3	Impact on Materials Budget	132
Table 8-4	New Book Delivery Service Chain Performance against Target	133

Table 8-5   New Book with Hold—SDA   134
Table 8-6   New Book with Hold—AST   134
Table 8-7   ORL SDA Benefits   135
Table 8-8   Holds Service Chain Turns Available   137
Table 8-9   Holds Service Chain Turns Available—Lean   137
Table 11-1   Branch Performance Gap Analysis   160

Foreword

How many of us have as much budget as we need? We have a long list of unfunded projects and new technologies to purchase. Economic times *demand* that every dollar be "well spent." Technology has moved ahead at light speed, and library users have embraced it. The ability of mobile devices to access massive amounts of data has left many believing that a library is unnecessary or redundant. Some of these believers are politicians and decision makers who have control over library budgets and see libraries riding off into the sunset in favor of an all-digital information world.

Your prime motivation to apply the lessons and ideas in this book is simple and fundamental: they save time and money that you can then use in more creative ways. *Lean Library Management* is a way of thinking that embraces the leanness of motion and efficiency and enables staff time to be devoted to less clerical work and more professional activities. By applying the lessons in this book you will better utilize your staff's talents, eliminate job monotony, and increase staff retention. It is simply good business.

As a society we have become universally impatient; for example, when our computer takes sixty seconds to boot, when our lunch order takes more than three minutes. We have come to expect "instant gratification" from service providers, be they electronic or human. If the casual Internet user or the student assumes that they can get everything they need on the Web, almost instantly, with little effort, why should either need a library? To survive, libraries must maintain a competitive edge in our immediacy-driven society and our live processing, instant sharing electronic world. We can accomplish this by aggressively searching for ways to slim our back-of-the-house and service methods. This will allow us to redirect staff abilities to do a better job marketing how our professionals know how to access authoritative information and how they *can* make a difference to our customers.

I've been a longtime devotee to the concept of kaizen—making small continuous improvements to reap efficiency. *Lean Library Management* empowers this school of thought by energizing staff members who know services inside and out. John Huber's book focuses staff creativity and brainpower by challenging mind-sets.

My first encounters with a "productivity expert" were in the County of Los Angeles Public Library and later the City of Scottsdale (AZ) Public Library. These encounters weren't greeted with the best mental attitude. Who is this person to come "fix" us? What does this "expert" know of libraries? I am now a convert. Although John Huber helped me with numerous projects, I'll share one example. John came to the Tulsa City-County Library to address a longstanding bottleneck of delivery service to the then twenty-three libraries. Branches and customers complained about the slow turnaround time, errors of incorrect books received, and misdirected personnel or payroll documents. The growth in volume had impacted the effectiveness of our process, causing high turnover in delivery drivers due to backbreaking work with negative coworker comments about poor service. Library service and operations were adversely impacted at their most fundamental level. No one wanted to take this on. It meant "criticizing" staff who had done their level best to make the current system work. It was complex. A fresh view was needed to untangle the bottleneck that impacted every service and function. This story had a happy ending. The new Lean methods reaped ergonomic benefits for branch staff and delivery drivers, reduced staff turnover, improved morale, and internal and external customers received their books, organizational mail, and documents in a timely manner. Positive comments were heard throughout the library system.

As you can see, Lean-minded principles are about methods for service improvements, not about hurting feelings or making anyone feel less valued because change is suggested. Lean-minded improvements require periodic audit. Clinging to what works and has served us for years will eventually work against us. We must stand back and look at the big picture—survival of library service is dependent on our response to this immediacy-driven society. Library boards and city or university administration want to see how dollars invested reap results. The Lean principles can provide you with tangible hard data and monitored results.

The fear of cutting staff positions if improvements are made is probably at the core of why people resist change. However, with these Lean improvements, you have many more options than before. Use this opportunity to make some shifts in workload to ensure that the most critical tasks are accomplished. Staff can be cross-trained for better coverage and job descriptions rewritten to meet the organizational needs. Often positions are vacated through natural attrition and bring you the opportunity to reevaluate staffing needs. It is all a gradual evolution. There was no drive to reduce staff levels, but we did provide our staff with more time to service the customer rather than service the processes. And remember, reductions in hiring and training new staff, in industrial injuries with loss of work time and productivity, and in staff complaints are also organizational cost savings.

Do the Lean methods work everywhere? You need to assess where they apply and what improvement will make the greatest difference for your organization. If changing the size and location of a book return cart can make it easier and faster for staff to check in books, service is improved times your number of branches times your numbers of books received. A small improvement can reap big results. Finding bottlenecks is easy. They are legendary among your staff; just ask. The bottleneck might be one of your pet ideas. Focus on the result, not on who thought of the idea. Times change and so do methods. Slow down and experience your expectations as a customer when shopping, using the bank or a personal service. Does your library meet this same high standard for ease in use, delivery times, and feeling of being well served? Every dollar spent in the quest for Lean methods is more than repaid in results and happier staff. Whether a circulation clerk, librarian, or delivery driver, libraries attract and hire smart people. All of us want to be utilized at the highest skill levels possible. It adds purpose and value to our jobs. Let go of the routine or rote tasks. Employees who feel valued bring crowd-pleasing internal and external customer service and begin to see other ways service can be tweaked or enhanced. Libraries as a place are so much more than the thoughts expressed here. In these times of fast-changing digital connectivity options and stressed budgets, the use of Lean methods to redirect staff resources to unleash and offer services your library is known for is even more critical. Even the most well-run libraries with healthy budgets can profit from Lean methods. Good luck on your Lean journey!

Linda Saferite, CEO
Tulsa City–County Library, 1996–2009

Preface

Increased customer expectations coupled with tough competition, changing technology, slashed budgets, and reduced staff—sound like today? Yes, but the year I'm referring to is 1981. Inflation approached 11 percent, the unemployment rate reached nearly 10 percent, IBM launched the personal computer, and overseas manufacturing companies were winning the hearts and minds of the American consumer. U.S. manufacturing, once the envy of the world, faced an uncertain future. Some industry leaders fell back on old traditions and familiar solutions, while others responded by looking for new and innovative management techniques.

Today's threats to library service are similar. RedBox and now Blockbuster are providing kiosk delivery of $1.00 DVD rentals; Google provides easy-to-use, one-click engagement search tools; Amazon.com delivers books within twenty-four hours; McDonald's now offers free Wi-Fi service; Amazon's Kindle e-book sales are zooming; and Apple has upped the ante with the release and upgrades of their iPad. This is all occurring while library budgets are under pressure and staffing levels are slashed. Your customer expectations for fast, friendly, and effective service have certainly not diminished; in fact, due to the competition and a struggling economy, customer expectations have never been higher. In the face of this challenge, some library leaders will retreat to old and familiar techniques, while others will search for new and innovative ways to respond.

The parallels between the manufacturing industry of the 1980s and libraries today are numerous. Can libraries rich with history and experience learn survival techniques from the manufacturing industry? I believe they can, and that is why I wrote *Lean Library Management: Eleven Strategies for Reducing Costs and Improving Customer Services.*

Nearly thirty years ago, I was a part of history. I had joined a small band of young engineering consultants working for Accenture Consulting (formerly Andersen Consulting). We were challenged to introduce a breakthrough management concept developed by the Toyota Motor Company called the Toyota

Production System to a reluctant U.S. manufacturing industry. The Toyota Production System was the forefather of what is now called Lean Manufacturing. This small band of consultants not only had success but also sparked what would change the entire U.S. manufacturing industry. Lean Manufacturing is now the cornerstone of nearly every manufacturing company's operational improvement strategy, not only here in the United States, but throughout the world. It is no longer an option but a requirement for survival.

Lean is a very simple concept: constantly strive to reduce the distance between you and your customer by eliminating all of the waste in your service delivery cycle. Lean accomplishes this by attacking the waste that lies hidden behind poorly designed process flows, outdated business models, ineffectual organizational structures, inflexible software systems, and stagnant procedures. Waste is defined by any delay or nonvalued activity in the process. Reduce this waste, and the distance between you and your customer is reduced. In addition, your costs will go down. Specifically, by eliminating wasteful delays and nonvalue activities in your service cycle the speed, accuracy, and quality of service to your customers will dramatically improve. Therefore, Lean provides a vehicle to improve customer service and at the same time reduce your costs.

After applying Lean concepts to more than 100 of my manufacturing clients, I have had the privilege to work with many different types of libraries across North America. In this book I will help you understand and apply the concepts of Lean to your library environment.

Lean Library Management begins with an introduction to the transformational power of Lean by comparing it to a smooth-flowing river as opposed to a twisting/turning river with dangerous white-water rapids. I define Lean in terms of its history, its philosophy, and the benefits it can provide. The book's chapters provide eleven strategies that you can use to cut waste and costs dramatically while improving customer service:

- Strategy One shows how libraries can embrace the business side of their endeavors and recognize, benchmark, and measure their performance against for-profit competitors, such as Amazon.com and Google.
- Strategy Two discusses why organizations of all types (including libraries) tend to resist change initiatives, and it provides specific ways you can transform your organization to a culture that embraces change.
- Strategy Three reveals an essential key to Lean transformation: the realization that libraries are actually a series of delivery service chains (also called service delivery chains), not an amalgam of separate departments.
- Strategy Four examines these delivery service chains in terms of performance metrics and shows you how to use these performance metrics.
- Strategy Five focuses on the book delivery service chain and dives deep into a library success story to illustrate how you might transform your own book delivery performance.

- Strategy Six covers another common problem area: the holds/reserves delivery service chain.
- Strategy Seven encourages you to abandon your budget cost control management style and embrace the Lean philosophy of cost reduction by eliminating wasteful activities that create gaps between you and your customer.
- Strategy Eight discusses how one overall performance measure can capture how Lean your library can become.
- Strategy Nine shows how Lean can be used to provide digital materials to customers.
- Strategy Ten uncovers the power of Lean's "pull" demand philosophy versus the common "push" demand philosophy most libraries incorporate.
- Strategy Eleven focuses on branch service performance and how the design of the physical branch can dramatically affect how the customer interacts with your library. A case study in which a library would have been better served to think Lean prior to pouring the concrete makes this concept a reality for all readers.

The book ends with an appendix that features additional valuable tools you can apply in your Lean transformation effort.

Libraries today are under unprecedented pressure to lower costs and expand digital services. Librarians are also facing increasing competition in both services and available funds. Lean strategies can be invaluable in facing this environment. In a time of shrinking budgets and more demanding customers, you may find that Lean is the right tool at the right time for your library.

Acknowledgments

I would like to thank Linda Saferite of the Tulsa City–County Library (TCCL); Charles Shannon, former operations director at TCCL; Jon Walker, the former director of information technology at TCCL (the current director of the Pueblo City County Library); and, especially, Josh Ashlock, the former facilities director at TCCL, who all were instrumental in implementing the breakthrough concepts of a Lean delivery system and processes in a library environment. It would not have happened without them.

I would like to acknowledge the entire staff of the TCCL technical services group; they deserve a great deal of credit for embracing the concepts of Lean and transforming their new book delivery service chain:

Charlotte Frazier
Sarah Simpson
Barbara Meehan
Tamala Pruiett
Eve Tang
Carolyn Greene
Linda Yaffe
Sharon Leach
Beverly Brady
Kim Goode
Alicia Stickney

Denise Lange
Jan Coffman
Sandra K. Smith
Jane Hannah
Micah Wulfers
Nancy Kattein
Linda Morgan
Shonta Cobb
Stephanie Lunsford
David Dias
Terry Stemkowski

I would also like to acknowledge the TCCL collection development group:

Laurie Sundborg
Rosemary Moran
Mary Waidner
Robert Sears

Sally Kotarsky
Kelly Jennings
Myles Jaeschke

I am very thankful to all of the libraries over the past ten years who have invited me into their workplace and helped me feel welcomed as well as helped refine the application of Lean in the library environment:

Baltimore County Public Library
Brooklyn Library
Carnegie Library of Pittsburgh
Johnson County Library
Kansas City Public Library
Lakeland Library Cooperative
Mid-Continent Public Library
New York Public Library
Okanagan Regional

Oklahoma State University Library
Ottawa Public Library
Southern Maryland Regional Library
    Association
Tucson/Pima Library
Tulsa City–County Library
Tulsa Community College Resource
    Learning Center
Youngstown Mahoney Library

Introduction

After providing consulting services to the manufacturing, distribution, and retail industries for more than twenty-five years, I can now say with confidence, I really like working with libraries and librarians. Your bathrooms are much cleaner than those of my manufacturing clients, your personal hygiene is much better than some of my shop floor friends, and you are a highly educated group of people who share my love of books.

Most important, I have a great deal of fun working with libraries. Before we dive deep into the serious business of Lean, as a form of introduction, I would like to share with you a couple of stories from my favorite libraries and the great camaraderie I have witnessed working with the library community. To begin, I would like to tell you a story about the first time I was invited into a library to serve as a process improvement consultant.

As a consultant, I have worked for steel mills, airline manufacturers, furniture manufacturers, consumer product assembly plants, high-tech electronic manufacturers, and automobile component suppliers, and I even served as the director of operations for a biotech research, design, and development company. My experience with libraries was primarily a typical customer point of view. I had no idea what went on behind the circulation desk or in those hidden rooms.

About ten years ago, when I received a call from Linda Saferite, the former CEO of the Tulsa City–County Library (TCCL), requesting my assistance to improve their customer service delivery performance, I was hesitant. I was a manufacturing, distribution, and retail consultant. What did I know about libraries?

I met with Ms. Saferite, curiously enough, on September 11, 2001, at 9:30 a.m., less than one hour after the World Trade Towers attack. It was a day none of us will forget, but for me it was also the day I started a new area of practice, library consulting.

After Ms. Saferite successfully battened down the hatches, she explained to me their dilemma. A few years ago they had added a feature to their integrated library system allowing customers to create Internet holds from their home or office and have the books delivered to their chosen branch. The service was so popular within the Tulsa community that TCCL's delivery system was bombarded by demand and they were falling further behind in their deliveries every day. As I listened to her, all I could think was, "What do I know about libraries?"

However, as we toured the facility, I began to see some very familiar scenarios. As compared to my manufacturing clients, the acquisitions department served as the purchasing department, the technical services department reflected a manufacturing assembly line, the circulation department looked like an operations inventory control department, and the shipping department echoed the distribution and logistics arm of most of my manufacturing clients. Finally, the circulation desk looked exactly like a retail checkout counter.

Who knew? Behind the desks and hidden walls of a library lie a purchasing group, a manufacturing assembly line, an inventory control department, a distribution operation, and a retail shop. I was not only home, but all my skills and experiences were being expressed in this one organization. It was the Super Bowl for this manufacturing consultant: all of the issues and opportunities of my separate manufacturing, distribution, and retail clients wrapped up in this one complex organization.

Over the next three months, we applied the concepts of Lean to TCCL's delivery process, starting at the time a customer requests a book until the book is delivered to the hold shelf. The results were dramatic. Prior to the project, TCCL had two delivery drivers (who also served as sorters) and two vans to support an annual circulation of more than 4 million and nearly 400 thousand hold/reserve requests. They were behind four to five days in their shipments and falling behind more and more every day. By applying the concepts of Lean, we replaced the archaic use of tote boxes with book trucks, upgraded the vans to box trucks, and created the innovative hold shelf ready, sticky label concept. We reduced TCCL's overall delivery lead time by 60 percent, eliminated the backlog, improved delivery capacity by 110 percent, and improved staff productivity by 30 percent. On top of this, the delivery group was able to meet a 48-hour delivery target 95 percent of the time. We did all of this without increasing staff; in fact, we freed up circulation and branch staff to spend more time on customer service activities. This is what Lean is all about: improve a process, reduce lead time, reduce costs, and improve customer service.

A year later we presented our results to over 300 librarians at the Seattle PLA conference. At the end of the presentation, many of those in the audience rushed the stage seeking more information. (It was very cool.)

Now, nearly ten years later, TCCL's circulation has grown by 50 percent and their customer holds/reserves have grown by 25 percent, and only recently have they considered adding a third delivery truck and driver. Over the past eight years, we have applied the concepts of Lean throughout TCCL's entire service delivery chain, including circulation, branches, acquisitions, technical services, cataloging, processing, outreach, bookmobile, and even gift book processing. I believe TCCL's efforts to streamline their processes and improve customer service is one of the reasons they were voted a Five Star Library by the *Library Journal*.

My second story happened a few years later after I had gained much more experience working with libraries. I believe this story puts an exclamation mark on my statement, "I like working for libraries!"

I was invited to Baltimore, Maryland, by James Fish, Director of the Baltimore County Public Library (BCPL). I was asked by Mr. Fish to help his group evaluate and improve their customer service delivery performance. On my first-day commute, as I often do, I turned on my rental car radio to get a taste of the local flavor.

"Arrggg, ye matie, ye be on the air," said the Baltimore disk jockey.

"Ahoy, ye scurvy dog, argggggg," the caller responded.

This "Pirate Talk" continued until I pulled into the parking lot of BCPL's Central Library. Obviously I discovered Baltimore had some interesting local flavor.

First days can be tough. You are never quite sure how the day will go. Most first days go great, but on occasion things can get a bit dicey. For example, a few weeks prior to my Baltimore trip, I had an interesting experience with a library out west. The director had invited me in but had not informed the staff why I was there. Understandably, the staff was a bit suspicious and defensive about who I was and what I was about. It took a day or two for them to get comfortable with me and, more important, enthusiastic about the project. In the end we had a successful project, but it was a tough first day.

Because of this recent experience, I entered the front doors of the Baltimore County Central Library a bit more apprehensive than usual. To prepare myself, I rehearsed the day's agenda in my head. First, meet with Mr. Fish, understand his project purpose and objectives, arrange for a five-dollar tour, and then meet with a select few of Mr. Fish's team to organize the project, cross-functional team members, and project structure. I felt at ease as I found my way to the front receptionist. It was a good plan.

"Good morning," I said. "I am John Huber. I have a meeting with Mr. Fish."

"Yes, Mr. Huber; we are expecting you."

I looked for Mr. Fish's office as she guided me toward the back offices when, surprisingly, she took a hard right turn into a large conference room where about twenty people sat around a conference table.

The group stared me down as I was guided to one of the two remaining empty chairs. My mind scrambled. I had not had my second cup of coffee and I was not quite ready to kick off the project to this large group from the word "Go."

After a moment though, I was ready. I had done this hundreds of times before but, nonetheless, meeting a room full of people for the first time and winning their confidence can be tricky. As I began to speak, a man dressed in a pirate outfit—hat and eye patch included—entered the room and headed right for me.

"Ahoy me heartie," he said as he shook my hand, " 'Ave these scallywags offered ye a pint of me special ale yet?"

Well, to say the least, I was taken aback. "Coffee, please," I replied. Turns out, September 19 is *Talk Like a Pirate Day*.

(I learned later that Talk Like a Pirate Day was started by a couple of guys in Portland, Oregon. The story goes that each afternoon, they liked to play racquetball together and they also liked to *hit* each other with the racquetballs. Each time they were hit they would yell, "AAARRRGGG." This started the pirate talk. Apparently the pirate talk carried over to the local bar to impress the girls with colorful pirate approach lines. After years of this banter, these two industrious gentlemen sent a letter to Dave Barry, the Pulitzer Prize–winning columnist with the *Miami Herald*. The letter introduced the concept of Talk Like a Pirate Day and Mr. Barry fell in love with the idea. He wrote an article suggesting that on September 19 everyone in the entire country should talk like a pirate. Apparently someone in Baltimore read the article.)

What a wonderful tone this librarian set for our project. The project resulted in a strategic shift for BCPL's delivery philosophy, and the improvement results were dramatic. We also had a great deal of fun making it happen. (I don't think any of my manufacturing clients would have walked into a meeting wearing a pirate outfit.)

Tulsa City–County Library showed me that my library clients and my manufacturing, distribution, and retail clients have a great deal in common. Baltimore County showed me that libraries have a wonderful, fun, and welcoming culture.

Thirty years ago I helped introduce the concept of what is now called Lean to a reluctant manufacturing industry that eventually transformed that very industry. With this book, I feel privileged to introduce the concepts of Lean to your library. In this book, you will learn the concepts, philosophies, and tools of Lean. You will learn how to apply these concepts to your library and you will learn how to dramatically reduce the service gap between you and your customer by improving your customer service delivery chain while reducing costs, inventory, and service delivery lead times.

Prologue

The Power of a Lean Transformation

In this chapter you will be introduced to the transformation power of Lean. You will learn that Lean is simple in concept, powerful in practice. You will also learn that transforming your library to a Lean culture can be managed, controlled, and implemented with a standard Lean Transformation Methodology.

Understanding Lean

To understand Lean, I would like you to visualize a river near you. Is it a smooth-flowing river with straight banks? Or is it a river with twists and turns, white-water rapids followed by dry mud-filled beds and stagnant water? If you understand these two types of rivers, you can understand the transformation power of Lean.

For example, let us imagine there are two teams in a river raft race. Each is equipped with the same type of rubber raft, oars, etc. Each is to navigate a river that is twenty miles long. One team will float a river called the River Lean; the other team will float a river called the Snake River. The River Lean has straight banks, smooth-flowing water, and no hidden rocks or obstacles along the way. The Snake River has extreme twists and turns, white-water rapids, and hidden rocks. To raise the stakes, the two teams are in competition. The team with the best time at the end of the twenty-mile mark will win a valuable five-year contract from a customer they have both been pursuing for years.

In the end, there is no contest; the River Lean team completed the race in half the time as the Snake River team. The River Lean team felt energized by the experience while the Snake River team was exhausted fighting the river as well as themselves. The River Lean team had so much extra time they were able to work on their rowing techniques so that the next time they rafted the river they would be even faster.

Doesn't seem fair, does it? Why should one team in a competitive race be able to raft a river that has smooth-flowing water without obstacles while the other team must paddle through difficult waters and avoid hidden rocks?

In Lean Management terms, the Snake River results in long service delivery times, unpredictable overtime, an exhausted and dispirited workforce, poor-quality products and services, and, most important, many unhappy customers.

So here's the question to ask: Is your library navigating the Snake River or the Lean River? Can your library transform your delivery service process to reflect more closely the Lean River? This is an important question, as it directly reflects your library's capability to provide excellent customer service. In this book I will help you answer that question. Based on my experience with libraries over the past ten years, I can predict that you are likely closer to the Snake River than you are to the River Lean, which means you have tremendous service and cost improvement potential in front of you.

A Brief History of Lean

Lean has its roots in the Toyota Production System, commonly referred to as TPS. The Toyota Production System not only revolutionized Toyota but the entire Japanese manufacturing industry. In the 1970s, after decades of producing cheap and poor-quality products, Toyota realized their delivery service chain (the river) had too many twists and turns, too many delays, too much imbalance, and too many obstacles to allow them to build a low-cost, high-quality product. They realized they were expending too much time, too much energy, and too much money trying to navigate such a poorly designed process. They were determined to smooth out the flow, eliminate the obstacles, and straighten out the twists and turns of their river. The Toyota leadership team charged their employees and management team with the task of transforming their manufacturing and business processes. The result was the Toyota Production System. TPS lowered costs, shortened lead times, and provided better customer service, not to mention better quality to their customers. U.S. customers, once loyal to American car companies, now saw their friends driving higher-quality and lower-cost cars from Toyota, and it did not take long for the message to spread: Japan was no longer building low-quality products but was instead setting the standard for low-cost, high-quality products.

During the late 1970s, an Accenture Consulting manager named Roy Harmon, who worked in the firm's Tokyo office and witnessed firsthand the revolutionary TPS in action, saw clearly the significant impact of TPS on Toyota's productivity and service lead times. He convinced the U.S. partnership of Accenture to add the TPS approach to their consulting services. As a result, Accenture for the first time hired a small group of industrial engineers to be on the front line of the U.S. manufacturing response to the Japanese challenge. I was one of those recruited, and I can proudly say that this small group of industrial engineers helped to spark the "TPS/Lean" manufacturing revolution in the United States.

Thirty years later, nearly every successful manufacturing company in America has embraced the concepts of Lean Manufacturing, seeing it as a fundamental tool for survival. Working with libraries across North America, I have discovered that Lean is just as powerful for the library world as it was and still is for the manufacturing industry. Many public service–driven libraries may be reluctant to compare, contrast, or learn service lessons from a profit-driven manufacturing industry, but I believe it is critical that libraries do so, if for no other reason than because your competitors already have.

Jeffery P. Bezos, founder and CEO of Amazon.com, wrote in a letter to shareholders, "Everywhere we look (and we all look), we find what experienced Japanese manufacturers call 'muda' or waste. I find it incredibly energizing."[1] I believe libraries must embrace the concepts of Lean to remain viable and competitive in meeting today's customer expectations, especially considering the likes of Google, Amazon.com, Apple, and Barnes and Noble.

The Principles of Lean

Throughout this book we will examine the principles and tools of Lean and how you can apply these techniques to your library. The following key Lean principles will help guide your journey:

- Lean is based on simple concepts: Anything that does not add value to a service or product is wasteful and separates you from your ability to better service your customer. All waste must be attacked and eliminated. As waste is eliminated, costs are reduced, quality improves, and customer service lead times are reduced.
- Lean seeks to create the smoothest and quickest delivery path to your customer. The smoother the flow, the less disruption, the fewer peaks and valleys, and therefore less delay.
- The fewer errors and wasteful activities in the process, the better the product and, most important, the better the customer service.
- Lean teaches us that the shorter the service delivery time, the less cost incurred.
- By reducing lead times, Lean allows an organization to respond to changing customer demand requirements more quickly and with more flexibility.
- If you commit your organization to eliminate disruption, delay, error, and wasteful activities, your library will improve customer service *and* reduce costs.

The Benefits of Lean

What can you expect to achieve through the transformative power of Lean? It is important to note that the following metrics directly reflect customer service level improvements. Many of these achieved benefits will be presented in the case studies throughout this book.

* 50–75 percent reduction in new book delivery lead time/backlog
* 50–75 percent reduction in customer reserves delivery lead time
* 20–45 percent reduction in service delivery costs
* 25–40 percent improvement in book service days available
* 10–80 percent reduction in overtime
* 25–90 percent reduction in injury-related tasks
* 25–90 percent reduction in internal book damage

The Eleven Lean Transformation Strategies

You can take various approaches to transforming your library to a Lean environment. Based on my experience with more than 100 manufacturing clients and more than a dozen library clients, I have developed and honed my own Lean library transformation methodology, which can be summarized in the eleven major strategies that your library should embrace:

Strategy One: Recognize that service performance is the key to customer retention.

Strategy Two: Transform your change-resistant culture.

Strategy Three: Understand that measuring your delivery service chains drives your library's performance.

Strategy Four: Set your library's Lean transformation priorities based on service performance gaps.

Strategy Five: Transform your new book delivery service chain.

Strategy Six: Transform your customer hold/reserves delivery service chain.

Strategy Seven: Transform your budget cost control philosophy to a Lean service improvement philosophy.

Strategy Eight: Transform your overall performance metrics to service days available.

Strategy Nine: Transform your digital content delivery service chain.

Strategy Ten: Transform your "push" demand philosophy to a Lean "pull" demand philosophy.

Strategy Eleven: Think Lean before the concrete is poured.

These transformation strategies, illustrated by actual library case examples, will help guide you on your Lean journey.

Lean Transformation Review

You should now understand the potential power of a Lean transformation:

- Lean is simple in concept; like a river, it attempts to flow smoothly, without unexpected twists and turns, large peaks and valleys, stagnant water, or dry river banks.
- Wasteful activities, delays in the process, service peaks and valleys, and errors all increase delivery lead time and costs. The larger the gap, the poorer the customer service performance, and the greater the likelihood that your customers will look elsewhere to meet their needs.
- Lean has transformed the world's manufacturing companies as well as your competitors and is now viewed as a fundamental competitive strategy. In the same way, Lean can and must transform your library to help you remain viable.
- The benefits of Lean are dramatic, including reduced service lead time, lower costs, and improved service performance. Lean also creates a safer work environment and a more engaged workforce that is motivated to reduce costs and constantly improve customer service.
- You can transform your library to a Lean environment by following this proven culture-changing methodology.

Note

1. Bezo, Jeffrey P. 2009. "Letter to Shareholders." In *2008 Amazon.com Annual Report*. Scribd. http://www.scribd.com/doc/14670406/Amazon-Annual-Report-2008.

Strategy One

Recognize That Service Performance Is the Key to Customer Retention

A few months ago, I was asked to present our proposed Lean delivery improvement design to the board of directors of one of my library clients. I began my presentation by emphasizing the importance of service and competition. I presented one particular slide that argued that libraries compete with Amazon.com and Barnes and Noble, not to mention used booksellers, Netflix, and the rest.

One board member took great exception to my point. He stated confidently, "We provide free services; you cannot expect us to be held to the same standards of service and delivery as these commercial business enterprises." But can't I? Can't I expect libraries to be held to the same standard as a for-profit enterprise? Can't I call a library a business?

Libraries consist of a merger of purchasing, manufacturing, inventory control, distribution, warehousing, and retail. Libraries are not only a business, but a complex business. For libraries to pursue the concepts of Lean successfully they must first recognize that they are complex businesses and should be managed as such.

I will begin with a basic definition of a business. The Investopedia website defines a business as "an organization or enterprising entity engaged in commercial, industrial or professional activities."[1] Librarians are professionals engaging in a professional activity, and many libraries not only provide free books, but they provide research assistance, sell used books, charge fines, and sell the occasional cup of coffee. On top of this, by purchasing, preparing, and delivering books and digital media to customers, they are engaged in a professional and industrial activity.

The BusinessCoachingPedia states further, "The owners and operators of a business have as one of their main objectives the receipt or generation of a financial return in exchange for their work and their acceptance of risk."[2] Car manufacturers carry a great deal of financial risk. They risk years of effort and

7

a significant amount of money designing and manufacturing cars. Years from now, it is their best hope consumers will buy the product they are now designing at a high enough volume that they can make enough money to pay their employees and make a profit (or at least break even) for their shareholders.

Libraries carry a great risk as well. They select and invest a significant amount of money in physical and digital materials in the hope that their customers will borrow them. While libraries are a not-for-profit business, they must work within the funds allocated to provide successfully the goods and the services their customers demand. If not, circulation (or use) goes down. If over time, circulation growth and budget containment do not meet the library's governing body's requirements, management will be replaced, or libraries will be shut down. This is the same for a for-profit business; if sales and profit performance do not meet the board's requirements, management will be replaced or operations will be closed or go bankrupt. Certainly sounds like a library is a business to me.

I will go even further and add my own definition of a business: An entity that provides needed or desired goods or services that competes with other entities that provide the same needed or desired goods or services. Now it gets interesting. Do libraries compete with other entities that provide the same goods or services? The answer is quite obvious: of course they do.

I have spent countless hours flying the friendly skies. One of the great things about flying the friendly "sky" is that you have a great deal of time to read. Prior to my library work, I was an avid customer of Barnes and Noble, Amazon.com, and Borders. Apparently I am not alone. In the year 2008, book sales for Borders, Barnes and Noble, and Amazon.com totaled $13.7 billion dollars. (Amazon.com enjoyed a growth rate of 45 percent from 2006–2008).[3] Another $8 billion from Wal-Mart and other supermarkets bring U.S. book sales to around the $22 billion mark. That's a lot of books.

For more than twenty years I did not borrow a book from a library; I was more than willing to use the convenience of the airport bookstore and spend the $15 to $20 to own the book, even if it took me just one plane trip to read it. For the past nine or ten years I have bought only a few books and borrowed dozens upon dozens of books from my local library. Once I was fully exposed to my local library's Internet delivery capabilities I found they could successfully compete with the likes of Amazon.com and Barnes and Noble. In fact, the library provides me services that an on-site retailer does not. For example, I am now reading *Moby Dick*, and it was available on a hold shelf waiting for me to pick up in less than twenty-four hours at a location about a mile from my home. I use the library to support my reading habit, I receive services comparable to those for-profit retailers provide, and I save a great deal of money. I was once an avid customer of Barnes and Noble; now I am an avid customer of my local library.

Your circulation depends directly on your ability to take customers away from your commercial competition. Circulation is your lifeblood. Providing better service than your competitor is a business survival necessity. You might say that I did not use the library because it was not marketed to me properly, and you may have a good point. However, I would argue that they won me over because of their new customer service capabilities. I now use the library because it is convenient for me to do so. I can, at my leisure, from the comfort of my home or office, research the book I want, reserve it, and have it delivered to a library near my home. My library's performance fits into what I call "my service window of expectation."

Libraries must recognize that they have competition, and as such they must benchmark their service performance against this competition. They must manage themselves as if they were competing for each and every customer. To state it more clearly, they must reject the notion that a library cannot be held to the same standards as a for-profit business, specifically because these businesses are aggressively attempting to take customers away from them.

In every library project in which I am engaged, I constantly remind myself of the client's main competition. For example, I was involved in designing a new circulation desk for the Kaiser branch of the Tulsa City–County Library. My first step was to make many trips to the Borders down the street for comparison. How are they performing the same task? How long is the waiting line, and how is it controlled? Where is the computer? Where is the scanner? What is located around and under the desk?

I also look at the bigger picture. What new services do they offer? How fast is their delivery service? How easy is it to use their service? How many hours are they open? This exercise can lead to many interesting questions. For example, could a library branch be opened in an airport? It might be crazy, but it sure makes you think out of the box for a moment, and that is what a successful business enterprise must do—outthink and outperform the competition.

Looking at the bigger picture, academic libraries are facing stiff competition with Google to provide easy-to-use, reliable, and up-to-date research materials. While most would argue that academic libraries still have the advantage on peer-reviewed research materials, some would argue that Google's search tools are far easier to use. Academic libraries must, therefore, respond to Google's challenge to remain viable.

I will talk more about a library's ability to deliver books, as well as online research materials, but the lesson I want you to take from this strategy is the following:

> *Whether you are a small, medium, or large public or research library, you work in and support a very complex business that competes with for-profit enterprises.*

Through its retail, inventory management, manufacturing, research, and distribution operations, all libraries provide goods and services at great financial risk, and they must compete aggressively with other commercial entities to provide those same goods and services.

If you are convinced that libraries should *not* be held to the same service standard as Amazon.com or Barnes and Noble, let me ask you one last question: Do you believe Amazon.com and Barnes and Noble perceive your library as a competitive threat? Answer: You better hope they do.

Strategy One Review

Before you embark on your Lean transformation journey you must embrace the first strategy of Lean Library Management. You must recognize that you work in a very complex business environment and that your toughest for-profit competition is aggressively pursuing your customers. To remain viable and competitive your library leadership team and staff, no matter the size, must embrace this concept and respond aggressively to improve service to reduce costs.

Notes

1. Investopedia. 2010. "Business Definition: What Does Business Mean?" Investopedia. Accessed November 12. http://www.investopedia.com/terms/b/business.asp.
2. BusinessCoachingPedia. 2010. "Welcome to BusinessCoachingPedia—The Business Coaching Encyclopedia: Business." BusinessCoachingPedia. Accessed November 12. http://www.businesscoachingpedia.com.
3. Foner Books. 2010. "Book Sales Statistics: Amazon, Barnes&Noble, and Borders Sales Numbers Annual Update." Foner Books. Accessed November 12. http://www.fonerbooks.com/booksale.htm.

Strategy Two

Transform Your Change-Resistant Culture

In Strategy Two we will recognize that a Lean transformation of your library cannot happen without developing and nurturing a culture of change. In the first section we will examine why organizations and libraries in particular resist change. In the second section we will walk through key Lean principles that can help you create a culture of change.

Note: Many of you are familiar with organizational change theory and methodologies, and if you so desire you may skip reading Strategy Two and move on to Strategy Three. However, I might recommend you quickly review the sections of Strategy Two, as they will establish a common frame of reference throughout the rest of the book.

Libraries Must Create a Culture of Change

I hear one common refrain in every library I have ever worked with: *Our staff does not like change.* Libraries, like most organizations and most people, do not like change. People and organizations like routine; they like comfort; they like things to stay the same. The issue of course is if there is no change, there is no chance for improvement. Most certainly without a culture of change a library or any other organization will not be successful in their Lean endeavors.

During my travels, as I attempt to create a culture of change and as I pursue the Lean ideals, I hear many common rebuttals. I have heard the following comments more times than I can count:

- If it ain't broke, don't fix it.
- If we mess with it, things could get worse.
- I have done it this way for thirty years.
- We tried that before, and it didn't work.
- Sure, change things, but they will just go back to the way they were.
- Management talks a good game, but they will not support it.

- It's just one more program that will fail.
- Why should I help? Management will take all the credit.
- Our customers seem happy, so why should we change?

The following sections provide three stories about change.

Dinner to Go

One day after we both arrived home from work, Kathy, my wife, started making dinner. Now before I tell the story, you must understand that I have a degree in industrial engineering and management; my job is to observe and evaluate how machines, materials, and people work together and develop ways to improve these processes. In other words, I live the Lean philosophy all of the time, a philosophy that says: eliminate all non-value-added activities and streamline the process. It is hard for me to turn it off.

That particular night, a year or so into our marriage, I sat in the kitchen talking with my wife as she prepared spaghetti. She went to the refrigerator to retrieve the hamburger. Then to the pan drawer to get the frying pan. Then to the spice cabinet to get the salt. Then she began cooking the hamburger. Then she retrieved the onions from the refrigerator. Then she got the pepper from the spice cabinet. Then she got the cutting knife from the utensil drawer. Then she put the onions in the frying pan. Then she went back to the spice cabinet for spices. Then back to the refrigerator for the spaghetti sauce. Well, you get the idea.

After watching this for a while I offered my trained and expert opinion: "You know, honey, if you plan out all of the things you need before you start cooking dinner you could save yourself a lot of time."

Well, I did save her a lot of time, because she stopped making dinner, at least for a few days. (She eventually took over after I made a Hamburger Helper meal three days in a row.) But I did learn a valuable lesson: people don't like it when you mess with their kitchen.

Libraries are your kitchen, and I understand this. Change does not come easily, and I understand this as well. People don't like to be told how to change. To be a successful "change consultant" I had to learn a lot more about the change process and how best to make it a successful endeavor. The dinner incident was nearly thirty years ago, and I dedicated myself from that day on to learn all that I could about how to create change successfully while engaging the very people who must create the change. I am still happily married, and I have a successful management consulting firm, so I must have learned something from that night in our kitchen. (And I have since learned to cook more dishes than just Hamburger Helper.)

The Two Sides of Karen

During one library project I found myself having a fruitful discussion with a nice lady we will call Karen. One of Karen's responsibilities was to receive and sort the books to be shelved at her library. As I held my video camera, she enthusiastically explained all of the innovations she had designed that helped her receive and sort the books. She had done a really good job, and I was very impressed. In fact, she had done such a great job I felt she would be a great resource for our Lean team as we planned to re-engineer the library's delivery process. She had so aggressively initiated change in her own process that I assumed she would be open to hearing some of my ideas. I was also hoping she would help me determine how best to introduce these concepts into their library system; after all, it was *their* kitchen. As I explained some of the changes we had made in other libraries, the smile on Karen's face slowly turned to a frown, her body stiffened, and her brow furrowed.

For every idea I offered, she countered with why it would not work. She resisted me at every turn. As the discussion continued her arguments became more nonsensical. I had a hard time believing this was the same person. At one point I felt that if I said the sky was blue she would say the sky was yellow.

"I'm confused," I said. "All of these changes you made in your process are fantastic. You have a real grasp on how to streamline a process, eliminate the non-value-added activities, and reduce the costs of an activity. All of the ideas I have discussed with you will do the same for the entire delivery process. Why are you so resistant to these ideas?"

She replied, "I'm the union steward, and the ideas you are suggesting will change people's job titles."

She was right, and it was her responsibility to represent the union employees and, in her thinking, protect them. In an instant she went from a reasonable, energetic agent for change to a huge obstacle to change. Whether your library is unionized or not, this same issue exists for your group as well. People do not like their job tasks or titles changed. As soon as they see that jobs may be combined, or pay scales merged, or department walls torn down, resistance grows in leaps and bounds.

Cindy versus Shy Sally

Recently I was working with a group of women in the technical services department of one of my library clients. These women had worked together for years. Some of them had been there for more than thirty years. Things had not changed dramatically for them since bar coding was introduced.

At the time of the engagement the department had more than two months of backlogged books to be received and checked in. This was not acceptable to management, and I was asked to come in and help. The plan was to apply Lean principles to improve the productivity of the group by redesigning their workstations and the overall process flow. I met with the manager of the department to discuss the formation of a cross-functional design team.

"Who is the most negative person in your group, the one who is the most resistant to change?" I asked the department manager.

She did not hesitate, "Oh, that would be Cindy." (Names and specifics have been changed to protect my health.)

"I would like her on my team," I said.

"No, that wouldn't be a good idea," she replied.

Now you might ask: Why would I want the most resistant, negative person on my team? Am I asking for trouble? Well, not really. I could argue the old adage to keep your friends close and your enemies closer, but there is much more to it, as I will explain in a later strategy. I relented in the end, and we did not include Cindy on the team, which I later regretted. The next day I kicked off the project with our cross-functional team without Cindy.

A week later we began to define and document the current processes and layout. This is when I flowchart the process and film the operation steps. This helps me and the team members evaluate each process step and identify opportunities to eliminate waste and create improvements. The group was very welcoming as I stood in the middle of the technical services area and filmed how they unpacked and checked in CDs.

"Is this going to end up on YouTube?" Carol asked.

"Let me fix my hair before you film me," Roberta said.

"You need to film Carol; she loves to be in front of the camera," Mary said.

I encourage this type of friendly banter because it helps people cope with the fact that some stranger is filming every move they make. Carol was checking in a box of CDs. After about ten minutes of filming, I observed her using a box knife to cut the plastic wrapping off a CD case. Now, if you have ever tried to unwrap a DVD or a CD case, you know why this captured my attention. In front of me was an expert on how to do it efficiently; after all, she did this hundreds of times a day. This had become personal.

"That's interesting; you cut along the spine," I said.

"Yes, it is easier for me because I can get a good hold on the case while I'm cutting, and there is a groove to follow," Carol explained.

"That seems like a good way. I could use that at home," I replied.

Like placing a spark on a bunch of dead leaves, I had started a brush fire. All of the ladies but one jumped up from their workstations and gathered around Carol to see how she was cutting off the CD wrapper. Seeing how someone else performed the same task as they did suddenly intrigued them. (Curiously, they had never shared with one another their preferred best practices techniques before this day.)

"I didn't know you did it that way," said Roberta.

"I usually cut it down the front," said Mary.

In the corner at a workstation sat a lady named Sally who had not left her station. Sally said, "I saw a tool at Borders that was designed to easily cut wrappers off CDs." Now I got the impression that Sally was very shy and very rarely said anything, much less voiced her opinion out loud.

Up until that point, things were going exactly to plan. The group was now sharing with one another how they performed their tasks, something they had never done before. This is the first step to accepting change and adapting to new best practices. The shyest person in the group was even offering new ideas that could improve the process, something I did not expect for another few weeks or even months. I was feeling very good about how things were going until Cindy weighed in.

"Those things don't work. We tried them before," said Cindy. With those eight words, all the good progress we had made was squashed.

A number of reasons might explain why Cindy jumped on shy Sally. First of all, Cindy does not like change, any change. She had been doing her tasks her way for more than twenty years and she had no intention of changing. Anything that threatened her routine was not good. Second, Cindy had been there much longer than Sally and was at a higher pay grade. This may have influenced her negative reaction to Sally's suggestion.

For the rest of the project, I could never get poor shy Sally to say much else, and when she did she tended to be more negative than positive. Cindy's words had not only shut her down but also turned her a bit negative. Whether Sally's idea was good or not is not the point—the point is that an idea was thrown out and immediately chastised, and it reduced the potential creativity of the team. If I had had Cindy on my cross-functional project team from the beginning, had helped and coached her to be a part of the solution and not the problem, she would have become not only an agent for change but also one of the best agents for change. By the end of the project, Cindy did come around, not necessarily as a change champion, but she did adapt and eventually like the changes that were made.

It is very important to embrace the negativity of people when creating change. At times these people are actually the most motivated people in the department. Their bad attitudes often reflect years of trying to be heard but finding no one to listen. Give them a vehicle to be heard and to make a difference and they will eventually change their stripes. Furthermore, the impact of the most negative person changing his or her stripes is dramatic. After all if Cindy, the most negative person in the room, is all in, then this must be a really good thing.

Negativity, cynicism, and the resistance to change is a powerful force not easily dealt with. Sometimes you need to embrace it and the results are always surprising. Cindy is not uncommon; there is a Cindy in every department and every organization I have ever worked for, including my library clients.

This brings us back to the subject of this chapter: *Libraries do not like to change.* The following items contribute to this "antichange" culture:

- Many people who work for a library make a career of it, which means many librarians and staff have been part of the same organization for ten, twenty, thirty, or even forty years. This amount of experience can be a formidable force against new ideas.
- Libraries by nature have very repetitive tasks performed every day. After a few months, years, or decades of a person doing the same task the same

way, suggestions on how he or she might change can be very threatening to their comfortable routine.

- Even though every member of a library system is part of one continuous service flow, libraries are set up into departments. Walls form between departments both literally and figuratively, which makes communications between those departments more difficult, and power struggles between departments often occur.

- Departments become protective of their turf and can be resistant to outside influences and suggestions for change.

- Education levels, pay grades, and titles hold a lot of weight in libraries. Any changes that might alter or combine tasks from one pay grade to another must be negotiated and approved by either the union or the department managers and their employees. Regardless, everyone is resistant to the idea of changing job titles or responsibilities.

- Library management often segment tasks in terms of skill level and pay grade. A higher paid individual does not want to perform tasks he or she believes a lower paid individual should do. Therefore, seeing and streamlining the entire customer delivery process as a whole can take a backseat to the smaller objective of matching skill level with pay grade. This can result in saving pennies rather than dollars.

- To be called a professional librarian, you must achieve a higher education in library science, often a master's-level education. Many university libraries have a tenure track for their PhD librarians. A large gap in education can exist between professional librarians, clerical staff, and volunteers. In some environments asking a professional librarian to perform a task that a volunteer or a clerk could or should perform can seem inappropriate.

- People are tied to their job descriptions, and changes to these descriptions can be difficult for people to accept, and unions are often driven to protect these job descriptions at all costs.

- Finally, it is human nature. People love routine; change is a threat to that routine, and it is very natural for us to resist. *Stay out of my kitchen* is familiar to all of us.

Every academic and public library culture is different, but I believe if you look closely you will find that some of these items exist in your library culture. There is a paradox, however. While libraries do not like to change, libraries have been on the forefront of using and adapting to technological advancements for decades. Mike Dean of Learning Resources Center (LRC) at the Tulsa Community College writes:

> In many instances it was the library/LRC that purchased (in the campus environment) the first fax machine, or where CD-ROMs were first used for data. Authoring software for producing computer-based learning modules often appeared first in the library/LRC media departments, as did new media formats. The library/LRC may have been the first place on campus to

install and use a satellite dish for teleconferencing or to operate an electronic bulletin board. Librarians in some community colleges in the early 1990s were finding ways to gain access to a totally new entity called the World Wide Web and found ways to gain access to it even in its early, pre-browser form to locate information for their users.[1]

While libraries can be very resistant to change, they have proven they can embrace and adapt to new technology. Just as libraries embraced and benefited from technological advances, I believe libraries can also benefit from the tools and philosophies of Lean.

How to Transform Your Change-Resistant Culture

If your library staff does not embrace a culture of change, they will never embrace a culture of improvement. Therefore a fundamental part of your Lean transformation is to understand how to create and nurture an organization that not only allows change but embraces it.

To create an organization that embraces change as well as to drive your Lean transformation, I recommend your management team embrace a methodology that I developed over my thirty years of consulting. I use this methodology on every Lean project to create, manage, and guide a culture toward an environment of change. You may be familiar with this approach or have a change methodology of your own; however, for the purposes of this book we will use this methodology as our common framework. The primary steps to the methodology include:

- Understand and embrace your organizational purpose
- Practice a top-down and bottom-up driven management style
- Practice process change ownership
- Initiate projects to drive change
- Develop gap driven performance metrics
- Drive change through your cross-functional teams
- Develop and share economic, cost–benefit projections and results
- Implement flexible job descriptions
- Celebrate current and past accomplishments

Understand and Embrace Your Organizational Purpose

I often ask my library clients to share with me why they chose the library profession. This helps me understand what my clients' purposes are, and it helps me focus my efforts to help them achieve their purpose. One client with a library in southern Maryland said she had become a librarian because the librarian she had as a child was very mean to her and it made a significant impression on her. She recognized how important a librarian can be to a child.

Her purpose was to take advantage of this power to become a positive influence for the children in her community. She knew as a librarian she could make a difference. I wondered whether her coworkers knew this about her. If they did know, would they be inspired to help her achieve her purpose? Did she know the purposes of those around her? Would she be motivated to help them in return if she did?

It is human nature to want to be a part of something bigger than yourself. People want to find a vehicle to contribute their skills, their ideas, and their hard work. They want to contribute to a larger purpose and be appreciated for their contributions. Every person wants to wake up in the morning and be excited about going to work that day.

The reality, however, is often quite the opposite. Many people feel less than enthusiastic about going to work. They arrive at work to find their ideas dismissed, their skills underappreciated, and their hard work measured simply by a paycheck reward system. In the end, the purpose of their life's work is measured by what they can buy with the money they earn or how many days off they get.

Most people want more from their job than a simple paycheck. People who work for libraries choose their profession for a reason. When they chose the library profession they expected to go to work each day and find a place where they can fulfill a purpose.

When my children were younger, I coached youth baseball and basketball for many years. I looked forward to the practices and games all week. I was motivated because I had a purpose: to help the kids on my team reach their full potential, even if they were not athletically or socially inclined. To fulfill this purpose I often sought out the kids whom no one else wanted. If I had not, many of these kids would not have been able to join a team. I received great joy seeing those kids whom others thought had no potential succeed. You might think that my teams never won, but in fact they did very well; some of my basketball teams were undefeated. In some ways I have the same type of purpose for my management consulting firm.

J Huber and Associates' Organizational Purpose

J Huber and Associates exists to help people and their organizations reach their full performance potential so that they can fulfill their personal and organizational purpose. We want to create a culture for our clients where people go to work each day and are excited for what awaits them.

Just like my coaching experience, this is what gets me excited to get up in the morning. It is the thing that motivates me to get on a plane and travel across the country to work with organizations such as yours. Libraries are well positioned to explore this concept of organizational purpose. For example, when asked why she became a librarian, Pamela Price, associate professor and director of library services at the Mercer County Community College Library, wrote:

I still have not worked one day (during my twenty-seven year career) even though I often work ten, twelve, and fourteen hour days. Then, what do I do for the hours I am in the office? I share, give, guide, learn, inspire, heal, and connect people to literal and virtual information windows of opportunity, hope, and personal and professional fulfillment.[2]

To motivate your workforce and help your organization reach its full potential, you must learn and understand what not only motivates you but those around you. Too often organizations rely on systems of reward and punishment to motivate performance. To create a culture that seeks change and a desire to improve you must tap into what makes your library staff want to go to work each morning beyond simple reward and punishment.

Can an organization have one overall purpose even though each individual has his or her own unique reason for going to work each day? Most librarians share a common purpose. Perhaps each has his or her own flavor, but in the end, I believe Ms. Price might have shown us the way: "Share, give, guide, learn, inspire, heal and connect people to the literal and virtual windows of opportunity, hope and personal and professional fulfillment."[3]

Whether you are adding jackets to books, working at the reference desk, delivering books in a delivery van, working in the outreach department, assisting university students with their research, driving a book mobile truck, or working at the circulation desk, these words resonate. You are part of a chain that is fulfilling a purpose. If you recognize that you are a part of this chain and those around you recognize, respect, and appreciate your role in fulfilling the common purpose, then you and your organization can do only one thing: succeed. Furthermore, if we all understand, respect, and appreciate the part we play in fulfilling this purpose, then we as a group are motivated to do this to the very best of our ability.

A library can embrace and reflect their organizational purpose in many ways. Vision and mission statements, for example, are excellent ways to bring a common organizational purpose to your staff. The following are some of my favorites:

- The New York Public Library—Mission Statement
  "The mission of The New York Public Library is to inspire lifelong learning, advance knowledge, and strengthen our communities. To deliver on this promise, we rely on three great resources—our staff, our collections, and our physical and virtual spaces—as well as on a set of core values."[4]
- Carnegie Library of Pittsburgh—Mission and Vision Statements
  "To Engage our Community in Literacy and Learning"
  "Carnegie Library of Pittsburgh will inspire in the citizens of our region respect and responsibility for life-long learning, citizenship, and civic participation."[5]

- Tulsa City–County Library—Mission Statement
  "The mission of the Tulsa City–County Library is to provide service that is high in quality and timeliness while promoting the joy of reading, research, literacy, and access to information for people of all ages.

  "In support of this mission the Library provides community outreach, materials in a variety of formats, programs on a variety of topics, current technologies, and free and equal access to information."[6]

- Oklahoma State University Library—Mission and Vision Statements
  "We exist as a resource to expand the learning potential of students and citizens of our state and to enhance the teaching and research capabilities of our faculty.

  "We will be the best performing land-grant university library as measured by resource access and use by OSU students, faculty and the citizens of the state. We will deliver these resources in a user-friendly and service-oriented manner. Our constituents will consider us the preferred provider of learning and research information."[7]

These are all well-written statements. Each is an effective means to communicate to their community and employees their common organizational purpose. However, mission and vision statements are only a beginning. You must embrace your common organizational purpose in all of the activities of your library, including your change initiatives. If your organization has a purpose, and it has a desire to reach its full potential, change is no longer a choice; it is a necessity. Therefore, any resistance to (or fear of) change quickly falls in the face of this desire.

Periodically, you and your coworkers should share and remind one another of your individual purposes as well as your common purpose and your desire to accomplish it together. After all, it is why you get up in the morning.

Importance of Metrics in the Change Process

About twenty years ago I took up golf. It is an extremely difficult sport. At first I was terrible, and I saw very little progress. Every year about forty of my friends and I would gather at a local golf resort for our annual golf tournament. The teams would be organized so they would be evenly matched. Each team would have an excellent player called an "A" player, a good player called a "B" player, an average player called a "C" player, and, finally, a pretty awful golfer called a "D" player. I was a "D" player. I really hated being a "D" player among my friends.

Last week I shot a 73, which is one stroke over par, one stroke from shooting a perfect round. (Of course you can do even better than perfect, but that is not the point.) I accomplished this amazing feat playing with some of the same friends I played with ten years ago when I was a "D" player. Many of them commented on how I used to be such an awful golfer and they were amazed to see how much I had improved. One of my friends asked me how I did it. I replied by saying that I was very motivated to improve and I was willing to change my swing every day if that was what it took to get better. After all, if my old swing was not getting the results I desired, I had to change it.

Change requires three components: a purpose, a desire to improve, and a desire to get feedback. My purpose was to be recognized by my friends as an "A" player, I had a great desire to improve my performance, and I had score-cards to provide me feedback. Change was not a choice for me. My scorecards made it very clear to me that I had to change to improve.

If your library is truly motivated to better service your customers and your community, you should also be motivated to acquire feedback on not only where you are now but how far you have to go to achieve your desired purpose. This requires scorecards, or stated another way, performance metrics. Every change effort must embrace your common purpose, and you must understand how large a gap exists between where you as a group want to be as opposed to where you are.

Practice a Top and Bottom Management Style

Do you ever get frustrated with the historical and ongoing debate between politicians regarding the trickle-down versus bottom-up stimulus debate? I do. I get frustrated because I know that it is not an either/or choice. The answer is obvious: it takes some of both. Why choose one over the other?

The same is true about creating a culture of change and pursuing a Lean transformation of your library. No change effort or project for that matter can be successful without the full support and commitment of top management, but it is just as important to receive the full support and commitment of the workforce as well. Otherwise the project or change effort will fail.

When you want to initiate change in a change-resistant culture it must come from the top. Management must be committed to the effort; they must fund it, support it, and proactively remove the obstacles that might prevent progress. Add the full support of those who will be most affected by the change—the "bottom-up" employee group—and this transformation will not only be successful but long lasting and enthusiastically embraced.

All managers face resistance to change, and they have a choice on how they will respond to this resistance. They can force change by a top-down management style or they can try a bottom-up approach. A top-driven management style is about control. Decisions are made at the top; directives are issued and implemented without question by the workforce. This is the military style of management. The bottom-up approach preaches self-directed work teams. This management style sees an organization as many small businesses, each with its own set of customers and vendors. Each unit forms a team, and the team makes all of the decisions. Priorities do not come from management. The team sets priorities, and the team even has the responsibility to interview and hire anyone new. Improvement suggestions do not come from the top; they come from the team, and the team makes the decision whether to pursue the changes.

It appears to me most organizations see this as an either/or choice. Will our management style be a top-driven military style of management? Or will we have a bottom-up, self-directed style of management? QuikTrip, a highly successful Tulsa-based convenience store company, is a great example of a well-blended team-driven organization with top-down leadership. The majority of the leaders of QuikTrip started out as clerks working at the checkout register of the convenience store. It is a matter of policy that promotion comes from within. Therefore top management has a perfect understanding of the day-to-day responsibilities of their workforce. Because of this the leaders of the organization are able to effectively work with and inspire their workforce because they have been there before. They understand the importance of engaging those on the front line because they know no one is closer to the process issues and customer service challenges than the frontline clerks. Libraries have a great deal in common with this organizational philosophy. At QuikTrip, nearly 90 percent of top management started as entry-level clerks, just as most library directors and managers started off working at a circulation desk.

Libraries have a wonderful organizational culture to build on, but do they take advantage of it through their management style? To create a change culture and pursue a Lean transformation of your library, there has to be leadership. This leadership must set a direction, establish parameters, and set priorities. Management must be committed to the plan; they must fund it, support it, and proactively remove the obstacles that might prevent progress. However, management must recognize that those on the front lines understand better than anyone else the process and customer service challenges they face every day. Management must also recognize that without the full support of those who will be most affected by the change, no change will ever be successful.

Management should embrace both a top-down and a bottom-up management style to actively involve the workforce on issues that may lead to change. Ultimately management must set a strong direction, and they must make the final decisions, but developing a means for your organization to be a part of the process (and organizational purpose) is critical. I believe the most effective means to merge these management styles is a series of management-initiated projects driven by cross-functional teams.

Practice Process Change Ownership

To create change in a change-resistant culture, or any culture for that matter, those most affected by the change must be active participants in developing the change. They must understand what the problem is, and they must have ownership of whatever solution is developed. Those leading the change and those who will develop and implement the change must work together to create long-lasting improvements successfully.

This lesson is the most important lesson I can teach you. It is my primary philosophy. It is so important that I often start my discussions with every new client with the following question: There are two approaches we can take:

1. I can accomplish the objectives you have established by using my skill and experience from the many projects I have worked on, combine it with information I gather from your employees, and design and implement a 95 percent perfect solution for your company.
2. I can accomplish the objectives you have established by forming a cross-functional team of those employees who will be most affected by this project, involve them in every design task, and actively develop their ownership in the effort. The effort should result in a 75 percent perfect solution for your company.

Which option would you have me take?

Without a doubt, option 2 is the best choice. While option 1 may present a near-perfect solution, it will eventually fail. Why? Because the people most affected by the change do not have ownership of the actions that must be taken to make the effort a success. They will not support it, and they will eventually allow it to fail. Perhaps not overtly, but over time it will not be supported. Without the support from those who must do it every day it will fail.

Option 2, while not the perfect solution, will be very successful. Why? Because those people who actually must make the change happen are key parts of the change process. They understand why the project was initiated in the first place. They helped uncover the issues and obstacles that were in the way, and they were a part of the design of the solutions to be pursued. My experience tells me that while the first solution they develop as a group may not be perfect, they will adjust, adapt, and commit to finding that 95 percent solution, and they will not stop there. They will strive and adapt to the conditions around them to continue to improve the process, eventually reaching a best practice model.

Over the past twenty-five years I have learned that change does not occur from employee surveys, management edicts, or motivational posters. Change is a process, a process that starts small and like a seed must be nurtured. Over time this process grows, eventually reaches critical mass, and then becomes a part of the culture. The change process I use is centered on the concepts of Lean. Once the Lean process is part of the culture, so is change. I have seen it happen for my manufacturing clients, and I have seen it for my library clients as well. The primary means to create ownership in those most affected by the change is to engage them in the process. In a Lean transformation, I accomplish this using cross-functional project teams.

Initiate Projects to Drive Change

Consider the following benefits of using a project-based approach to create change:

- A project allows you to start the change process in an incubator environment using a series of small pilot projects.
- A project can be initiated to close the gap in performance from where you are and where you want to be.
- A project allows you to form a cross-functional team across departments and pay grade barriers.
- A project has a beginning date and an ending date.
- A project has specific objectives to accomplish.
- A project has performance measures that determine success and failure.
- A project can lead to spin-off projects across the organization.
- A project can be given special priority and attention.

Creating change in a change-resistant culture requires a process. I have found that using a series of projects is the best means to facilitate the transformation to a culture of change. I like to organize my Lean transformation projects as shown in Figure 2-1.

It is important to note that every Lean transformation team will be a little different depending on the size and character of your library. For large libraries a steering committee as well as a cross-functional design team is recommended. For smaller libraries, the steering committee and the cross-functional team may well be one and the same.

A project approach is the best vehicle to drive change while engaging those who are on the front lines of the process and customer service issues. It also provides a vehicle to acquire the critical ownership of those who will be most affected by change. The following sections provide a summary of the project team members' responsibilities.

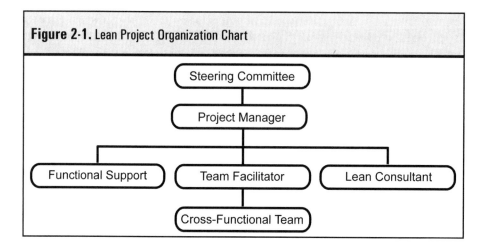

Figure 2-1. Lean Project Organization Chart

The Steering Committee

In a new library construction project, management must provide the vision, the funding, and the removal of all barriers that might prevent success. A leadership team or steering committee is often formed to keep management engaged on the project's progress as well as to resolve any issues that prevent that progress. The same is required in any Lean change effort. The primary job of the Lean steering committee is to spark a flame, nurture the fire, add fuel when required, and provide a protective cover from the rain when needed. The steering committee must make sure no one tries to smother the flame.

In a construction project, the architects, general contractor, and subcontractors are driven by a construction plan with specific milestone dates that must be presented and updated to the steering committee. These milestone dates drive the measurement of progress. Steering committee meetings are a powerful incentive to stay on schedule; no one wants to go in front of the steering committee and report project slippage. The same holds true in Lean transformation projects. When a change project team knows that they must present an update to the steering committee, it sparks great motivation to make progress.

Project Manager

The project manager is typically the primary customer of the project. For example, if a project is focused on the technical services department delivery service chain, the project manager should be the manager of the technical services department. In a construction project it is important that the project manager is skilled in project planning, staffing, budgeting, milestone date tracking, and status reporting. In a Lean project the project manager is also the primary person responsible to nurture the change culture. If the project manager does not have a great deal of experience leading projects this gap can be filled with an experienced team facilitator or the Lean consultant.

Team Facilitator

Management, represented by the steering committee, is the driving force behind any change. To ensure the change effort crosses all department and hierarchical levels, the management group should also assign a team facilitator. The team facilitator represents management's commitment to the change effort. This person should be enthusiastic, have good communication skills, be a good listener, and have a good rapport with the staff and management. The team facilitator should be empowered to communicate with anyone up and down the organization to remove any barriers to progress. It is not critical that the team facilitator comes from the department or delivery service chain on which the project is focused.

It is best if this facilitator has had some experience leading teams through a continuous improvement type project. I have served this role for many of my clients. My goal is to train team members to become team facilitators themselves. Once a series of projects is complete, many of these team members are capable of leading their own team. This is how you initiate the Lean transformation process and keep it growing.

The team facilitator should become familiar with the principles and tools of Lean and be strongly committed to reducing costs while improving customer service. The primary responsibility of the team facilitator is to coordinate the mapping of the delivery service chain, work with the project manager to guide the service performance expectations, coordinate the measurement of the current library's service performance, assess the gap in performance, establish improvement priorities, approve design changes, and initiate new Lean transformational projects.

Lean Consultant

A person experienced in the tools and concepts of Lean can help you establish the foundation and groundwork of your transformational efforts.

Functional Support

Lean projects will, from time to time, require specialized skills to overcome specific technical barriers, develop cost–benefit analyses, and implement the physical changes required. It helps to have specific people assigned to the team on a part-time or as-needed basis. Typical support functions would include the systems, accounting, and maintenance groups.

Cross-Functional Team

A cross-functional team is made up of those most affected by change. A cross-functional team is your vehicle to obtain the needed ownership for success and to educate your staff on the current process, the gap in performance, and the need for change. The team should consist of people who represent all the components of the process. This is true whether you are a multibranch library or a stand-alone library. A well-balanced team will emphasize to each member the importance of the overall service effort and their particular link or contribution to it. Take out any of these links and the delivery service chain falls apart. The best example of this is the delivery driver. Mostly out of sight and out of mind, he or she is one of the most critical links in the chain. I have formed many cross-functional teams that include a delivery driver. Often this is the first time many of the library personnel actually meet the driver. Make sure you assign to your cross-functional team at least one member from each link of the delivery service chain affected by this effort. These members will create the ownership from the bottom up that is required for success. We will discuss the service delivery chain in great detail in a later strategy.

A cross-functional team should have between four and eight full-time members; any less and it is difficult to develop out-of-the box ideas; any more and it is difficult to coordinate the team in one direction. It is the responsibility of the leader and the team to keep other staff not assigned to the project involved and engaged. This can occur through project status reports and larger brainstorming sessions. Each person who may be affected by the change should be involved in brainstorming.

Develop Gap-Driven Performance Metrics

Change occurs for a reason. Someone has recognized that the current state of operation is not meeting expectations or has not reached its full potential, so it must change. Anything can be improved, and nothing ever reaches its full potential, so change is always required. For example, the great thing about golf is that there is always the potential to score better. But if you did not know what you scored the last time you played, how would you know whether you improved?

If you embark on a journey of improvement and you do not know where you started from, how will you know what you accomplished? In the same light, if you do not fully understand or measure the thing you are changing, how do you know whether it was actually changed for the better by your actions? Performance metrics is a key management tool to help understand the need for change and to evaluate the impact of that change. It is also a very effective tool to get your staff engaged in the change process. For example, imagine two scenarios:

Scenario One

The director of the library informs the technical services manager that it is taking too long to get new books onto the branch shelves once received and wants her department to find ways to improve. The technical services manager writes a memo to her staff stating, "We are taking too long to get new books to the branch shelves. I would ask all of you to try to get more books out each day so we can perform better."

Scenario Two

The director of the library meets with her staff and they discuss that new books are not getting onto the branch shelves soon enough. The director states she would like to get new books on the shelf to be competitive with Borders. The technical services manager calls a meeting with her staff and informs them of the issue. She explains the plan to close the gap between their performance and the competition's, that the competition is getting new books on the shelf the same day or the next day they receive them. She asks her team to come back in two weeks and tell her how long it takes for a new book to get to the branch shelves in their current environment. The staff works together, and after two weeks they meet with their manager to report the results. They have discovered it takes them fifteen working days on average to get a new book from the dock to the branch shelf.

In the second scenario the staff knows two things: where they want to be and where they are now. Not only that, the staff is the group that reported to management how big a gap exists between where they want to be and where they are now. They are already a part of the change process. They have a full understanding that there is a gap, how big the gap is, and that to close that gap something must change.

Many of you may say that establishing Borders' performance as the target is too high a standard for your library. After all, you must receive, catalog, and process a book, where Borders books are for the most part shelf ready. This may be the case; however, you should set your goals high, because then and only then will the big ideas be found. If you believe the reach is too high, then create another target you are comfortable with. Perhaps a forty-eight-hour target, or a ninety-six-hour target—the point is that if you define where you are now and where you want to be you will recognize that a gap exists between the two, and you will know specifically what that gap is. If the gap is recognized, then the need to close that gap is also recognized, and therefore the need for change is recognized. Without this recognition the commitment to change greatly diminishes. If those who recognize and report the gap are the very people who will be most affected by the change, then it is the staff that is stating and perhaps even recommending the need for change.

In the first scenario, management wants improvement but they have not defined where they are now nor where they want to be. Therefore, they do not know how large a gap exists. The staff knows or interprets the desire to improve only as an edict to work harder.

Recognizing the size of the gap in performance between where you are now and where you want to be establishes benchmarks. These benchmarks are fundamental success factors in the change process. They allow you to establish performance metrics to see how successful you were in making the change. This feedback will help you learn what works and what does not; it will help those involved with the change engage in the recognition of the problem and share in the achievements of their hard work. Finally, with before and after gap performance metrics, management has the means to justify and support the funding of the effort through a cost–benefit analysis.

Drive Change through Your Cross-Functional Team

Change must start at the top, and no change can be successful without bottom-up support. A cross-functional team is the best means to accomplish this. A cross-functional team removes the departmental walls, titles, and pay grades that in the past may have inhibited communications. Many library personnel spend their entire careers working within the same department or the same branch. They have a complete understanding of what they do every day. Often they do not have a good understanding of how their particular piece of the puzzle fits into the overall service supply chain. A cross-functional team provides each member of the team an opportunity to see the delivery service chain as a whole. They can see how their link fits in the chain. Effective change cannot occur without understanding how one fits into the entire delivery service chain. Cross-functional teams remove the blindfolds and the earplugs so all the team members (all the links in the chain) can row together in sync toward one direction, with better customer service and lower costs the results.

Develop and Share Cost–Benefit Projections and Results

Scientific studies have shown that teenagers are more apt to take risks than older adults. It seems, therefore, as adults our brains are more conditioned to avoid situations and circumstances that are unknown, unpredictable, and risky.[8] Often what we fear is what we do not know. The best scary movies are all about not knowing what is beyond that door.

Change can be a scary thing because we do not know what change will bring. Will it change what I do every day? Will I still have a job? Will my friend still have a job? Will my skills become obsolete? What new skills will I need to learn? Will I lose control of things I now control? When the results of change can be predicted and communicated, change is no longer an unknown. It no longer has to be feared. If done properly, the impact of change can be fully understood by those who will be most affected by the change. The persons impacted by the change will know precisely how it will affect their jobs, their day-to-day responsibilities, and the things they control. To help a change-resistant culture accept change you must be totally transparent. Having those most affected by the change involved in the project is the best transparency.

Most often changes brought on by the Lean philosophy are changes that make processes and jobs more effective and more productive. These changes can be predicted. A process flowchart can show the flow of the current process, including its overall lead time, overall labor costs, and current task assignments. The new process can also be predicted, showing the new process flow, overall lead time, new labor costs, and new task assignments. A dollar value can be assigned to the changes. The difference between the before and after flowcharts shows the elimination of non-value-added tasks and delays. Eliminating these wasteful activities will result in more time to work on tasks that add value to your customer and a reduction in labor costs.

Lean does reduce the amount of labor time required to complete a task, and a library could choose to use these savings to reduce staffing levels. My experience, however, is that most of these savings are twenty minutes here and twenty minutes there; rarely does it result in the elimination of an entire job in one event. The best way to use these freed-up labor hours is either to fill the gap of areas where service levels are suffering or to accumulate these savings within the staff as a whole and reassign, cross-train, or consolidate job responsibilities to other areas. In the end if the time savings accumulate to a full-time person then the library could choose to reduce their staffing levels. The best means is to use natural attrition to absorb the savings.

Some Japanese manufacturers have taken this to the ultimate level. To eliminate all fear of change and to encourage employees' participation in the creation of change they have guaranteed lifetime employment. If improvements change jobs, these workers are reassigned, some of them to full-time jobs dedicated to improving other processes. They see labor as an investment to be retained, nourished, and improved.[9]

Full transparency to those most affected by the change must be first on the to-do list of the management team. If those affected by the change are involved in the design of the change itself, they are much better prepared to understand and accept the change and become a supportive voice for the effort. Finally, if they can see how these changes will affect the ability of the library to better serve their customers and they are a part of making the change, you have helped them tap into their primary purpose for working for the library in the first place.

Implement Flexible Job Descriptions

Lean process improvement involves streamlining the service process by improving the interaction between processes, people, systems, materials, and equipment. Invariably these improvements will eliminate non-value-added tasks, reorder the sequence of these tasks, and even change which department performs the task. The following words can be a death knell to any attempt to streamline a process to improve your organization: *It is not in my job description.*

Organizations place great value and personal worth on job descriptions. Hierarchical organizational charts with specific titles, descriptions, and pay grades structured within departmental walls create huge obstacles to change. Job titles and pay grades are meticulously negotiated into contracts and are often a firewall to any job title changes.

One library I work with had a separation of duties and job titles between those who receive and link books and those who process books. However, we discovered that the peaks and valleys of demand between these two groups occurred at different times. It was obvious that if the two departments cross-trained their staff and shared personnel they could better handle the shifting demands and improve their delivery lead times. However, due to different job titles and pay grades, this was not an option. Allowing pay grades to drive how a department runs can prevent an organization from improving its customer service performance. In other words, in many environments, pay grades and titles are more important than customer service.

If changing job titles and pay grade is difficult, then the current organizational structure is for the most part static. If the current organizational structure cannot change, then the processes behind this organizational structure are also static. If processes cannot be changed, then there is no change at all. Therefore, by building internal structural resistance to changing job titles an organization has created a stagnant organization that will eventually falter or fail. To improve a process, the interaction of who does what when must be able to change, and the job descriptions must be flexible enough to allow change.

If your organization already has flexible job descriptions you are well prepared to make improvements throughout your organization. However, if your job descriptions are defined in great detail or defined specifically in a contract, you have already discovered changing anything in your organization is very difficult because "it is not my job" stops progress in its tracks. If your organization is one of those unfortunate enough to have specific job descriptions, what do you do? You must change or renegotiate how job titles and job descriptions are defined and make them more flexible and adaptable to change. These job descriptions should reflect how the person can support the delivery service chain as opposed to one particular job task in a department. We will discuss the delivery service chain in great detail in Strategy Three.

Celebrate Current and Past Successes

When a new library opens it is a celebration. Important people in the community attend. A great deal of work went into building the library, beginning with the hard work to obtain the funding to the final piece of furniture placed. A celebration is certainly in order. In the same way, each time a Lean transformation team has made progress, a celebration is in order. You may not need the mayor, donors, or celebrities, but it certainly deserves the attendance of the Lean leadership team.

Celebrating at the end of a project is important to keep the momentum of change moving, especially in a change-resistant culture. It is also important to remember and celebrate past successes. If you have a great success in your pocket, you can rebut every one of these change-resistant arguments listed at the beginning of the chapter. Success breeds success. Change breeds change. Celebrate your current and past successes and you will find change becomes an expectation, not a fear.

Strategy Two Review

Libraries resist change. The keys to success for creating a culture of change lie with the people who will be most affected, whose everyday lives will change. Ownership is everything when it comes to changing a change-resistant culture. Ownership is everything to achieving success. Change is hard. It requires a common purpose, a desire to reach your full potential, an understanding of the gap between where you are now and where you want to be, and a well-disciplined project management vehicle to manage and measure the change process. It requires flexible job descriptions that support the service process and not just departmental functions and pay grades. It needs an adaptable work force and a team that can recognize and celebrate past and future successes.

Notes

1. Schreiner, Rebecca L. 2007. *"It's All About Student Learning: Managing Community and Other College Libraries in the 21st Century"* [book review]. *portal: Libraries and the Academy 7*, no. 3 (July): 392–393.

2. Price, Pamela. 2010. "Me? A Librarian?" Central New Jersey Library Cooperative. Accessed November 12. http://cjrlc.org/home/becomealibrarian/MeALibrarian .htm#PamelaPrice.
3. Ibid.
4. New York Public Library. 2010. "NYPL's Mission Statement." New York Public Library. Accessed November 12. http://www.nypl.org/help/about-nypl/mission.
5. Carnegie Library of Pittsburgh. 2010. "Mission and Vision." Carnegie Library of Pittsburgh. Accessed November 12. http://www.carnegielibrary.org/about/ mission.html.
6. Tulsa City–County Library. 2010. "Mission Statement." Accessed November 12. http://www.tulsalibrary.org/about/mission_statement.php.
7. Oklahoma State University. 2010. "Mission Statement; Vision." Accessed November 12. http://www.library.okstate.edu/about/mission.htm.
8. Nauert, Rick. 2010. "Teen Brains Wired for Risk." LiveScience.com. Accessed November 12. http://www.livescience.com/culture/teen-brains-risk-100604.html.
9. Tabuchi, Hiroko. 2009. "In Japan, Secure Jobs Have a Cost." *New York Times*, May 19. http://www.nytimes.com/2009/05/20/business/global/20zombie.html.

Strategy Three

Understand How Delivery Service Chains Drive Your Library's Performance

In Strategy Three you will learn that while libraries are organized along department lines, the customer services libraries support have very little to do with departmental organization. You will discover that your library actually consists of a number of service delivery chains that cross departments, pay grades, and supervisory boundaries. Any improvement effort must be focused on the entire delivery chain, not just on individual links in the chain. While you may optimize one link (a department), you may actually be hurting the performance of the overall delivery chain.

The Five-Dollar Tour

In my younger days as a consultant, my first day with a client would normally start with a tour of the manufacturing plant floor. At the completion of the tour, the plant manager providing the tour would almost always say, "That was your nickel tour; where's my nickel?" I always had a nickel in my pocket to respond.

To fully understand the delivery chain of service (the river), I have learned over the years that the nickel tour is not sufficient. Nickel tours tend to be geographic—you simply go from one department to the other as they happen to be connected. To fully understand an operation and how it can be improved, you must understand how the operation works from a process flow point of view; you must follow the rafters down the river through the twists and turns, over the rocks, past the stagnant water, and to the finish line.

Supply chain management is a very popular concept in the world of Lean manufacturing. I prefer the phrase *delivery chain of service*. I believe this term will soon become a popular concept for librarians. Its roots can be found in the Toyota Production System mentioned in the Introduction. Toyota recognized that their customer service performance was only as good as the weakest link. Therefore, one must understand the entire delivery chain and each of the links to improve customer service.

In the 1970s, 1980s, and even part of the 1990s, most organizations viewed their operations only as separate and distinct groups, such as outside vendors, purchasing, warehousing, fabrication, assembly, distribution, and retail suppliers. Each group or department worked individually to accomplish their internal departmental goals. This is certainly reflected in the nickel tour. Organizations see themselves as departmental, so if you give a tour, you give a tour of the departments.

Lean states that there are no departments but instead a series of links in a chain that together provide a service or a product. This delivery chain of service exists whether you are a multibranch library system or a stand-alone library. This delivery chain of service is not supported by departments but by a series of processes. Each process required to service a customer is a critical link in the supply chain. Each link works together toward the same goal: to provide the customer the best product or service, at the lowest cost, and in the shortest lead time possible.

Now, before I take a tour with any of my first-time manufacturing or library clients I take a five-dollar bill out of my pocket and say, "Instead of the nickel tour, may I have the five-dollar tour?" The five-dollar tour is given from a product viewpoint, specifically from the viewpoint of the product's individual components, until they are assembled into the final product. For the purposes of this book, I will focus on the library's internal delivery chain of service.

Join me while I re-create a tour with one of my Midwest library clients. I explained to my tour guide, the deputy director, the difference between the five-dollar tour and the nickel tour, and she immediately understood. I asked her if she would walk me through the life cycle of a typical book from the very beginning to the very end. We began our tour in the acquisitions department, where the book is first identified for purchase by a selector. We walked to the congested receiving dock, where new books are received, and we followed it to a staging area in the back corner of the receiving area. We noted that a large number of boxes were backed up in the staging area and that each box was marked with the date it was received at the dock. We also noted that some of the dates on the boxes were over four weeks old. We followed the path to a desk where the books are received and checked in, and then moved on to the cataloging department. We noted that a large number of full carts sat in front of the catalogers waiting to be processed, and many books sat on the shelves surrounding the catalogers. The dates on some of the books were less than a month old and some were more than two months old. We left the cataloging department and followed the path back to the receiving area, where a person was linking the book to the system and branches. I followed my tour guide then to the processing department, where we once again saw a large amount of full book carts waiting to be processed. Out of processing we followed the book's path to the sorting and shipping area, where many tote boxes were waiting to be sorted. We followed the tote boxes as they were lifted multiple times into the delivery truck, got in our car, and followed the delivery driver to his first branch delivery. As we drove we wondered how anyone could lift that many tote boxes day after day after day. We followed the tote boxes to a staging area and then to receiving and check-in desk. The deputy director explained how the books were sorted to one of the various book carts, and we followed the books to their final destination, the shelf.

I asked the deputy director to continue the tour by walking me through the next links in the delivery chain of service: the customer holds/reserves delivery. She showed me how a customer makes a hold request online and through the printing of the paging (pick) list report. We went to the printer to pick up the paging report containing the list of books and media that customers have placed a hold on, then to the shelf where we pull the hold, then back to a desk where the hold request is processed. A staff member wrote the destination on a sheet of paper and placed it in the book. We followed the book back to the tote box to the staging area where the delivery driver will pick it up the next morning. We drove back to the sorting area where the book was sorted, and once again followed the delivery driver as he delivered the book to the destination branch where the book is staged, checked in, has a hold slip taped to it, staged again, and then finally placed on the hold shelf. We discussed how long the customer had to pick up the book and how long the book waits on the shelf before the customer picks it up. We then followed the path of the book as the customer returns it to the book drop, checked in, staged, and picked up by the delivery driver to be returned to sorting the next day.

Then we walked through the final days of a book when it is determined it will be pulled from the shelf, discharged, delivered to the used book sales processing area, and either donated, discarded, or sold in the used book sale. We reminded ourselves that all these steps were required to support delivering one book to one customer.

The five-dollar tour the deputy director provided us follows the true process flow, the delivery chain of service. The actual library, however, is organized along departmental lines, each with their departmental responsibilities, functions, performance measures, and walls. Most librarians and library staff see a library and their services departmentally. These departments understand and focus on the performance of their own particular link(s) in the chain contained within their four walls, but they might have very little knowledge about how their link fits or affects the overall performance of the entire chain.

As I have mentioned, I continue to find that libraries have a great deal in common with my manufacturing clients. Specifically, my manufacturing clients are also organized by departments, each department having their own budget, performance measures, and culture. Physical as well as virtual walls separate the departments. These walls create barriers to communication, and with these barriers come blindfolds and earplugs that must be overcome.

These walls and the clear demarcation of departmental responsibilities they represent can create an "us versus them" atmosphere and an environment of protectionism and competitiveness. Who are these departments competing against? Outside competition? No. Often it is other departments or even one another in the same department. They compete for budget dollars and they compete for recognition.

The Lean delivery chain of service (the river) does not recognize departments, walls, or departmental goals or budgets. It recognizes only the series of links in the chain that provide a service or product to a customer.

As the Pittsburgh library tour illustrates, libraries have many links in their delivery service chain. Nearly all the links of the chain are internal to their organization and within their control. This includes purchasing, manufacturing, distribution, and retail. Very few organizations do it all; libraries are special in this regard because their business model is a merging of many business models, providing many opportunities for improvement.

An organization that sees itself as only departmental will often look within the individual departments for improvement initiatives. At times the improvements in one department actually may hurt another department's service capability. Once an organization sees the overall delivery service chain, all efforts go toward improving the service and productivity of the entire service chain, not just the individual department's performance. In fact, some departments might have to lose a little productivity to allow the entire service chain to gain in overall performance.

Your library is made up of a number of separate delivery chains of service. While the following list may not be comprehensive, it should reflect the majority of the service chains that exist in your academic or public library. *Note*: When I use the term *book*, it is meant to capture all physical materials.

- New book delivery
- Customer holds delivery
- Customer self-checkout delivery
- Digital content delivery
- Circulation desk delivery
- Children's programs delivery
- Customer book return delivery
- Customer information research delivery
- Donated book receipt and delivery
- Book end-of-life delivery
- New journal issues delivery
- Document requests delivery
- Research results delivery
- Interlibrary loan delivery

A Lean library would be driven to identify and reduce the service lead time and the costs associated with each of the delivery service chains they support.

The following were the two major delivery chains of service for this Midwest library:

* New book delivery
* Customer holds delivery

The flowcharts presented in Figures 3-1 and 3-2 provide an overview of the major steps and links for these two service chains.

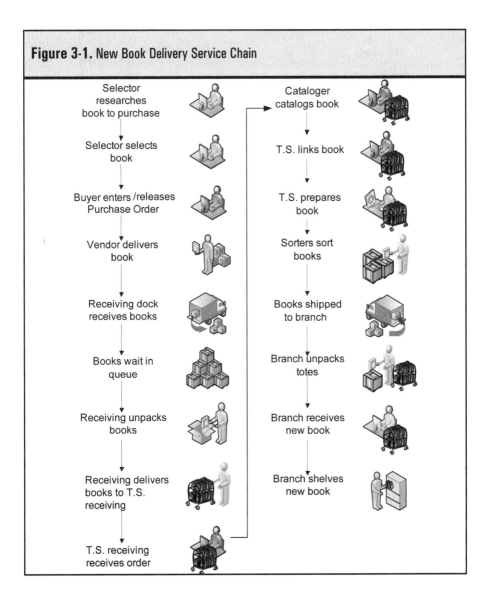

Figure 3-1. New Book Delivery Service Chain

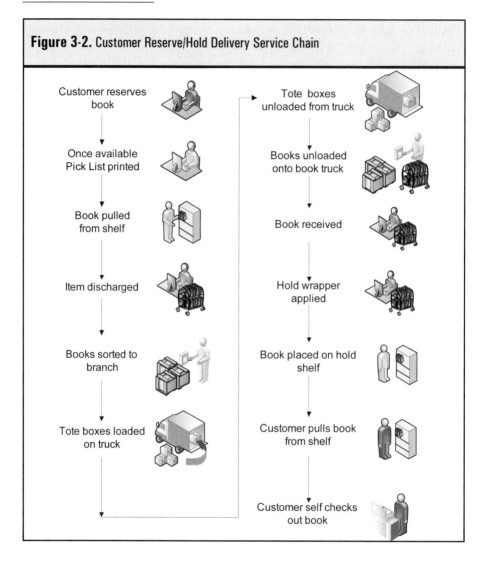

Figure 3-2. Customer Reserve/Hold Delivery Service Chain

Customer reserves book

Once available Pick List printed

Book pulled from shelf

Item discharged

Books sorted to branch

Tote boxes loaded on truck

Tote boxes unloaded from truck

Books unloaded onto book truck

Book received

Hold wrapper applied

Book placed on hold shelf

Customer pulls book from shelf

Customer self checks out book

Walk through the process and make a mental note on which departments in your library are responsible for the various links in the chain. Notice for the new book delivery and customer holds delivery that in each delivery service chain process several departments may be involved (not to mention the number of branches).

To break down the department walls a Lean library must recognize, optimize, coordinate, and manage the delivery service chains that cross department boundaries. By doing this they help their workforce remove the blindfolds and the earplugs that the walls create. The Lean transformation of your library focuses on transforming each of your delivery chains of service, but how do you do it? You have already learned one of the techniques to streamline your service delivery chains: the change methodology presented in Strategy Two. As such, you now have two legs of the stool—the service delivery chains and a methodology to change it. Now you just need to learn and apply the Lean tools that will expose and eliminate the wasteful activities, delays, stagnant water, and peaks and valleys hidden in your service delivery chains. The rest of this book is dedicated to helping you create, understand, and implement this third leg of the stool.

Revisiting our river raft race, we recognize the importance of a team working together, paddling in time and in the same direction. I am sure all of you have seen the motivational poster of the rowers in their boat during a sculls race. The premise of the poster is to recognize that all the rowers must be exactly in sync to create the highest level of performance for the entire team. If one of the rowers is a little off, the entire team suffers. Imagine if each rower had viewed the race as an individual competition rather than a team event. The boat might very well go in circles. By focusing everyone on your delivery service chains, everyone will row toward the same objective.

Strategy Three Review

While libraries are organized and managed within departments or functions, this does not truly reflect the actual flow of services you provide to your customer. In fact, department walls can actually inhibit your ability to provide low-cost, high levels of service to your customer. The survival of any business lies in its ability to effectively service their customers and to do it in the shortest time at the lowest cost possible. When the separate processes that link together to create this service are separated and managed by different groups, the forest can easily be lost among the trees. Lean teaches us to ignore the department walls and organizational chart and recognize and document what the true service delivery chain is. Then and only then can you apply the change methodology and the Lean performance tools and techniques required to improve the entire service delivery chain. Now wasn't that worth five dollars?

Strategy Four

Align Your Performance Metrics with Your Delivery Service Chains

What You Measure Drives Your Performance

On my first visit with a library client, usually in the middle of the five-dollar tour, I am often asked to go to lunch with the director of the library. Like all first social meetings the conversation usually follows the same track: weather, kids, and hobbies. Once the common and familiar topics are covered, the conversation eventually gravitates to the topic at hand, the library's service performance. In one particular lunch meeting with the executive director of a regional library in Kelowna, British Columbia, I asked her the question I ask all my clients: "So how is your library doing?" It's a simple question, broad and open ended enough to invoke all kinds of answers.

"Our circulation is up. Our budgets are tighter," Leslie responded. This is the typical response I get every time I ask this question.

This Lean lesson states:

> *What you measure drives performance; therefore, what you do not measure must not be important.*

The corollary of the lesson then would be:

> *What you measure gets most of the attention and therefore drives your priorities.*

Based on my travels and discussions with library management and staff I feel comfortable in my conclusion that budgets and circulation are the primary performance drivers of your typical library.

I researched the annual reports of a number of libraries to see what other metrics may be driving libraries. The following is a list of the common performance metrics included in a typical public library annual report:

- Number of items circulated
- Number of items in the collection
- Number of cardholders
- Number of library visits
- Number of website hits
- Number of interlibrary loans provided
- Number of interlibrary loans received

Similarly, the following are common statistics found on academic/research library annual reports:

- Number of items circulated
- Number of visitors
- Number of website visits
- Number of help desk queries
- Number of items in collection
- Number of serial subscriptions
- Number of e-resources owned/leased
- Number of reference transactions
- Number of laptop/device loans
- Number of e-reserves
- Number of items reshelved (in-house use)
- Number of electronic database searches
- Number of circulating collection volumes repaired

These are all good numbers to track, but are these really the core factors that should drive your customer service improvement goals? Do these measurements properly measure the success of your delivery service chains? Do these metrics motivate your library's workforce to improve the library's service performance?

The answer is no. These numbers are volume statistics and reflections of service performance. To drive your improvement efforts and motivate your staff, you need to know the key performance factors that actually drive customer service performance and measure the competitiveness of your library.

One of the quirks of being a process and service improvement consultant is that wherever I go, I evaluate the customer service performance of everything around me. When I visit a restaurant, grocery store, or retail outlet, I notice how long the lines are and how quickly the line moves. I look behind the counter to see how well the team works together, how many people are standing idle or talking. I evaluate the flow of the traffic, the congestion around the entrance, how they manage and store their inventory, and even where and how the supplies and support condiments are stationed.

McDonald's has caught my attention on a number of occasions. I have visited many, many McDonald's across the country. Sometimes it is by choice, and other times it is for a clean bathroom. There is a consistency to the McDonald's chains, either good or bad. Over the years I have watched McDonald's service performance both improve and degrade. Many factors have influenced their service performance: new cash registers, new kitchen designs, drive-through changes, and changes in the size of the menu are a few of these service factors. They have also changed the look and feel of the service counter personnel. Whether you like McDonald's or not, they are a great success story. In the mid-1950s McDonald's sales were around $350,000 a year. In the year 2007, McDonald's sales were $22.8 billion.[1] Can a business like McDonald's be compared to libraries? It is not as far-fetched as it seems. Let me begin by briefly exploring what drives their success.

McDonald's marketing director Joe Talcott cites brand loyalty as McDonald's most valuable asset. According to Talcott, speed of service, staff attitudes, cleanliness, and taste all have a role to play in building loyalty to the McDonald's brand. "Everything we do touches the brand,"[2] he says. "The brand is a promise; if you break that promise, you damage the brand." I decided to do my own consumer research on McDonald's. I asked a number of people I know what they thought made McDonald's successful. The most common answers were low cost, fast service, consistent from store to store, clean public bathrooms, and close by. These service factors directly influence what Talcott says is the key to building brand loyalty and, ultimately, sales growth.

While the management of McDonald's recognizes these key performance metrics and meticulously measures each one of them, they do not always meet their service benchmarks. I have seen unclean bathrooms and unprofessional service counter personnel. I have also seen the growth of McDonald's menu choices negatively impact their fast service objective. What is important, however, is that McDonald's recognizes that certain service performance factors impact their competitiveness and that when they do not meet those benchmarks, brand loyalty and sales are impacted.

At the core of these service performance drivers is fast and effective service. Did you know that McDonald's has established a service goal to fill each customer order within sixty seconds? When they fail, management reassesses their business strategy. Can McDonald's service business model and a library's service business model be compared? They do have a number of things in common:

- Libraries have low costs.
- Libraries have reliable, clean public bathrooms.
- Libraries are close by.
- Libraries are consistent from one to another.
- Libraries provide free public WiFi.

Do libraries build brand loyalty by focusing on speed of service, staff attitudes, and cleanliness? I can testify to their cleanliness and to staff attitudes. In fact,

McDonald's would be well served to look at the library world on these two service factors. Do libraries focus on speed of service? Is this an important service factor to libraries?

Speed of service was at the heart of my inquiry when I asked the library director, "How is your library doing?" How would you answer the question "Does your library provide fast and effective service?" I have asked this question to libraries across the country. The typical response I get is: "What do you mean by *service*? What do you mean by *fast*?" "What do you mean by *effective*?" It seems a simple enough question, but for most libraries it is a very difficult question. It often depends on what department you work in. Service can mean a hundred different things to different people. Even when talking about customer service specifically, many libraries struggle to define it. The following story provides us a good example.

Book Now Program

I was hired by a library to help improve their delivery system and customer service, particularly how fast they deliver books to their customers. I formed a cross-functional team represented by all those who participate in the delivery service chain. We had a technical service representative, a delivery manager, a delivery driver, a sorter, a branch manager, and representative branch personnel. "Does your library provide fast and effective service?" I asked the group, expecting the *"What do you mean by customer service?"* question in return. "Oh yes," the branch manager said. "Our Book Now program is designed to assure fast service."

I was thrown a bit off track. They had a ready answer to my question, and it was driven by this Book Now program. "What is this Book Now program?" I asked. "Why don't you visit my branch tomorrow and you can see for yourself," the branch manager replied. The next morning, with coffee and video camera in hand, I was ready to see the Book Now program in action.

The branch manager guided me toward an information circulation desk near the middle of the library. She pointed to a staff member behind the desk. "Any customer can call us on the phone at any of one of our branches," she said, "and we will immediately see if the book is available and go pull that book for them while they are on the phone. They can then come in and pick it up."

At first I thought this was an interesting concept. What better service can you provide than immediate results over a phone call? Even McDonald's might be proud. The branch manager introduced me to the employee working at the information desk and then left me to observe the Book Now program. As soon as she left, a line formed at the desk.

Putting the video camera down to make the employee more at ease, I sat down at a chair behind the desk and watched the events unfold. Two people were waiting for assistance. She helped the first person, who left satisfied. The second person stepped to the front of the line when the phone rang. The employee picked up the phone.

"Book Now, may I help you?" she said to the caller. She nodded her head. "Yes, let me check to see if it's on the shelf." She propped the phone to her ear and checked the computer for the status of the book the customer had requested. The man in line had a confused look on his face.

"Yes, we have it on the shelf. Could you hold for a moment while I go get it?" she said. She wrote the information down on a slip of paper, left the information desk, and went in search for the book. The line grew to three people. The man in front of the line looked very frustrated. She returned to the phone after searching the shelves while patrons waited.

"I'm sorry. The book is no longer on the shelf. Could I find another book for you?" She asked. "Okay, thank you, and please call Book Now again." She turned her attention to the man waiting in line. As she was helping him, the phone rang again: "Book Now, may I help you?" she said. "Yes, let me check." She repeated her previous routine while the waiting patrons grew more frustrated.

The line had now grown to four people waiting. After retrieving the phone customer's book, she checked it out, printed the hold slip, wrote the customer's name on the slip, opened the book, placed the hold slip in the book, closed the book, wrapped a rubber band around the book, and placed it in a pile to be placed on the hold shelf later. Then she turned her attention to the first man in line, the one who had waited more than five minutes for her attention. He did not look very happy. As she helped him, two of those in line gave up and left the library.

That night I examined the library's circulation data. What I learned surprised me. In nearly every library system I have worked in, the number of customer holds/reserves represent on average 13 percent of their total circulation. This particular library's online holds/reserves were about 2 percent of their total circulation. The only assumption I could make was that the Book Now program was so effective and successful that no one wanted to use the online reserve system.

After further investigation I learned that the Book Now program had originally been put in place for those who had a hard time using the computer, specifically the elderly. This made sense to me, but what I learned next did not. The Book Now program was a free service; the online reservation system cost a customer twenty-five cents per hold. Many customers probably searched for their book online and then called in their request.

Twenty-five cents is not a lot of money, but apparently it was enough to change the habits of nearly all of their library customers. How else can you explain the 2 percent usage rate versus my other library clients' average of 13 percent? How fast was this library's customer service? Clearly this is a complex question.

Did they provide fast customer service to the individual on the phone? Yes, they most certainly did. Did they provide fast service to the individuals waiting in line for help? No, they did not. Are they delivering books to their customers faster with the Book Now program as opposed to the online reserve and delivery program? I would offer that they are not. Is the Book Now program a more efficient and effective delivery system than the online reserve system? I would say, most definitely not. It would be as if McDonald's decided to have the same person take your order, fry the burger, warm bun, put the dressing on it, wrap it up, ring it up, and hand deliver it to you. This individual certainly would have provided me great individual attention, but it would have taken a very long time. If McDonald's adopted this approach they would have to hire ten times the people and ten times the equipment they have now. It certainly would not meet the sixty-second rule.

The library's cross-functional team and I evaluated the Book Now program and the online reserve program and we determined that in the end, customers would be better served by discouraging the Book Now program and encouraging the online reserve program. The amount of staff time it took to answer the phone and immediately pull the book off the shelf was sucking the air out of the service system. The paging process for online reserves coupled with a division of labor concept was a much more effective service model. This ultimately provided better and faster service to their customers at a lower cost. Prior to these changes, this library's circulation was on a downward trend, dropping 5 percent from 2003 to 2007. Since changing the policy (as well as going to a floating library concept) this library has completely reversed the trend, with circulation growing 5 percent in just one year. The number of holds filled has doubled in the same period. I applaud their original objective; however, overall customer service was better served by shifting the focus to the more streamlined, more effective online reserve system. But let us get back to our question.

How do libraries define fast customer service? For the most part, nearly every library system I have worked with does not define nor measure customer service. Many do, however, ask their customers for feedback through a voluntary questionnaire survey. One survey asked this question: How would you rate the quality of service we provided you: (1) below my expectations, (2) met my expectations, (3) exceeded my expectations.

The Association of Research Libraries has taken the survey approach to a new level using the LibQUAL+ program. The survey asks a series of thirty-five questions to gauge and compare customer satisfaction. Questions on the survey include, for example, "Does the staff of your library instill a high level of confidence?" and "In general, are you satisfied with the library support for your learning, research or teaching needs?" The survey ranks from one to nine, strongly disagree to strongly agree. While this is useful information to your library and well worth the effort, does it actually define for your library what drives your future success? What do you do with this information? What corrective actions do you take if we are below expectations? If the survey says your customers are mostly satisfied, does this mean you should not try to improve your current service levels?

Libraries must do much more than conduct generic customer surveys; they must dive deep into their delivery service chains and identify those key events that drive customer loyalty and customer satisfaction. Libraries must go beyond measuring just reflections of customer service with surveys and volume statistics; they must measure what actually drives customer service performance, and this is best represented and defined by using the delivery service chains.

Define Delivery Service Chain Performance Measures

Effectively delivering high-quality services or products to your customer should be one of the most important topics of any viable business. It is the primary event that drives success or failure. However, if you are measuring only reflections of what truly drives your performance are you truly being effective in changing behavior? If McDonald's measured only one thing—total customers served—would that help them improve customer service? What if total number served dropped this year versus last? Would they know what had caused this drop? Would they know whether they truly were effectively and competitively servicing their customers? Could they identify where they were falling short?

Delivery service chains represent the actual series of processes that support your customer service activities. Therefore, measuring the performance of the delivery service chains should directly measure how well you are servicing your customers. But how do you measure your delivery service chain performance? The first step is to define each of your delivery service chains paths to your customer (see Strategy Three, pp. 36–38). For each of the delivery service chains you need specific performance measures to tell how each one is performing.

In some cases delivery service chains will take different paths to get to the customer, and in those cases the chains may need to be split and segmented to be properly measured. For example, the customer holds delivery chain can take three separate paths once the book is on the hold shelf:

- The customer takes the book from the hold shelf and uses the self-checkout.
- The customer takes the book from the hold shelf and takes it to the circulation desk for checkout.
- The customer goes to the circulation desk, asks for a book, and a branch staff member finds the book on the hold shelf located behind the circulation desk and checks the book out for the customer.

You must therefore define your delivery performance metrics along each of these paths, as shown in Figure 4-1.

The main trunk of the tree can be defined as a service delivery chain, and each branch of the tree can be defined as a service delivery chain as well. Combining the results would provide you with a picture of the entire service chain.

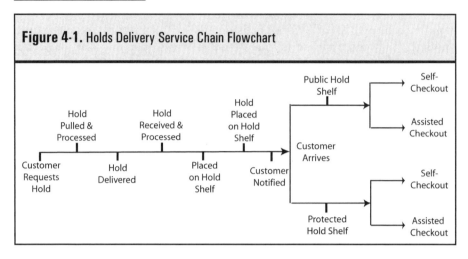

Figure 4-1. Holds Delivery Service Chain Flowchart

Now that you know how to define and present your delivery service chains, how will you define what performance measures you want to capture? To accomplish this I use one of my favorite Lean tools, the balloon diagram. I have used the balloon diagram technique for more than twenty-five years, and I believe it is the simplest and most effective tool Lean offers. I use the balloon diagram to guide my cross-functional teams to break down a complex problem into simple concepts and elements. In the middle balloon I state the issue or question I am interested in and I ask the team to populate (pop) as many balloons as they can. I do not let the team stop until at least five balloons are populated. See the sample shown in Figure 4-2.

For example, while working with the New York Public Library (NYPL) I used the balloon diagram to help them define what kind of performance they expected out of their delivery system, specifically from an internal view. Remember this was a cross-functional team with branch personnel, drivers, technical services staff, collection development staff, and circulation staff. The following internal delivery balloon diagram, Figure 4-3, presents the results.

Obviously, the group did not stop at just five balloons; they kept going until they had filled sixteen. They were very motivated to improve their delivery performance, and they appreciated the opportunity to not only define the delivery issues they were dealing with but to identify how they wanted the delivery system to perform. This was a good session, and it helped the team get into the flow of the change process. I asked the team to look at the delivery process from an internal point of view. It is not surprising to see internal issues such as number of totes, reliable vehicles, coordination, and delivery timing mentioned. These are common themes. We eventually addressed each of these internal issues because either contributed or impeded on their ability to service the customer. However, my objective at this point was for NYPL not just to look from an internal view but an external view as well, specifically from the customer's perspective. Following the same approach, I asked the team to pop-

Figure 4-2. Balloon Diagram Sample

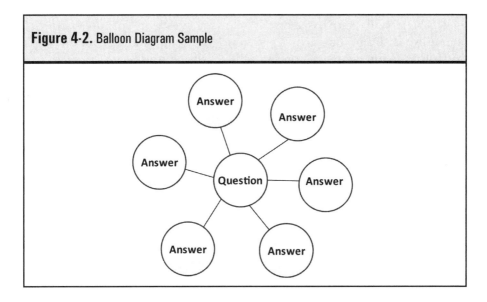

Figure 4-3. Delivery Service Balloon Diagram

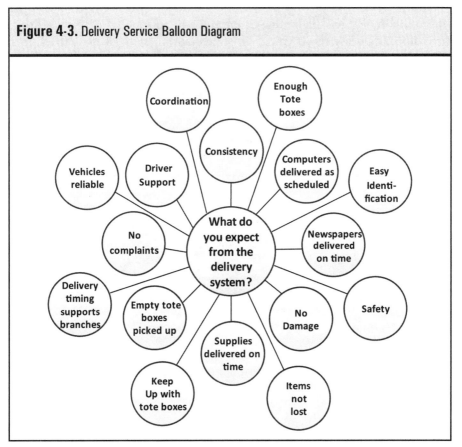

ulate a balloon diagram based on the following question: What does your customer expect from your delivery system? The following customer delivery balloon diagram, Figure 4-4, presents the results of this session.

Of course it would be most effective to have this session with a sampling of customers, but because we were under a tight time frame we moved forward using the perception of what the customer wanted. (Often the perception can be tougher than reality.) The list by NYPL is a good start; however, to be a truly effective Lean metric, each of these measurements must be defined in terms of a true measurable target. In addition it needs to be aligned with a delivery service chain such as the one presented in Figure 3-1 in Strategy Three. Over the past ten years I have conducted numerous sessions similar to the NYPL session, and as a result I have been able to develop a list of common measurements that are aligned with the delivery service chains of a typical library.

To help you define your service performance measurements I will take a few of the service chains discussed in this book and tell you how to measure them. As you read through the list, I must caution you that these measurements are for guidance only. You should develop your own list, defining what customer service means to you in your own unique library environment, and your cross-functional team must develop the list through their own series of brainstorming sessions to gain full understanding and ownership of your library's performance metrics.

Notice that each measurement defines a specific objective or target, a measurable unit of performance, and at what percentage performance the task is to

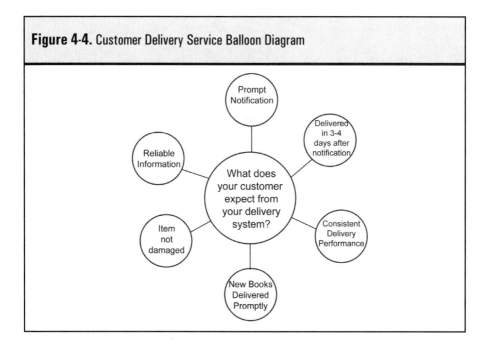

Figure 4-4. Customer Delivery Service Balloon Diagram

be achieved. Also note, for each of these performance metrics, "book" refers to any item that needs to be delivered to a customer.

Customer Hold Request Delivered to the Hold Shelf
- Customers can find and reserve a book online and select the branch of their choice within five minutes 95 percent of the time.
- Information regarding the book's availability and delivery status is accurate and up-to-date 99 percent of the time.
- Information on where the book can be found on the shelf is accurate 98 percent of the time.
- Once a book is available, the book is delivered to the branch of choice within forty-eight hours 99 percent of the time.
- The book is delivered in the same high-quality condition in which it was pulled 99 percent of the time.
- Holds received from delivery are on shelf within four hours 100 percent of the time.

Customer Self-Checkout Books Pulled from the Hold Shelf
- Customers can quickly and easily find their book on the hold shelf in less than thirty seconds 99 percent of the time.
- Customers can quickly and easily check out their items within sixty seconds 95 percent of the time. (Grouping six at a time.)

Customer Assistance at Circulation Desk
- The 3:1 service standard is achieved 95 percent of the time. (No customers will have more than two customers in front of them in line.)
- Once at the circulation desk, customers can quickly and easily have their items checked out to them within sixty seconds 95 percent of the time. (Grouping six at a time.)
- Customer questions at the circulation desk are handled correctly within three minutes 95 percent of the time.

Book Returned Is Received and Delivered Back to Owning Branch
- Internally owned items received are returned to the proper shelf within eight hours 100 percent of the time.
- Items returned are processed and placed on the next-day delivery truck 98 percent of the time.
- Returned items to be sent to other branches are returned, delivered, and shelved within twenty-four hours 99 percent of the time.
- Books with activity in the past two years match computer records 98 percent of the time.

Many of these items address services that most public libraries perform, but what about academic libraries? For a research/academic library, the service metrics take a slightly different focus. Flinders University Library in Adelaide, Australia, provides a great example of embracing Lean performance metrics. The following metrics are presented in Flinders' annual report.[3] *Note*: Flinders is not a client of mine, but I was thrilled to find a library embracing the concepts of Lean performance measures.

- New course books will be displayed on "new book" shelves forty-eight hours from receipt.
- New journal issues will be processed within twenty-four hours 100 percent of the time.
- Alterations to journal holdings will be processed within twenty-four hours 100 percent of the time.
- Loans will be reshelved within twenty-four hours 97 percent of the time.
- Document delivery requests from our patrons will be ordered within twenty-four hours 98 percent of the time.
- Document requests from external libraries will be processed within twenty-four hours 98 percent of the time.
- Flexible delivery requests will be processed within twenty-four hours 98 percent of the time.
- Catalogers will process twenty-two volumes on average per day.
- Book orders will average five weeks' delivery lead time from major suppliers.

Flinders has developed a great list to drive their performance, but I would like to add a few of my own to guide research/academic libraries who want to embrace the Lean transformation journey. Lean performance measures must go beyond the walls of the library and embrace the customer's window of service expectation. Using a balloon diagram approach, you can add on to the excellent list from Flinders, but with a customer's viewpoint. The following performance measures can be added to the list:

- Online research tools will be available 24/7 both on and off campus 100 percent of the time.
- By using common language and terms, peer-reviewed articles will be made instantaneously available to customers using a one-click search box 98 percent of the time. (For more discussion, see Strategy Nine.)
- If the information customers seek is not available, with one click customers will be directed to other information sources that will provide them the information they seek 85 percent of the time.
- Critical physical materials not currently available to the customer through the library will be provided to the customer within five days 95 percent of the time.

The 3:1 Standard

I previously mentioned the 3:1 service standard regarding circulation-assisted checkout. The 3:1 standard originates from the QuikTrip Corporation. QuikTrip is a convenience store with its headquarters in Tulsa, Oklahoma. If you do not have a QuikTrip in your hometown, I am truly sorry. When I travel the thing I miss the most (with the exception of my family) is the convenience of my local QuikTrip store.

Growing up, my friends and I rode our bikes to the corner QuikTrip. Just like McDonald's, I have watched them grow since I was a kid. There is no retail organization that I am more impressed with than QuikTrip. They have repeatedly been voted on Fortune's 500 Best Corporations to work for. In the nearly thousands of times I have visited a QuikTrip I have never been disappointed by their service.

I would highly recommend you read Chester Cadieux's book *From Lucky to Smart, Leadership Lessons from QuikTrip* to learn what has made them successful. Mr. Cadieux summarizes a key service performance metric that drives their corporation: the "3 to 1" standard:

> The "3 to 1" standard is a measurement of the number of visible employees, the number of employees at the register(s) and the number of customers at the checkstand. We strive to staff (and perform) to prevent any customer from waiting behind more than two other customers. An integral part of the standard is servicing 3 customers in 1 minute or less. We've done studies of the transactions that we know that making change on an average cash transaction takes approximately 2 seconds while the average credit card takes 5 seconds if the customer is required to sign a receipt. Of course, speed should never take precedence over accuracy and attitude. We know that customers don't mind waiting in line a reasonable amount of time as long as people at the registers are hustling.[4]

Again, I can personally testify that QuikTrip takes these service performance metrics seriously. I would recommend your library tailor your own 3:1 standard into your service performance metrics.

Percentage Measurements of Achievement

You may have noticed that your benchmark performance metrics always end with a statement such as "98 percent of the time." You might ask, why not 100 percent? It is a great goal, but it does not recognize the times when a customer is better served if you do not just focus on being fast. As Mr. Cadieux says, "Of course, speed should never take precedence over accuracy and attitude." This is what I call "service tolerance." Each library must decide how much tolerance they want to add to a particular service metric. You certainly do not want to send the message to your circulation staff that no matter what, they must check out a customer in sixty seconds. There are circumstances in which customers are better served if more than sixty seconds are used. However, for the majority of time, perhaps 95 percent of the time, you do want to effectively and courteously check the customer out within sixty seconds.

However, there are metrics where you do want to achieve 100 percent. For example, delivering holds within forty-eight hours 100 percent of the time might very well be a realistic service goal. Anything less than 100 percent reflects a missed opportunity or a problem in the process.

Some of you may be resistant to the idea of using metrics in your library. After all, you are an organization dedicated to customer and community service; using metrics to statically reflect the kind of services you provide the customer may not tell the whole the story. For example, I worked with one branch manager who emphasized customer relations above all else. She believed the personal touch was the key to good customer service. This personal touch often led to conversations about family, vacations, and the weather. The checkout times often exceeded two minutes and at times approached five minutes, and the number of people in line often exceeded QuikTrip's 3:1 standard. Their customers may be better served with a faster checkout process. However, this is not for me to decide—each branch and each library system must find the balance they are most comfortable with and the one that most affects how well they service their customer. Regardless of how you define good customer or community service, developing a means to measure these elements will provide you feedback and a means to improve this particular service effort. Metrics should not be seen as a cold, harsh management technique but a tool to empower your staff to improve the value of the service you provide your customer and community.

In this section I have discussed the importance of service metrics and examined how your library can define these metrics. Any good Lean measurement should be tied directly to the delivery service chain; this is the process that is providing your services to the customer. I have not focused on department performance measures but on overall delivery service chain performance. In some cases the measures are department specific, but management should never lose sight that the delivery service chain crosses all walls, functions, and boundaries.

Even though you now understand how to define Lean performance measures aligned with your delivery service chains, you are far from done. What good are these measurements if you do not actually measure them? The next section will provide you effective Lean tools to measure your newly defined service performance metrics.

Measure Delivery Service Chain Performance

This strategy is driven by the following Lean lesson:

What you measure drives performance.

Thus far in Strategy Four you discovered that your performance metrics should be defined along the terms of your delivery service chains. By defining these measurements you are sending a signal to your staff that these service measurements are important. Now you must not only define these measurements; you must actually measure them. The good news is that delivery service performance metrics can be easily measured by one of four techniques: service chain time logs, process performance audits/logs, time studies, or mystery shopper feedback. The following sections describe each of these measurement techniques and provide examples of how these techniques can be applied to your delivery service chain. Implementing these measurements may seem daunting, but they are in fact fairly straightforward.

Service Chain Time Logs

The service delivery chain crisscrosses departments, branches, and delivery personnel. How can you possibly measure the entire service delivery chain? How can you determine if you are actually delivering customer requests within forty-eight hours 95 percent of the time? Measuring the performance of an entire service delivery chain is a bit more complex than a single event time study. It requires a log that travels with the targeted service item and a coordinated effort from everyone in the chain. By using a traveling event time log, this actually is not too difficult to accomplish.

As we defined on page 48, delivery service chains can take different paths to ultimately deliver a book to the customer. Specifically, for the customer holds request and delivery service chain, the path splits after customers arrive to check out their books. Nonetheless, there is a beginning point (customer requests hold) and an ending point (book is checked out to customer). You may choose to simplify your collection log by capturing only these two events. By doing so, you will have collected the data to determine whether you are delivering customer holds to your customer within forty- eight hours 95 percent of the time. You may also choose to collect information for each path of the chain as well as each link in the chain. The more detailed the information you collect the more valuable the information will be for you and your team. Once again, detailed or not, it is not too difficult to accomplish. Working with the Baltimore County Public Library (BCPL), our team did a wonderful job developing and implementing a holds/reserves log tracking system. Here are the steps we followed:

Step 1

After reviewing priorities of service, BCPL management and I selected the holds/reserves delivery service chain as our first measurement project.

Step 2

We flowcharted the holds/reserves delivery service chain. We used this flowchart to identify the key touch points in the service chain. The flowchart for the holds/reserves delivery chain was presented in Strategy Three. These were the touch points we identified for the log:

- When the pick list (pull list) is printed
- When the item is pulled
- When the item is sorted
- When the item is received at the branch

- When the items hold slip is applied
- When the item is put on the shelf

For simplicity's sake, we did not include the time the customer placed the hold and when the customer actually checked out the hold. We decided to use a worst-case assumption for the front end, which includes the assumption that the customer placed the hold right after the pick list was run. We also decided to measure the customer checkout process as a separate delivery service chain, as the book can sit on the hold shelf for days before being checked out. Once again, you should tailor the log to your specific environment and where you want to place your focus and message of importance.

Step 3

I helped BCPL acquire a set of repositionable sticker labels. These labels are like Post-it notes, but they have the glue applied to the entire back of the label. The labels stay firm on the item, can be easily removed, and do not leave a sticky residue on the book. Caution: Some removable labels out there will leave a residue, so be careful which ones you use.

Step 4

We developed a template on Microsoft Word to produce the information we wished to collect. The template was printed on a sheet of sticky repositionable labels. Figure 4-5 provides a sample of the service log label we used.

Figure 4-5. Service Log Label

```
Pick List Printed:          Received @ Branch:
Initial:                    Initial:
Time ___:___:___            Time ___:___:___
Date ___/___/___            Date ___/___/___

Item Pulled:                Hold Slip Applied:
Initial:                    Initial:
Time ___:___:___            Time ___:___:___
Date ___/___/___            Date ___/___/___

Item Sorted:                Placed on Hold Shelf:
Initial:                    Initial:
Time ___:___ ___            Time ___:___:___
Date ___/___/___            Date ___/___/___

Notes:
```

Step 5

We developed and communicated the rollout plan. BCPL's Technical Services Manager sent out a memo to all branches and departments supporting the holds/reserves delivery service chain stating the objectives of the service logs and what was expected from each group. She instructed those in the circulation group who pull the books to apply a label at the time they pulled the book. Once applied, the label became the collection log driver. Whenever anyone in the delivery service chain found a label on a book, it would tell them they needed to log the time they first touched the book. We decided to randomly apply labels to 10 percent of the daily pull totals each day for two weeks. For example, if we had two hundred holds per day, we would randomly apply twenty labels to the items in that run.

Step 6

Run a pilot. For the pilot I suggest using 5 percent of the number of pages. So if your pick list averages two hundred pages, you would initiate ten collection labels. Track the ten as they go through the process and refine your procedures accordingly.

Step 7

Run the study. For two weeks BCPL applied the labels. The technical services manager was on standby to answer any questions that might come up. She randomly visited the various touch points, making sure the logs were being completed properly.

Step 8

Collect and report the data. I developed the spreadsheet to collect the data and to summarize the performance measurement results for each touch point as well as for the overall performance.

With this information we were able to determine how well the BCPL's holds/reserves delivery service chain was performing against their stated objectives. Figure 4-6 presents the result of the service performance study.

BCPL had established a goal of a twenty-four- to forty-eight-hour delivery performance 95 percent of the time. BCPL understood there was a gap between where they wanted to be and where they were; however, after this study they fully understood how large the gap was. Specifically, they delivered books in less than forty-eight hours 46 percent of the time, within seventy-two hours 88 percent of the time, and 12 percent of the time they took more than seventy-two hours. This did not include the added one to twenty-four hours between when a customer placed a hold and the pick list was printed or how long it took for the customer to check out the book from the hold shelf. The BCPL management team was not satisfied with this performance, and we focused the team on how we could do better.

You may be fortunate enough to have an integrated library system (ILS) that actually tracks the key collection points in your holds/reserves delivery ser-

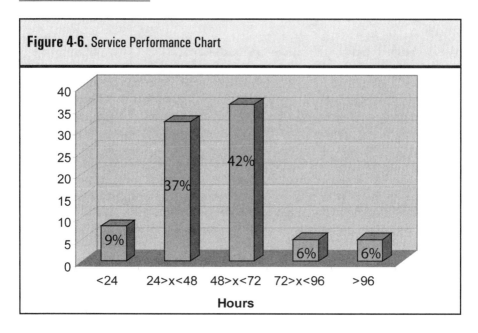

Figure 4-6. Service Performance Chart

vice chain, thus eliminating the need for a log. This was the case at NYPL. Working with the ILS group we developed custom reports to determine NYPL's actual delivery performance. Figure 4-7 presents the actual results of the in-transit aging study.

Once again, the NYPL management team knew they were not meeting their stated objective, which is why the improvement project was initiated. However, after these performance metrics were developed they realized the gap was larger than they expected, and it became a major priority to close that gap. (What we measure is important; what we do not measure must not be.) NYPL's goal was three to four days delivery 95 percent of the time. They were actually performing at six to eight days 76 percent of the time and seven to twelve days 20 percent of the time. Once again we set out to close the gap.

These are two examples of how to measure the overall lead-time performance of delivery service chain. The following key performance measures can be measured using this approach:

- If a book is available, the book is delivered to the branch of their choice 99 percent of the time within forty-eight hours.
- The book is delivered in the same high-quality condition in which it was pulled 99 percent of the time.
- Books received without a hold are returned 99 percent of the time to the owning branch within forty-eight hours of being returned.
- Books with a hold are transferred to the targeted branch within forty-eight hours.

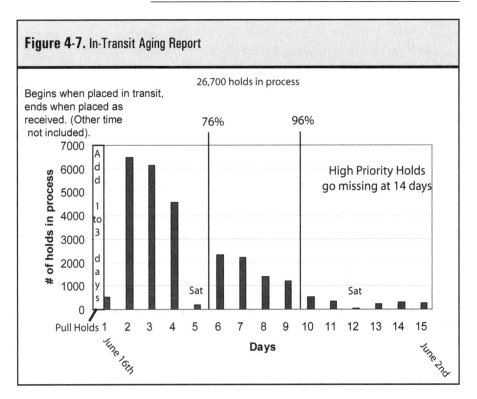

Figure 4-7. In-Transit Aging Report

- Books received without a hold are returned to the owning branch within forty-eight hours of being returned 99 percent of the time.
- Holds received from delivery are on shelf within four hours 100 percent of the time.
- Returned items are returned to the proper shelf within thirty-six hours 100 percent of the time.

For an academic/research library the following key performance indicators can also be measured by using the delivery service chain time log approach:

- New course books will be displayed on "new book" shelves forty-eight hours from receipt.
- New journal issues will be processed within twenty-four hours 100 percent of the time.
- Alterations to journal holdings will be processed within twenty-four hours 100 percent of the time.
- Loans will be reshelved within twenty-four hours 97 percent of the time.
- Document delivery requests from our patrons will be ordered within twenty-four hours 98 percent of the time.

- Document requests from external libraries will be processed within twenty-four hours 98 percent of the time.
- Flexible delivery requests will be processed within twenty-four hours 98 percent of the time.
- Book orders will average five weeks' delivery lead time from major suppliers.
- Critical physical materials not currently available through the library will be provided within five days 95 percent of the time.

Process Performance Audits/Logs

I had the privilege of working with the outreach group at the Tulsa City–County Library. The objective of the project was to improve the number of clients they could serve without increasing the number of staff members required to support the increase. Using a balloon diagram we established our service goals and identified our major issues. During the project the outreach manager identified his number one issue: not being able to find the book on the shelf where the ILS system said it should be. This was greatly affecting their ability to service their customers. Not only were they not able to fill the customer request, they had to go back and do a great deal more work to cancel the request, work with the customer to select a new item, and, if they had time, determine why the book was not on the shelf where it should be.

We set out to find out how big a problem it was and what we could do about it. Our team knew that the shelf accuracy was creating a problem in their service delivery chain, and I surmised it was causing problems in the holds delivery service chain for the rest of the system as well. It was not about the trucks or the drivers. The problem was on the shelves themselves. The outreach group (or the circulation group) could not deliver a hold in their targeted time frame if the book targeted to fill the hold was not on the shelf where it was supposed to be. This is a major issue for many libraries attempting to meet the twenty-four- to forty-eight-hour delivery 95 percent of the time. If the book is not on the shelf in the first place, then they lose the service opportunity before ever getting out of the service gate.

We all knew that shelf accuracy was our problem, so we decided to perform a shelf audit. Shelf audits should be a familiar concept to library management and staff. The difficulty with a shelf audit is that you are trying to take a snapshot of a moving target. The more movement there is, the more blurred the image. If the ILS system says a certain book is on this shelf but it is not there, then it could be that a customer is sitting in the lounge reading it (which is why it is always good to do the audit and to work your pick list before the library opens). Everything is tied to the accuracy of the ILS system. If your ILS system tells a customer a book is available and it is not available, you have failed in your customer service promise.

Our cross-functional team performed a sample audit of the number of times a hold could not be filled (see Figure 4-8 for results). After a few days of work

Figure 4-8. Audit Results

Audit	Science Fiction	Fiction		Total
Total Collection	78	3967		4045
Total Audited	78	195		273
On Shelf	67	182		249
Found	59	172		231
Not Found	8	10		18
Not Found %	12%	5%		7%
Required Search	11	48		59
RS%	16%	26%		24%
Missed Cataloged		6		6
MC %		3%		2%
Not in System	0	11		11
ET %		6%		4%

we found that 18 of the 273 (7 percent) could not be found and 59 of the 273 (22 percent) required a search. Therefore, nearly 30 percent of the items were not immediately found. We knew then that we had a serious shelf accuracy problem and that the only way to achieve our service goal was to fix that problem.

After further research we found that six items had been miscataloged and eleven items were not in the system, so therefore 6 percent were cataloging or system issues. The rest (78 percent) of the items had been misshelved.

I quickly learned that the misshelving issue was outside the control of the outreach department. The primary source for the outreach collection was the large print collection, which was shared with the central library circulation group. The outreach group was not responsible for shelving books; this was the responsibility of the central circulation group. This is a perfect example of a service delivery chain that crosses department boundaries and responsibilities.

Once we discovered how large a problem we had, we expanded the cross-functional team to include the circulation group and the catalog group. Once the catalogers reviewed and cleaned up the miscataloged items and the circulation manager retrained the circulation staff, the group's find rate increased to 90 percent. Not as good as it needs to be, but a vast improvement.

This example shows how a process audit can provide you performance measurement feedback on how your delivery service chain is performing. The following additional delivery service chains can be measured using the process performance log and audit approach:

- If a book is available, the book is delivered to the branch of choice 99 percent of the time within forty-eight hours.
- Information regarding the book's availability and delivery status is accurate and up-to-date 99 percent of the time.
- Online research tools will be available 24/7 both on and off campus 100 percent of the time.

Time Studies

As a college student I was hired as a summer intern for a local Oklahoma manufacturer. My job was to perform time studies to help establish their company's standard cost of production. For an aspiring industrial engineering college student, it was the perfect summer job. It was perfect except for a guy named Harry. Harry worked a big brake machine press in the lower shop area, and he did not like anyone with a stopwatch. Not surprisingly, I was assigned to the lower shop area and Harry.

Harry did not want to be timed, and he was good at avoiding it. When he saw me coming he would invent some kind of problem. The machine needed maintenance, the parts were not right, or he had to go to take a break. But I was persistent; I came day after day after day. He finally ran out of excuses and I conducted my time study. Harry, however, was not through with me yet. A few days after the time study I walked into the break room for lunch as firecrackers exploded all around me. For the next few weeks, when I least expected it, the fireworks show would repeat itself. Harry got a lot of laughs out of it, as did the production supervisors. Eventually, however, it did backfire on Harry. The plant manager caught him one day and that was the end of Harry.

If done correctly and with respect, time studies do not have to be painful, nor do they need to result in fireworks; in fact, they are easy to do, very informative, and even a bit fun. Figure 4-9 presents the result of a circulation desk checkout time study I recently completed for branches within the Tulsa City–County Library (TCCL).

Remember our goal of a sixty-second service cycle at the circulation desk? The sample data presented tells TCCL how well they are performing during a certain period of time on a certain day against that goal. How would your group perform this time study? Keep it simple and understandable. Here are some easy steps to guide you.

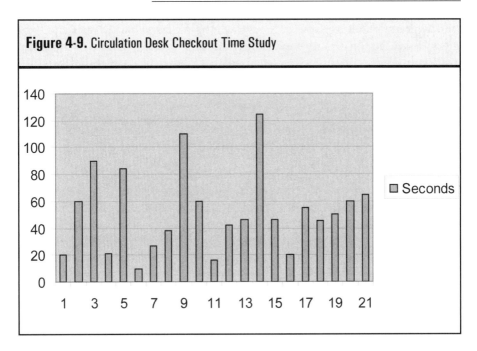

Figure 4-9. Circulation Desk Checkout Time Study

Step 1

Select a pilot. I would recommend you select the self-checkout station as your pilot. The pilot is intended to get you comfortable with taking time studies.

Step 2

Decide who is going to take the time study. One person should be assigned to do the time studies for all branches. This provides a level of consistency and independence.

Step 3

Develop your plan. Your time study should be as simple as possible. You do not want to try to collect too much information in one sitting. Many things are going to happen while you are taking a time study. For example, when I first attempted to take a time study, I was constantly starting and stopping what I was doing because a number of other things were happening at the circulation desk that I was not there to measure. People were waiting in line and asking for computer assistance and directions, the circulation desk clerk was being interrupted by phone calls, fines were being paid, and all of this was happening at three stations at a time. In fact, most of the tasks we established as performance goals were happening at once. I quickly determined that I had to stick to one type of service measurement at a time. I learned to focus my efforts to measure the time it took to check out items at one particular circulation station only. I could have measured how long someone waited in line before being serviced, or how long it took to pay a fine, or how long a person had to wait while the clerk answered the phone, but it is near impossible to capture all of this information in one setting. Once I measured that one station for about forty-five minutes I moved to the next station and repeated the process.

Step 4

Select a time. I would recommend selecting the branch's busiest time. For example, if Thursdays between 4:00 p.m. and 6:00 p.m. are the busiest times of the week, select that time frame. Why? Because I would want to know how the library performs in its toughest situation, not when everything is slow.

My mentor once said, "It is not how well you perform when things are easy; it is how well you perform when things are tough." If I get a good snapshot of this library's performance during the few hours it is the busiest, then I have a pretty good idea of how it is performing overall.

Step 5

You need a stopwatch. Many cell phones now have stopwatch capability.

Step 6

Notify the branch manager about the time study. Have the branch manager discuss the effort with their staff. She or he should explain the goal of the time study and what it will be used for. Even better, have them read this book. The staff should be encouraged to work at a normal representative pace.

Step 7

Select a location in the branch to observe. Find a table where you can easily see the area you are observing. Try to do the study without drawing attention to yourself. A library is a good environment where you can blend in, either at a work table or a computer station.

Step 8

Develop your time study log. You can tailor the log any way you want depending on what you are going to measure. An example log is presented in Figure 4-10.

Once completed, simply divide the total number of events that exceed the targeted performance measure by the total number of events, and you now have your percent service performance result. (If there are more than six items, divide the items into groups and divide the total time by the number of groups.)

For our sample on this station, we identify six events out of twenty-six samples that went over the sixty-second target. This translates into a 73 percent service performance. Time studies are an effective tool to the Lean librarian. The following performance measures can be collected using the time study approach:

Figure 4-10. Circulation Desk Time Chart

Branch	Observer	Approved		
Kaiser	John Huber	Glenda		

Date	Day	Station	Support Staff		Start Time
15 - Jan	Thur	One	Eric		3:00 pm

Obser-vation #	Total Time (sec)	# of Items	> 6 Split	> 6 Split	> 60 Sec
1	20	3			
2	60	4			
3	90	3			1
4	21	2			
5	84	5			1
6	10	1			
7	27	1			
8	38	3			
9	110	1			1
10	60	7	30	30	
11	55	3			
12	16	1			
13	42	5			
14	46	1			
15	125	10	63	63	2
16	46	5			
17	20	4			
18	55	5			
19	45	2			
20	50	3			
21	60	2			
22	65	6			1

- Customers can quickly and easily find their book on the hold shelf in less than sixty seconds 99 percent of the time.
- Customers can quickly and easily check out their items within sixty seconds 95 percent of the time. (Grouping six at a time.)
- At the circulation desk, customer wait time is less than three minutes 95 percent of the time.
- Once at the circulation desk, customers can quickly and easily have their items checked out to them within sixty seconds 95 percent of the time. (Grouping six at a time.)
- Customer questions at the circulation desk are handled correctly within three minutes 95 percent of the time.
- Responses to computer questions are completed correctly within three minutes 95 percent of the time.
- Catalogers will process twenty-two volumes on average per day.
- By using common language and terms, peer-reviewed articles will be made available to me using one click search box 98 percent of the time.
- If the information I seek is not available, with one click I will be directed to other information sources that will provide me the information I seek 85 percent of the time.

Once the data are out there, your branches may want to know how they are stacking up against one another and may get a bit competitive. Since this is most likely going to happen, let us discuss a few cautionary notes to avoid any fireworks:

- Make sure everyone understands the purpose of the time study.
- Explain which delivery service chain metric we are measuring.
- Give everyone fair warning to the time and day you will be conducting the study.
- Emphasize to those being studied to work at a normal pace. Do not try to speed up or slow down.
- Make sure whoever does the study does it fairly and consistently.
- Do not impede on the people trying to do their job while doing the study.
- Make sure you perform the study at comparable time frames, such as at peak load times or at the same times during the day.
- Communicate the results after you complete the study. Do not keep them a secret for only a few to know.

Mystery Shopper Feedback

Again I turn to QuikTrip for best practice benchmarking. Some customer service metrics, like "service with a smile," cannot be measured with a stopwatch or a time log. However, they can be measured through random observation and long-term sampling. QuikTrip does this with their mystery shopper concept.

Chester Cadieux states:

> Unlike most of our employees, we don't promote our Mystery Shoppers from within since we want them to view the stores purely from a customer's perspective. The identities of the Mystery Shoppers are unknown to the store employees. . . . Because our customers' needs and expectations are constantly changing, we update the Mystery Shopper inspection points at least once a year. Our goal is to make high quality customer service natural to our employees so they don't think twice about greeting people with a smile and asking them to come back. Inspect what you expect and pay for performance—it's actually quite straightforward.[5]

Since I am initially a stranger to many of my clients, at times I can temporarily serve as a mystery shopper. I try to visit one of the branch libraries before any engagement starts to observe the service culture of the library. I would highly recommend libraries institute their own mystery shopper program, allowing the service performance metrics you developed lead the way. Make your log in such a way that the metrics being observed can actually be measured, counted, and compared over time as opposed to performance impressions on a scale of one to ten.

Strategy Four Review

Congratulations! You have now defined the metrics that drive your circulation numbers and your library future success, and you now have the means to measure them. You have sent a clear signal to your library staff on what is really important to your library. You are well on the way to becoming a Lean library.

Notes

1. Druce, Chris. 2008. "McDonald's Reports Rise in Global Sales." Caterersearch. com, January 29. http://www.caterersearch.com/Articles/2008/01/29/318551/ McDonalds-reports-rise-in-global-sales.htm.
2. Ligerakis, Maria. 2001. "Making Your Marketing Count." *B&T Today*, December 5. http://www.bandt.com.au/news/a4/0c0098a4.asp.
3. Flinders University Library. 2010. "Annual Report 2006." Flinders University. Accessed November 12. http://www.lib.flinders.edu.au/pub/anrep/2006.pdf.
4. Cadieux, Chester. 2008. *From Lucky to Smart, Leadership Lessons from QuikTrip*. Tulsa, OK: Mullerhaus.
5. Ibid.

Strategy Five

Transform Your New Book Delivery Service Chain

To understand the Lean transformation strategy, we compared the Snake River to the River Lean. In this comparison, the river represented the service delivery chain, and we drew stark contrast between a service delivery chain that is difficult to navigate and a service delivery chain that is easy to manage. We discussed how the River Lean dramatically outperforms the Snake River in delivery lead time, safety, and, subsequently, cost.

In Strategy Five we will apply the principles and concepts of Lean to one of the most important functions of your library: the new book delivery service chain. Specifically, I will show you how the concepts of Lean can dramatically transform your technical services department performance. We will examine in detail how Lean can be used to attack those design and management issues that created Snake River in the first place.

Throughout Strategy Five I will refer to an actual project with Tulsa City–County Library (TCCL) during which we successfully redesigned and transformed their new book delivery service chain. This project is a perfect example of a library that once rafted the Snake River but now is enjoying the calm, steady waters of the River Lean.

Note: While Strategy Five is focused on a medium-sized multibranch library (twenty-five branches), the Lean concepts presented can be applied to multibranch and stand-alone libraries as well. To receive and process new books, the steps represented in this case study must be completed regardless of size. In addition, the lessons learned from this case study can be applied to processes throughout your library's delivery service chains.

Before we embark on the lessons of Lean in Strategy Five I will provide some background of the TCCL new book delivery service chain transformation project. Let us begin with the organization and kickoff of the TCCL project, including understanding the project objectives and common organizational purpose, practicing a top-down and bottom-up management style, initiating projects to drive change, and developing gap-driven performance metrics.

Establish a Common Organizational Purpose

At the beginning of every project I try to establish a clear understanding of the project objectives and organizational purpose, specifically what the client hopes to accomplish from the project. The management team of TCCL had plans to relocate the entire delivery and technical services departments from the central library to a separate location. The management team had asked me to help the department develop a new layout for the new location.

After a few days of working with the group I discovered the following:

- The technical services department estimated that they were more than a month behind in delivering new books to the branches, and this was causing great stress in the department as well as management (not to mention many unhappy branches and customers).
- The receiving department had experienced huge peaks and valleys of incoming new books at the dock. The department was not able to match staffing levels to the huge swings in incoming product. The collection development group was unhappy with the acquisition group's ability to receive the books they ordered, and the acquisitions group was unhappy with the peaks and valleys they were receiving at the dock. In addition, vendors were not happy because TCCL was behind in processing and paying invoices.
- Due to the nature of the department and the length of employment for many of the department's staff, management felt that creating change within this department presented some challenges.

Looking at it from a delivery chain of service point of view, I found this project was much more than a simple new layout for a new location. A new layout alone would not entirely address the core issues driving their current backlog. The focus therefore expanded to not only the layout and process flow but to smoothing the incoming peaks and valleys of the department and creating a culture of change, flexibility, and cooperation. Therefore, the driving organizational purpose for this project was not only to move to a new departmental layout in a new location but to dramatically reduce the backlog and transform their service performance capability.

Practice a Top-Down and Bottom-Up Management Style

Change cannot happen without the strong leadership and direction of the management team. It also requires a strong bottom-up approach and commitment of those who will make the change actually happen. Working with the management team, we established the project direction and organized a cross-functional project team to create both a top-down and bottom-up approach.

The objectives of the project were as follows:

- Identify opportunities to improve the current technical services work flow and processes that will result in a reduction in lead time, improved productivity, and the ability of the department to manage peak loads.
- Develop a new process flow and layout for the technical services department in preparation of the relocation.
- Create a cohesive delivery chain of service.
- Create an atmosphere of teamwork between the various groups and management.

We created a steering committee and a cross-functional team, and I acted as the team facilitator and lead design engineer. The steering committee consisted of the collection development division director, the technical services manager, the associate director of technology, the technical services supervisor, the processing supervisor, and the facilities director. The cross-functional team consisted of acquisitions staff representatives, technical services staff representatives—linking, technical services staff representatives—processing, collection development staff representatives, receiving/unpacking representative, and branch representative (part time).

Initiate Projects to Drive Change

To gain ownership from those who must support the change, we used the cross-functional team as the primary driving force in the project. The project approach was developed with the team as follows:

- Define the technical services group delivery performance goals.
- Understand the gap in performance between goals and current environment.
- Evaluate the current work flow, staffing, and process procedures as well as lead times, work flow, and productivity improvement opportunities.
- Understand and develop a "peak load management" plan that would plan and prepare for the large seasonal surges of incoming books to be processed. This would include evaluating the impact that the collection development selecting habits have on the ordering process and the fluctuations in the receiving process.
- Based on the previous accomplishments, develop a new layout and process flow for the new technical services facility.
- Evaluate and recommend new performance tracking measurements for the department.

- Develop a cost–benefit analysis of any recommended changes.
- Develop a work plan to guide the implementation.

Develop Gap-Driven Performance Measures

The most critical step of every Lean project is to establish a common understanding of where you want to be compared to where you are, thus defining the gap in current performance. In this case study the primary customers of the technical services group are the branches themselves. While the library patron is the ultimate customer of their work, the branches are the primary customer they deliver to (and hear complaints from). At our very first cross-functional team meeting I asked the group to help me define their customer service from the branches' perspective. Figure 5-1 presents the service balloon diagram results of our brainstorming session.

Each of these measurements is important; however, for the scope of this project and to address their backlog situation we focused our efforts on the internal delivery time of the technical services department itself. The group stated that they would like to receive, process, and deliver a new book to the branches

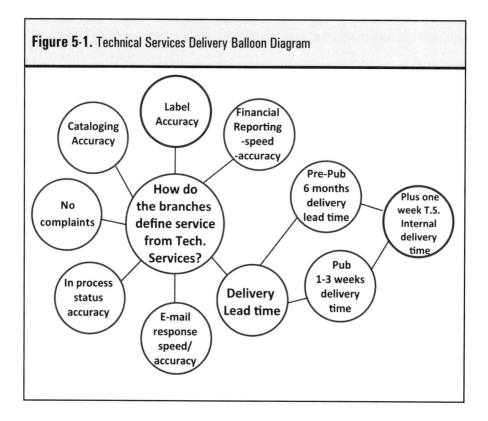

Figure 5-1. Technical Services Delivery Balloon Diagram

within a week. The question was, how large a gap existed between where they wanted to be and where they actually were?

The group, of course, knew they were behind, but they did not know how large the gap really was. They were desperately trying to get out of their backlog situation with methods they had used in the past. This project provided them an opportunity not just to make changes around the edges (such as overtime) but to change fundamentally how their processes worked and how their process design responded to delivery challenges. In this stressful environment, getting ownership to make the required changes while at the same time working long hours to eliminate the backlog situation would be difficult. I relied on my Lean Change Methodology and began by helping the groups understand in specific terms how their current performance stacked up against where they truly wanted to be.

Note: There is a very important management lesson in this project. Organizations often find themselves in backlog or "capacity bubble" situations. Many try to fight through it with overtime or temporary extraordinary measures. Management is often reluctant to add a core change project on top of this intense environment. My experience tells me that this "capacity bubble" time frame is exactly the time period you want to take on a project to correct the core issues, because you can fully examine the issues that caused the problem in real time. More important, the management and staff, even though a bit frazzled, are highly motivated to correct the issues so that they will never occur again. An outside project manager should be brought in to alleviate some of the project leadership pressure. This way management and staff can leverage their time using the outside project manager while handling the crisis. Part-time staff assistance can also be valuable during these periods of intense activity to help the staff cope with the backlog as well as the new project initiatives.

In this particular case study the gap was quite obvious and was represented by the number of carts waiting to be processed and the number of boxes yet to be unloaded. After the team established their service performance goal, I asked for my infamous five-dollar tour to get a better understanding of the issues and the backlog. As a part of the tour the supervisor of the acquisitions group gave me a quick walk-through of the department. She showed me stacks of boxes in the dock area, explaining that the delivery group was frequently complaining that the boxes were overflowing into the delivery work area and causing problems for the delivery group's work flow. She showed me the stacks of boxes in the technical services receiving area waiting to be unpacked. The receiving group had written a receipt date on each box. She showed me full carts of books and media in front of the first receiving station and in between each process step. The cataloging department had shelves full of books and media waiting to be cataloged. Full carts also sat in front of the processing workstations. She pointed out routing sheets that traveled with each individual book title or media item title. These routing sheets became the basis for our gap analysis study.

Using the routing sheets I examined each and every cart to develop a snapshot of where the books were staged and how long they had been in the process. Figure 5-2 provides a presentation of the staging areas I found.

Table 5-1 provides a time log of how long the carts had been in the process. The chart shows that roughly 4 percent of the in-process (staged) items were more than five months behind, 20 percent were more than three to four months behind, 23 percent were between one and two months behind, and 55 percent were three weeks into their cycle. It appeared that most items would eventually fall two to four months behind. If we had more time we may have created a

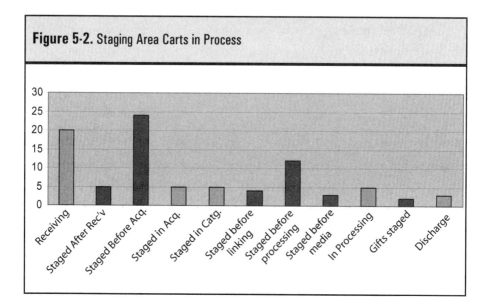

Figure 5-2. Staging Area Carts in Process

Table 5-1. Cart Backlog Analysis

Week In Process	% of Total
20–24	4
15–19	8
10–14	12
9–12	4
4–8	19
3	8
2	19
1	27

log showing the projected total lead time through the department for each set of books or media items, but this would have taken a great number of resources, and the snapshot was sufficient for our purposes in recognizing the size of the gap.

We also counted and dated the boxes waiting to be unpacked in the receiving area. This is presented in Table 5-2. The boxes represented 40 percent of the total items to be received and processed through the department. These boxes would not be unpacked until empty carts were made available.

From this snapshot of the department we learned a number of things:

- New books/items wait unpacked up to three weeks before their receipt is acknowledged. (Vendor complaints of late payments confirmed this issue.)
- Once unpacked, the books take from three weeks to five months to be shipped to the branches.
- Cataloging receives large carts of books to unload. They place the books on shelves and then batch them into like items to facilitate productivity. This added days and at times weeks to the process.
- Carts are not processed first in/first out but by preference of staff or priority of the book.
- The department's estimate of being only a month behind was inaccurate; they were actually two to five months behind.

While everyone knew that they were behind, seeing the gap documented on paper drove the point home. They now knew they were delivering books in months, not weeks. As overwhelming as it seemed, our team had taken a huge step in recognizing the need to make core process changes.

As this information was presented to the cross-functional team, a number of the members made suggestions for improvement, and some used the opportunity to vent their frustrations, which is a natural part of the process. I explained to them that we were developing an understanding of how the process performed and that the problem-solving part of the project would come later. I did not want them to start thinking of solutions until they had a thorough understanding of the Lean principles necessary for the solution phase.

Table 5-2. Unpacked Boxes

Week	% of Total
3	33
2	44
1	22

The following section provides a detailed discussion of each Lean principle I introduced to the team and used to transform TCCL's new book delivery service chain performance.

Implement Lean Design Principles

This section explains each of the Lean principles that transformed TCCL's Snake River into the calm, smooth-flowing River Lean. We will discuss:

- twists and turns (congestion in the flow path);
- stagnant water (staging areas);
- white water (large batches);
- large waves (peak loads);
- forks in the river (departmental layouts versus work cells);
- hidden rocks (imbalances); and
- dead-end coves (expediting).

Twists and Turns (Congestion in the Flow Path)

On the days I plan to take my five-dollar tour I do a great deal of walking. After reviewing the service supply chains presented in Strategy Three, you can imagine how much time and effort is required to follow a book's path to a customer. When I begin detailed analysis, I flowchart not just the overall flow but the flow of each individual product. I wear sneakers instead of business shoes that day.

The technical services department of TCCL provides a perfect case study to discuss the issues of Snake River versus the benefits of River Lean. After the department supervisor and I had successfully documented the current performance of the process and the team fully understood the gap in performance between where they were and where we wanted to be, we focused our efforts on better understanding their overall new book delivery service chain.

We flowcharted each product's delivery service chain within the context of the technical services department. Figure 5-3 presents the path of the pre-processed media materials as they flow through TCCL's technical services department. Follow the path and notice how the product twists and turns its way through the department. This was my first visual indication that this group was rafting the Snake River.

Snake River reared its ugly head for each product flow supported by the technical services department. Figure 5-4 presents the path of all the products flowing through the technical services department. It is not difficult to develop these flowcharts; in fact, I used PowerPoint. Or you can use pencil and paper to develop the flow diagrams. What is important is that you develop a visual understanding of your process.

Figure 5-3. Preprocessed Technical Services Flow

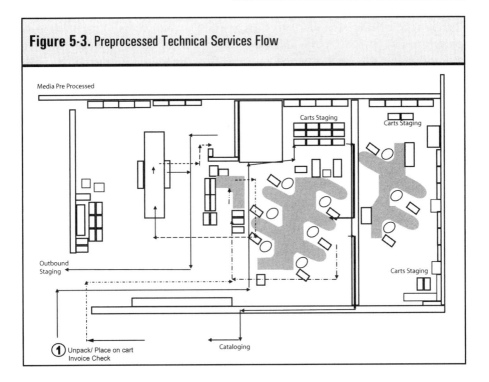

Figure 5-4. Tech Services—All Flows

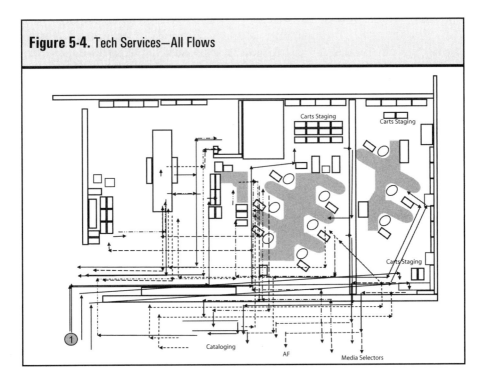

Just as it is difficult to navigate a river that has many twists and turns in its path, it is also difficult to manage a department that has many products twisting and turning as they flow through the department. As I showed the flowcharts to the department manager and her team, their eyes became wide, and a few even laughed. Their laughter was not an attempt to make fun of their department or themselves; it was recognition of what they live through every day. Up to this point there had been some resistance from the staff and some apprehension on changing a process they were comfortable with. Their current process was developed by a well-liked and respected member of the management team, and exposing the process to critical review created some apprehension from staff and tension in the management team. This is not unusual, and it contributes to a change-resistant culture. However, once the team could see a visual representation of what they were actually doing, this fear began to evaporate. The manager who was originally involved with the design embraced the changes enthusiastically, allowing the tension to be removed and the momentum to be changed. I give this manager a great deal of credit for the eventual success of the project.

I explained to the department manager and her crew that all the different products that flow through her department compete for limited staff time, book carts, and staging areas. As they compete they create bottlenecks, logjams, and peaks and valleys throughout the department, which are true indicators of Snake River.

Lean teaches us that you should be able to stand in the middle of a process and easily see where everything is. Managing the product and processes of this department was like trying to unravel sticky spaghetti on a slippery flat plate; it was difficult on a daily basis to predict what would flow into the department or what would come out. It could not be properly managed, no matter how skilled the manager. This complex process design was failing the staff, the management team, and the customer.

The first philosophy of Lean is to eliminate the twists and turns. A product should flow in a simple series of lines reflecting the path of a "U." Figure 5-5 reflects the ideal Lean U flow path.

An ideal Lean flow path starts at the bottom of the U and flows around the U, ending near where the product started. A manager or supervisor should be able to stand in the middle of the U and instantly see how the process is working and flowing. No twists and turns, but a visual understanding of the product paths and flows. The first objective of our new design was to have each product follow this U path as it moved through the department. The results of this effort are discussed in a later section.

Stagnant Water (Staging Areas)

In a library environment, stagnant water in Snake River represents staging areas. Staging areas allow the inventory of books to pool and become stagnant (and at times gather dust). Once a staging area is created it is an open admis-

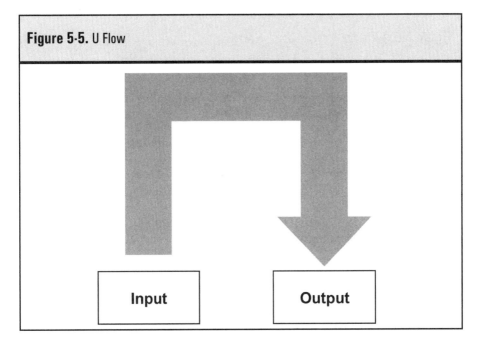

Figure 5-5. U Flow

Input

Output

sion by management that the department will be rafting Snake River, not River Lean. In Figure 5-6 the staging areas are highlighted in black boxes.

Notice that the staging areas for the carts take up as much space as the workstations. This shows that the product does not flow smoothly through the process. If the products were flowing down River Lean in a U flow, it would be in one smooth, constant flow, no stops and starts and no staging areas. Staging areas mean that the water will sometimes flow fast, sometimes flow slow. Staging areas hide inefficiencies and imbalances between workstations and staff, and they are an open admission by management that they have designed into the service flow imbalances and delays or, in terms of Lean, waste.

Working with the cross-functional team, we studied why each staging area was created and we attacked the causes of each, specifically imbalances between workstations, large batch processing, and poor scheduling. This is a difficult phase of any Lean effort. Staging areas are a means for staff and management to buffer themselves from core process performance issues. As long as these staging areas remain, the process falls into the "we can get by with moderately effective results" category. This is because factors contributing to mediocre performance are hidden by staging areas; in most cases no one even knows there are core performance issues to be addressed. At TCCL the contributing factors hidden by staging areas were large batch sizes and the large workload imbalances between stations, specifically between unpacking and receiving, acquisitions and receiving, cataloging and linking, and cataloging and processing. In addition, the staging areas were designed into the process to allow staff members to leave their desks and select the next cart they wanted to work on. This approach not only prevented the smooth flow of first

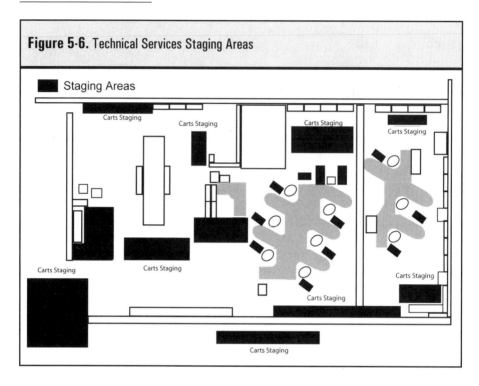

Figure 5-6. Technical Services Staging Areas

in/first out material but created potential for extended social events as they walked around the department (not a popular finding).

Lean teaches us to eliminate the staging areas, expose the workload imbalances and inefficiencies, and develop root-cause solutions to the problems that created the staging areas in the first place. In a Lean design a product flows into a process and continues to flow without being staged. There are no twists and turns, no staging areas. A Lean process flow has an input and an output and nothing stops or is staged in between.

For example, a book cart does not enter the U until the first station has finished with it, and the second station does not take the book cart from the first station until the first station is finished with it, and so on down the path of the U. The cart flows from one station to the next in one smooth line, never having to be staged. This is Lean's pull philosophy that we will discuss further in Strategy Ten. The scheduling policy for which individual staff members select which cart to work on next is the exact opposite of this first in/first out Lean principle. If one station is faster than the other it becomes immediately obvious and allows management to address how to balance the work flow better.

To eliminate these staging areas we must attack the imbalances between workstations, reduce batch sizes, and create a more flexible staff with flexible job descriptions that can adjust to the small surges that will naturally occur (even in River Lean). We will address these issues in the following sections.

White Water (Large Batches)

When rafting Snake River large waves can create a rough ride and can even overturn a raft, plunging the rafters into dangerous white waters. Lean teaches us that large batches have a similar effect on a process flow. Large batches are the number one enemy of Lean, and they prevent us from having a smooth, U-shaped process flow. Large batches force a process to have staging areas because large batches do not flow smoothly through any process. TCCL was significantly burdened by large batches.

During one of our cross-functional team meetings I explained to the team how large batches force them to raft Snake River and create staging areas that create long delivery lead times. It was a difficult concept to embrace, so we took some time to understand what Lean teaches about large versus small batches.

Lean teaches that there is a direct link between large batches and long lead times; the larger the batch size the longer the lead times, the smaller the batch size the shorter the lead times. To prove my point, I showed the cross-functional team a simplified version of their technical services department. I asked them to assume their group received and linked three types of items: item A, item B, and item C. I also asked them to assume our simplified technical services department had two departments: the first received and linked the items, and the second performed the physical processing. Figure 5-7 is the production schedule I presented to the team for our simulated large batch department.

Based on this schedule the group will deliver their first A items on Wednesday morning of the second week, their first B items the Friday morning of the second week, and their first C items on the Monday morning of the third week. In the large-batch scenario, the second department would not receive the A items from the first department until Monday of the second week, and they would not ship any of the A items until Wednesday morning of the second week.

Large batches lengthen the period of time between the different types of material events and therefore extend the time it takes for the different types of materials to be completed. However, small batches will create an opposite pattern. In Figure 5-8, I present a schedule that reduces the batch sizes from 500 As to 100, 500 Bs to 100, and 250 Cs to 25, and the result is shorter lead times.

You can see from the preceding diagram that smaller batch sizes create a different result from large batch sizes. Using a small-batch philosophy, the first department delivered A, B, and C items to the second department on the morning of the first day. The second department received, processed, and was able to ship all three items before noon of the first day. This is a 90 percent reduction in delivery lead times for all three products.

Lean teaches that you should constantly drive to reduce your batch sizes. Larger batches force items to be pushed back further and further away from the customer. The larger the batches you create the longer your delivery lead

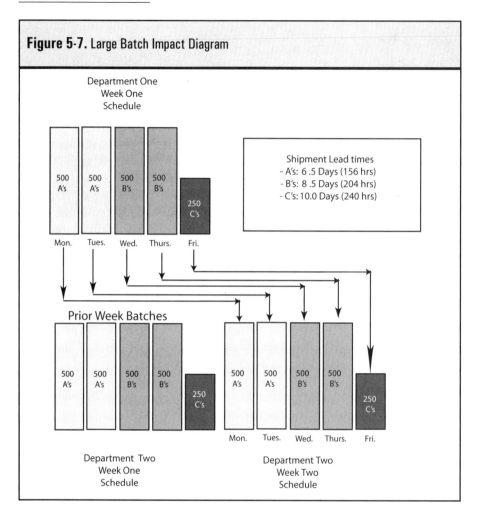

Figure 5-7. Large Batch Impact Diagram

times will be, the smaller the batches you create the shorter your delivery times will be.

What drives this desire to create large batches? The answer is labor efficiency. Most department supervisors and managers see output per hour as a key performance metric. The more you batch like items together, the argument goes, the more efficient you are and ultimately the more output per hour you produce. TCCL's cataloging department was adamant about batching items together because of labor efficiency. Even if this did improve efficiency, it does so at what cost? Would you trade a little less labor efficiency for a dramatic cut in delivery lead times, perhaps even a reduction in lead times by as much as 90 to 95 percent? Large batches are the result of placing too much emphasis on labor efficiency and not enough on delivery lead times or the performance of the delivery service chain as a whole. Don't get me wrong—Lean is all about labor

Figure 5-8. Small Batch Impact Diagram

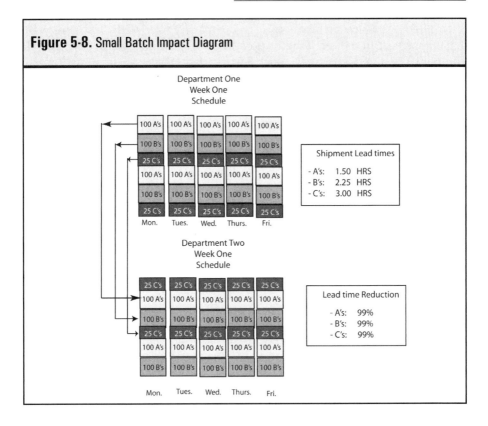

efficiency and productivity, but only after the process itself has been stream-lined, batch sizes reduced, and lead times reduced. Improving labor efficiency should become a priority only after flow paths, batch sizes, and lead times are improved, or, in other words, only after the entire service delivery chain performance is totally understood and streamlined.

Batching is a common occurrence in a library environment. Customer hold requests are batched to optimize the paging process. Books are batched during the check-in and delivery. Books from the drop box are batched, checked in, then batched again for shelving. Customer holds are batched before shelving. While batching items together may make sense in some cases, you should always ascertain if batching is extending service lead times. Have you ever considered that the first book dropped in a drop box will most likely be the last book taken out? And the larger the drop box the longer the first item will stay at the bottom. In a small drop box that first book will be processed quickly. The smaller the drop box the quicker the books will be processed.

The TCCL technical services improvement project provides a perfect case study of the impact of large versus small batches. During the project we brainstormed ways to reduce the large backlog of new books in the receiving area. There were close to fifty book carts completely filled with new items wait-ing somewhere in the receiving or processing work flow. This did not include the many unpacked boxes at the dock that had date stamps up to four weeks old.

The cross-functional team and I examined the process and found that in one example it took nearly a half day for one receiving staff member to receive and empty an entire book truck. We also found that the catalogers were experienc-ing peaks and valleys of workload based on the large batches flowing to them from receiving.

What was the solution? Lean tells us big batches are bad and small batches are good. I would like to take credit for our breakthrough, but I had nothing to do with it. During one of our cross-functional team meetings we discussed ways to improve the receiving and linking process. One team member asked whether we could stop putting books on the lower shelf of the book cart be-cause they were difficult to reach. She felt that productivity would improve if they did not have to bend over constantly. I liked the idea because, from a Lean perspective, reaching for the lower shelf as opposed to the higher shelf was a non-value-added activity as well as an ergonomic safety issue. The team and management agreed, and we decided to give it a try.

We asked the receiving staff in the delivery room to stop filling the bottom shelves of the book trucks, and they gladly agreed. (It kept them from bending over all the time as well.) After weeks of getting through the large bubble of backlogged carts already fully loaded, the team started processing the carts with only the top two rows filled. The results were immediate, obvious, and dramatic. Yes, the productivity of the receiving clerks (and the unpackers) im-proved slightly because they were not reaching and bending over as much, but what was really important was that the books were flowing faster and smoother to the catalogers and beyond (even with all the twists and turns still in their de-partment layout). We had inadvertently reduced the batch size that was flow-ing through the entire department. Suddenly books were arriving at each station more quickly, in smaller batches, and with fewer of the surges that large batches create. No longer were the catalogers being hit with a bunch of full carts all at once; now they were receiving smaller batches more frequently. More important, the books were being delivered to the customers faster, and the receiving clerks' productivity was much higher, an improvement that went beyond eliminating the need to reach to the bottom shelves. Perhaps it was the increased variety of work, or perhaps the staff paced themselves with larger batches. I am not sure of the reason, but I do know that small batches are good and large batches are bad.

Lean teaches us to process small batches in a first in/first out approach. By unpacking the boxes in the order they are received and by loading only two to four shelves of the carts, this group practiced the concepts of Lean, even though we did not know it at first.

Looking at the entire delivery service chain, the controlling batch—the larg-est batch in the overall service delivery chain—is the delivery truck. While we may create smaller batches in the technical services department, the delivery truck is making only one trip per day per branch and therefore is controlling the batch size at one day of full production. Does that mean you should process batch sizes of one day through the technical services department as well? If the receiving clerks accumulate one day's worth of items to process before sending them to the cataloging department it would re-create the large peaks and valleys that created Snake River in the first place. Even if the controlling batch is larger than the batch you are processing, it is okay. The smaller the batch size the better your department's links in the chain will perform. The objective of the technical services department is to deliver one day's worth of received books to the delivery department. This is accomplished by delivering a series of first in/first out smaller batches during the day. The fact that the delivery department eventually batches one day's worth of work onto the truck does not change the technical services objective of small batches. (This, of course, challenges you to reduce the batch size of the delivery truck by increasing the number of deliveries per week or even per day.)

The good news was that using some overtime and implementing smaller batches we started reducing the size of the backlog bubble. The problem, however, was that we did not fully address what was the primary creator of the backlog bubble in the first place: the peaks and valleys of product coming into the receiving dock. For example, if two weeks of production were received at the dock in one day, it did not matter how well our layout or small internal batching was, how well our product flowed, or how balanced our workstations were; product would be staged and backlogged before we could even get started.

Who controls the number of items coming into the dock on a daily basis? The collections development group does. Balancing the ordering pattern and the technical services processing capacity will be discussed in the next section. However, to set the plate, the ideal Lean scenario is that the selectors would deliver one day's workload to the receiving dock per day and the acquisitions, cataloging, and processing departments would process small batches throughout their departments to create smooth quick flows, delivering the items they received that day to the delivery truck the same day or following day. This is an aggressive goal, but goals should be aggressive.

This is a very important lesson of Lean. Your library should design into its process smaller and smaller batch sizes and balance those batch sizes across the delivery service chain to reduce lead times and smooth the flow. They should also aggressively attack the controlling batch size of the overall delivery chain to fully achieve ultimate lead time performance. It is a critical step to transform Snake River into River Lean.

Large Waves (Peak Loads)

Peak loads are exactly what they sound like, and they can have more of an impact than large batches do on creating backlog bubbles and longer delivery lead times. Peak loads are periods of demand that are far above the norm. Peak loads create more problems for my manufacturing clients than any other single issue. It causes just as many problems for libraries. There are many examples of peak loads in the library environment. Delivery drivers have peak loads on Monday and Tuesday due to the backlog of reserved and returned items on Saturday and Sunday. These peak loads create their own peak loads on Tuesday and Wednesday for the branches. Branches have peaks and valleys of customers from day to day and hour to hour. Libraries have peak loads of customer hold requests on Mondays followed by valleys on Wednesdays. For every library project I have worked on, peak loads is the one consistent and difficult factor. They are unfortunately accepted by most libraries as a way of life.

Lean states that there should be a smooth flow at all times. The smoother the flow, the more balanced the operation, and the shorter the lead times. Peaks and valleys cause backlogs, backlogs cause batching, and batching causes extended lead times and costs.

Continuing the case study, the team discovered that peak loads were one of the prime reasons they were rafting Snake River. At the end of the fiscal year the department was hit by huge peak loads of incoming books and media items that drove the technical services department further and further behind. When a large wave hit it created a bubble that remained in the system until they could eventually catch up during a long valley or by working overtime. In this case they were having great trouble overcoming the impact of the peak load and the bubble remained, keeping the delivery service chain weeks and months behind. As mentioned, I recommended that their goal be to receive a day's worth of production at the dock and deliver those same items the next day to the delivery dock. However, if they were receiving huge surges of materials at the dock to begin with, it was impossible to support this goal. In fact, at times the technical services department received more than two weeks' worth of production in just one day.

I met with the manager of the collection development group and explained the dilemma. Up to this point the manager and the selectors were focused on maximizing the productivity of their department, specifically how efficient and effective they were in selecting and ordering books. Once again efficiency trumped process flow, and while ordering books in seasonal large batches created a more efficient process for the selectors, it was not supporting the needs of the overall service delivery chain. The manager and I discussed the principles of Lean and the need to have materials flow smoothly into and out of the technical services department. She committed her group to helping find a solution. Together the cross-functional team researched the flow pattern of incoming new items to the technical services department. Figure 5-9 illustrates the number of copies ordered during the 2007–2008 time period, and Figure 5-10 presents the number of items received at the dock. Figure 5-9 shows large peaks followed by large valleys, as much as a 116 percent swing upward and 84 percent swing downward from one month to the next. Figure 5-10 shows the impact this ordering pattern had on the dock. You can see an amazing correlation between the two charts' peaks and valleys.

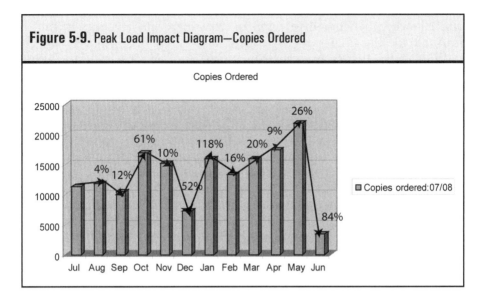

Figure 5-9. Peak Load Impact Diagram—Copies Ordered

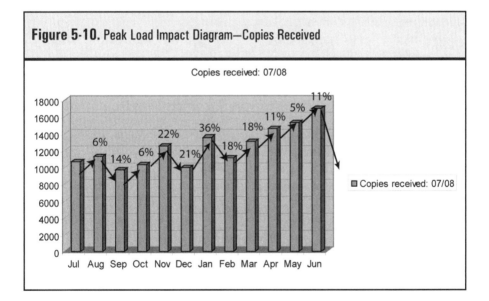

Figure 5-10. Peak Load Impact Diagram—Copies Received

The technical services department was not able to flex their staffing levels to meet these large peaks and valleys of incoming items. This becomes an even larger problem in smaller libraries that do not have a large staff. Management's prior response was to create larger batches to create better labor efficiency. The reasoning of management was that greater labor efficiency would translate into more output and more output would eventually reduce the bubble. The result, however, was months of unpacked boxes, large staging areas, frustrated staff, and long lead times.

Working through the cross-functional team, we engaged the selectors group to gain a better understanding of the ordering patterns. While publisher seasonality contributed to the problem, we discovered much of the ordering pattern was controlled by the selectors themselves. The selectors did not realize that their combined ordering patterns were causing problems for the technical services department. For example, the selector for children's books was assigned to reading programs during the summer months, so she ordered everything she needed prior to this time frame, creating a false bubble of production requirements. (This is a perfect example of how one department can optimize its process without understanding how it affects the overall delivery service chain.) The selectors went to work on shaving the peaks and filling the valleys and made great progress smoothing their ordering pattern. To keep the focus on this important link in the chain, I recommended they have monthly meetings to discuss how to coordinate the ordering patterns with technical services. For my manufacturing clients this is called master scheduling, and the goal is exactly the same. A master scheduler balances the sales forecast, production schedule, and staffing level to smooth the peaks and valleys hitting the production plant. It is so important to my manufacturing clients that the master scheduler is often a highly regarded full-time position. He or she is the conductor of the orchestra.

Peaks and valleys are often unknowingly self-inflicted, and every Lean library should try to identify the source and develop approaches to shave the peaks and fill the valleys when possible. This is a major step in transforming Snake River into River Lean.

The closer you are to smoothing out the receipt of items with production's capability, the better your lead time and delivery service performance. It may be a bit idealistic to assume that the acquisition department can smooth receipts to just one day's worth of production, but it is still an objective to strive for. Academic libraries are much closer to this ideal since they do not buy large quantities of the same item and order and process smaller batches as a part of their normal routine. Academic libraries should be able to prevent large peaks and valleys at the dock and therefore in technical services. There is no reason for an academic library to have longer than twenty-four- to forty-eight-hour delivery of new books to the shelf.

This is not to say that the technical services department is incapable of ramping up their labor force to handle seasonal peaks that the collection development group cannot control. The collection development group should, however, know when these peaks are going to occur, and it should work with the technical services department to prepare more resources in advance. Capacity planning tools should be added to current ILS systems. In the end, matching what is received at the dock and what the technical services department can process in one day should be the goal of a Lean library.

Forks in the River (Departmental Layouts versus Work Cells)

Prior to the Lean revolution in manufacturing, machine operations were often departmentalized. All of one type of a machine was located in one department, all of another type of machine in another department. Secondary operations had their own department, and subassembly and assembly had their own departments as well. It was assumed that it was easier to supervise machines and processes of the same type than of many different types. It also followed the false path of improving labor efficiencies through large batch processing. Large batches of inventory (perhaps 500 pieces) would be transferred from the first department to the second department. This large batch of 500 pieces would flow in large batches through one department to the next (similar to our simulated technical services batch discussion). This required a lot of storage space, many transport vehicles to move the inventory around, and many workers to run the transport vehicles. This created a very slow-moving and costly process. All these costs added no value to the product and therefore are defined by Lean as waste.

If you were to map the value stream of the process, you would find many staging areas and many pick-ups and put-downs and long delays. Once Lean changed the mind-set to pursue small batches rather than large batches, the concepts of separate departments no longer made sense. In the small batch concept in manufacturing, a few pieces would flow from one large machine directly to the small machine and then to subassembly. In a small batch configuration it no longer made sense to have these different machines apart from one another. What made sense was for these machines to be located next to one another, thus the birth of the work cell concept. In this example, a work cell would have one large machine next to one small machine next to a subassembly operation. Small batches (perhaps even one piece) would flow directly from one machine to the next and so on. The work cell concept had a positive impact on lead time, inventory investment, space requirements, and equipment and material handling. These non-value-added activities are primary targets for elimination by Lean.

Work cells are primarily a manufacturing tool, but as I discovered, libraries do have a manufacturing assembly component, so therefore work cells do apply. Work cells are a corollary to small batch sizes. The TCCL technical services department has many things in common with a manufacturing operation. They have a series of operations and a continual flow through those operations. For example, a perfect work cell in TCCL's receiving and processing department would have the unpacking, check-in, cataloging, linking, processing, sorting and shipping areas near if not right next to one another. The objective is a small batch of books (first in/first out) would flow through the work cell in a matter of hours, not weeks. Of course, much work has to be done to get there.

Work cells are designed to support short lead times and small batches and tend to be the natural approach for smaller staffs who are forced to perform multiple tasks at one workstation. However, the work cell may not reach the short lead time, small batch ideal for many reasons: imbalanced work flow, peak loads, and improper staffing are a few examples. The beauty of a work cell is that if you design it and implement it, these problems will quickly surface and force your team and management not only to recognize them but to correct them. In essence, if you build it, they will fix it. Another of my clients also had a large backlog in their new book delivery service chain, in some cases more than six months. One of the process steps included in their processing flow was a large laminating machine that for environmental reasons required a separate room. It was a large and expensive machine. I am sure when it was purchased labor efficiency was the primary concern. However, considering books had to be batched and transported to and from this separate room, it created longer lead times and higher costs. Our new design recommended that the new layout incorporate smaller, less expensive, and more focused laminating machines into the U work cell, therefore better supporting the natural flow of the process.

As mentioned, large batches and separation of workstations cover up and hide inefficiencies, imbalances, peak loads, and poor staffing levels. The large laminating machine was hiding imbalances from the workstation before and after the laminating process. The work cell is designed to create the best practice model and force you to reach it.

U flow is a continuation of the work cell concept. Work cells and departments as a whole should be designed with the U concept in mind. Once again, the left top of the U represents incoming product, the U itself represents the operations, and the right top of the U represents the outbound products. The value of the U design is that it is easily managed and supervised; the overall flow of material (and any problems that exist) is obvious.

A great test is the five-dollar tour. If you tour a process and your feet are tired at the end of the day, you do not have a Lean process or a U flow. If you can stand in one area and easily see the items flow through the entire delivery service chain, you have an effective Lean work cell process and a U flow. As the flow diagrams at TCCL showed, the technical services area had workstations scattered about or grouped into functions. It was difficult to see how one particular item flowed through the process, and it was difficult to see where the inefficiencies and imbalances were hiding. In a U flow, if book trucks are backing up in one particular area it becomes obvious where the imbalance is. Your team should look for opportunities to create U-shaped department flows and U-shaped work cells.

The work cell/U design also encourages a team philosophy. Remember, everyone is a part of the service chain. When the service chain work flow is represented as a U, everyone can see how they fit into the flow, and everyone can see how quickly the product is flowing in and out of the U work cell. It creates a sense of team rather than a sense of individuals.

Hidden Rocks (Imbalances)

Lean teaches us to reduce batch sizes to approach one-piece flow, eliminate the staging areas, and connect the links of the service delivery chain so items can flow from one step to the next without delay. The problem is that once you do this you expose all the rocks that have thus far been hidden by the high water levels of the river. Lean says we should lower the water levels so that we can see the hidden rocks. Then and only then can the rocks be eliminated, allowing the river to flow at a steady pace.

In our technical services example, once we eliminated the staging area and forced book carts to flow directly from one workstation to another, many rocks were revealed. Imbalances between workstations were exposed. Using our river example, we may have a 250-pound largely muscled man rowing on one side of the raft and a ten-year-old boy rowing on the other side. If the muscle man doesn't lighten his stroke, the raft will not go forward; it will go in circles.

In a similar way, if we have one workstation that works twice as fast as the next workstation, book carts are going to pile up. Lean teaches us to attack these imbalances. I often digitally record the targeted processes and break the process down to each step and movement, what Lean calls a value stream map. I look for the following types of opportunities to balance workstation times:

- Steps being duplicated
- Steps that can be eliminated
- Steps that can be moved "offline"
- Steps that can be changed in sequence
- Steps that can be moved from one workstation to another
- Steps that can be combined
- Steps that can be divided into smaller steps

- Excessive walking
- Excessive reaching
- Excessive bending
- Delays
- Steps that can be aided by tools, jigs, and fixtures
- Steps requiring a special skill that can be simplified
- Steps that can be automated within the context of the process flow

For your library, consider the following ideas when implementing your U-shaped flow patterns.

- Every time a staff member picks up a book presents a potential opportunity to improve the process.
- Tasks should not be pushed to other stations down the line if the task can be performed at that station. In other words, eliminate as many pick-ups and put-downs as possible. This is what I call the first-touch principle of a Lean library.
- Opportunities to use the systems capability to improve productivity should be actively pursued. A TCCL staff member suggested we examine the use of rapid receiving to lessen the workload of the linking station. This made a huge difference in the project and gave us greater flexibility in moving and balancing tasks from one station to another.
- As a last resort, split workstations into multiple stations to balance workload. Try to locate the workstations next to one another so the books can flow from one station to the next without having to load a cart to transport it.

- Look for opportunities to cross-train your department so staff can be more flexible in handling surges in incoming items.

You know you are successful when partially loaded carts flow from one station to the next without having to go to a staging area first, and when staff members do not sit idle waiting for the next cart to arrive. Once again, small batches greatly help to balance the load between workstations.

Shortcuts (Expediting)

Expediting means abandoning the first in/first out priority and thus abandoning the primary flow of the river because a book that is more important than another book is moved to the head of the line. This happens every day in technical service departments across the country. A popular, newly released book with a lot of holds is often received at the dock and given priority over all other books. By moving this book ahead we are abandoning our first in/first out philosophy. However, if the technical services department is already in a one-day turnaround mode, receiving and processing these books in a twenty-four- to seventy-two-hour time frame should be possible. It is when you are behind weeks or months that you are forced to expedite important books. This expediting further exacerbates the delays.

As you transform your process from Snake River to River Lean you will still be required to expedite new-release and high-priority books; however, once you achieve twenty-four- to seventy-two-hour delivery, be careful to plan ahead for those high-priority books and match the special labor requirements to the demand. A truly Lean library would be capable of scheduling for these events, pulling resources from various departments and branches to help if necessary and not creating staging areas and bubbles. A Lean library can do this because they have flexible job descriptions matched with the delivery service chain requirements, not the department requirements. When a large surge or an expediting event is coming, a Lean library will sound the horn, and cross-trained resources will come to the call from all directions. For larger-staffed libraries, a special group dedicated to high-priority books may also be considered.

From the prior sections you can see how easy it is for a process to fall into the reflection of Snake River. Twisted flow paths, planned staging areas, large peaks and valleys, process imbalances, and expedited items create a process that cannot be easily navigated or managed. Throughout the project the TCCL team became familiar with these concepts and developed an understanding of why they were rafting Snake River instead of River Lean. By applying these Lean principles, TCCL dramatically transformed their river. The following section presents the action items and results of our design efforts.

Apply Lean Principles to Transform New Book Delivery

As a result of applying the Lean principles to their new book delivery service, the TCCL cross-functional team and I along with the department manager and department supervisor developed the following new design concepts:

- Redesign the process to represent a U-shaped flow.
- Eliminate staging areas between the various steps in the process.
- Implement smaller batches by loading only the top two shelves of each book cart.
- Eliminate duplication of counting items against invoice.
- Implement Rapid Receive, a function of the III Millennium ILS system, to automate the receiving and linking of books and media.
- Check in items by cart/title against invoice rather then requiring an invoice pre-sort.
- Redesign workstations to be more flexible for right- and left-hand processing as well as two-cart work flow.
- Smooth the peaks and valleys at the receiving dock

Create a U Flow Process Design and Eliminate Staging Areas

Understanding the flow patterns of each product type, the TCCL cross-functional team and I developed a U-shaped work flow cell that could support all their product types. Once a book cart was emptied at the first workstation, then and only then did the design call for a new book cart to flow into the first station. That allowed for a smooth flow into and out of the department. Figure 5-11 presents the technical service department's U-shaped first in/first out design. Notice there are no staging areas and no twists and turns within the work cell. With this design and small batch processing, this department is now floating on River Lean. In this case we actually have two Us attached to each other.

Implement Smaller Batches to Reduce Lead Time

TCCL inadvertently reduced batch sizes by reducing the number of shelves that were loaded on the book carts, and it resulted in smoothing the flow throughout the process. It also reduced the number of items that were in process, allowing the carts to flow through the U without having to be staged. The most impressive impact was the near elimination of the entire backlog in the cataloging department. Once the smaller batch sizes were flowing through the department, the cataloging department had no trouble keeping up. The smaller batches allowed the U-shape design to be effective from day one.

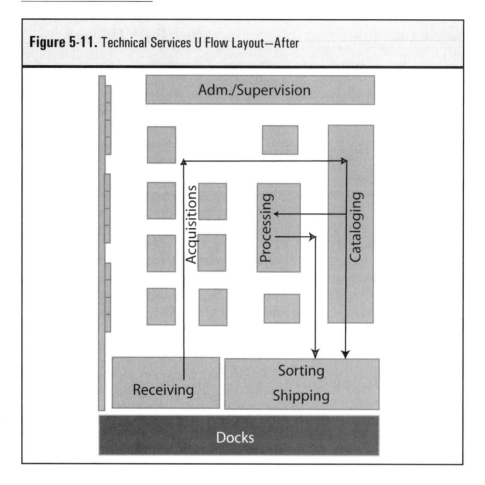

Figure 5-11. Technical Services U Flow Layout—After

Eliminate Duplication of Counting Items against Invoice

During the project we discovered that the receiving group sorted and counted the items in a box against the invoice. The acquisitions group was also counting the items against the invoice. Lean teaches us to eliminate duplication of effort. The reason the receiving department counted the items against the invoice was to make sure the items stated on the invoice were actually in the box. Books sat so long on carts between the time they were unpacked to the time they were processed in acquisitions there was a fear that the books would come up missing and the unpackers would be blamed. The team even considered placing book jackets over the cart to secure them. The answer of course was to eliminate the excessive time between when the book was unpacked and when it was received by acquisitions so the items did not have to be counted twice.

Management performed some research and discovered that the count provided by the unpacking group was very rarely different from acquisitions' count, so they told the unpacking group to stop counting and checking items against the invoice, which saved a great deal of time. They began only verifying the number of boxes received against the invoice, and if a discrepancy did come up, the issue was discovered soon enough to notify the supplier with the proper information. In fact, this saved so much time that the need for the unpacking position was eliminated from the process altogether and was integrated into the receiving work cell.

Implement Rapid Receive

Rapid Receive, as suggested by the acquisitions department supervisor, was a huge breakthrough for the team. The department manager told me that she had always wanted to try Rapid Receive but, considering the huge backlog, never had the time to. This project provided her a vehicle to push for the change, and we moved forward with a pilot. She describes the function as follows: "With Rapid Receive we make sure the bar codes are placed on the books in numerical order. We then enter the first bar code number and the number of copies, select the correct template, and the computer does the rest." This created labor savings in the receiving process and tremendous flexibility in resequencing and moving tasks around the work cell.

Redesign Workstations

Workstation design is the nuts and bolts of a process improvement effort. As a part of the detailed design we filmed each workstation that supported the individual links of the new book delivery service chain. After reviewing the film with the cross-functional team we examined and discussed the workstation designs, and, using the balloon diagram brainstorming approach, we identified key non-value-added issues that needed to be corrected. Figure 5-12 represents one of the receiving workstations and provides a good representation of how all the workstations were designed.

The team identified a number of non-value-added issues with the current workstations:

- Many workstations were designed for left-to-right processing, while most of the staff was more comfortable with right-to-left processing.
- The design of the workstation allowed room for only one cart, while the staff preferred the flexibility to work with two carts if needed.
- The book cart blocked access to the file cabinets.
- The printer and other items consumed much of the workstation's work space.
- The work area of the table was too large and created excessive reach situations.

Working with the team, we redesigned the workstations to allow right-to-left or left-to-right work flow, depending on the staff member's preference. We

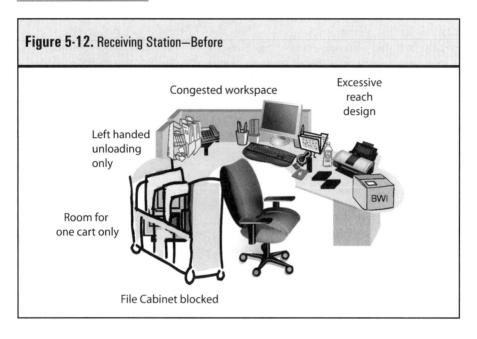

Figure 5-12. Receiving Station—Before

Congested workspace

Excessive reach design

Left handed unloading only

Room for one cart only

BWI

File Cabinet blocked

also created space for two carts rather then just one by changing the location of the file cabinets and redesigning the shape of the workstations. In addition, we built a platform to raise the printers, allowing more space on the workstation. Figure 5-13 presents the team's recommendation for the new workstation design.

This design created a more productive and comfortable work space for the staff, allowing tighter and more effective work flow, flexible unloading/loading areas, and supported one-cart or two-cart functionality.

Smooth the Peaks and Valleys Created by the Selectors Group

We discussed in great detail the impact the selectors' ordering patterns had on the peaks and valleys that the acquisitions group experienced. This was the major contributor to the backlog bubble. I worked with the associate director of collections development and her staff to develop solutions to smooth the peaks and fill in the valleys. The group developed and committed to the following actions to smooth the ordering pattern:

- Eliminate the conflict of summer reading program and selectors' ordering-time requirements.
- Institute regular management review meetings between selectors and acquisitions. Milestones will be set for encumbering funds.
- Milestone dates for Trust projects will be established, including a rolling completion schedule.

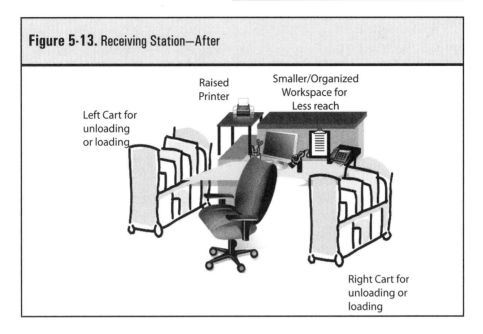

Figure 5-13. Receiving Station—After

- Schedule and balance projects with various department heads and selectors.
- Work with the business office to identify ways to get an earlier start on projects.
- Implement a priority system for orders coming from selectors.

As a result of these scheduling activity changes, the peaks and valleys smoothed out considerably. One remaining contributing factor to the backlog that has not been discussed and remains a small issue is the impact that fulfilling year-end material budgets has on the selectors' ordering pattern. This was originally such a large issue that I dedicated an entire Lean strategy to the topic. (For further information on budgets and the impact they have on performance, see Strategy Seven.)

Develop and Share Cost–Benefit Projections and Results

TCCL completed a Lean design for their new book delivery service chain, but we were not quite finished. The technical services cross-functional team was committed to the design, but change can be scary, and sometimes pure logic is not enough to drive the change. The team and management must be convinced of the benefits before taking the leap. You must quantify the projected benefits of your new Lean service delivery chain before moving to the implementation phase.

I worked with the technical services manager as well as the finance director in the business department to help develop the cost and benefit projections. We presented the design and projected savings to the cross-functional team and worked out any remaining questions and issues with the team. The following are the benefits TCCL achieved through this Lean redesign effort:

* 95–100 percent reduction in new book backlog
* Reduction of lead time during peak load periods by 70–80 percent
* 90 percent improvement in standard customer delivery lead time
* Improvement of productivity of 20–25 percent
* Productivity improvement valued at $20,000 to $30,000 per year
* 80 percent reduction in batch sizes
* Improved communications between selectors and acquisitions staff, resulting in improved customer and vendor service performance

For more information on how to develop the cost and benefit analysis refer to Strategy Four and Strategy Seven.

Once everyone was satisfied with the design and our projected benefits, the cross-functional team helped me present the overall design to the leadership team. Presenting the ideas and designs as a team showed that the departments and staff had full ownership of the changes. Even so, the closer we reached the point of implementing the changes, the more the staff became hesitant, if not resistant, until the technical services manager and supervisor implemented Rapid Receive and the small-batch philosophy of loading only the top two shelves of the book carts. Within weeks the department saw significant improvements in their process flow and a reduction in their backlog. These initial results eliminated any further resistance to the design changes, and they began looking forward to the new design in their new facility.

Celebrate Current and Past Accomplishments

I revisited this group a few months after the project design was completed. They had implemented most of the concepts we designed, with the exception of the physical U layout and new workstations, which was to be accomplished during the relocation to the new facility. To celebrate their accomplishments I delivered gold star cookies to everyone in the department. The backlog had been significantly reduced, the staging areas were much smaller, and the frantic looks of trying to keep up with the demand were gone. They appeared to be enjoying their jobs and work environment. I therefore felt that I had successfully accomplished my own company's organizational purpose.

My best memory centered around one particular staff member who was very reluctant to try an idea I had suggested regarding the sequence and approach she used to receive CDs at her workstation. Upon my return she pulled me aside and told me she had decided to try my suggestion after all and was now convinced it was the better way. I had suggested she place the CDs on the cart first, sort them together by title, then use the sequence of titles to check the items off the invoice (which was alphabetically presented and easy to use). In other words, it was easier to find the item on the invoice list as opposed to physically alphabetically sorting and sequencing the CDs. She discovered she was saving a significant amount of time and energy with the new approach. She was not ready to change until she saw the success of the other changes, proving that success breeds success.

I visited my TCCL friends again a few weeks after they had moved to their new facility. The team had successfully implemented most of the Lean concepts, a U-shaped flow, small batch sizes, reduction of staging areas, and first in/first out processing. This greatly reduced peak and valley surges. I was very pleased to see that their backlog had been eliminated, they were achieving one-week turnaround, and they had not only eliminated most of their overtime but had reduced the labor time required to support the process. Best of all, they have not stopped—they are still looking to fine-tune their Lean improvements because they have not yet reached their goal of a forty-eight- to ninety-six-hour turnaround time for new book delivery, nor have they addressed all the issues on the goals bubble diagram that they developed in the early phases of the project. I look forward to working with them in the future to help them reach their ultimate goal.

Strategy Five Review

Transforming any process in your library from Snake River to River Lean can be accomplished by simplifying the flow and path of items in the delivery service chain. By smoothing peaks and valleys, eliminating large batches, attacking staging areas, and coordinating the links in the chain, you can dramatically reduce the non-value-added, wasteful activities and dramatically improve your service and cost performance.

Strategy Six

Transform Your Customer Holds/ Reserves Delivery Service Chain

Strategy Five discussed how waste and non-value-added process issues such as twists and turns in flow, staging areas, large batches, imbalances, and peaks and valleys contribute to long lead times and poor delivery service. It explained how the principles of Lean can eliminate these added process issues and dramatically improve lead time and customer service for not only your new book delivery service chain but throughout your library service chains. Strategy Six will introduce a Lean design principle to improve your customer holds/reserves delivery. While Strategy Five focused on streamlining Snake River into River Lean, Strategy Six will focus on what I call the first-touch principle. The first-touch principle will make a dramatic difference in your delivery service chain's productivity, safety, and lead-time performance. You will learn once again that by attacking and eliminating non- value-added activities, service is improved while costs are reduced.

Delivery of customer requests is the heart and soul of multibranch libraries. If a library cannot deliver a book to a customer in an accurate and timely manner, that library is failing in its fundamental organizational purpose. Even in a stand-alone library, processing and delivering hold requests to the hold shelf in a timely manner is critical. I have worked with a number of libraries to improve how well they deliver a customer hold request to a customer. The solutions for each environment have varied depending on the number of branches they support, the size of their reserve volume, whether they are a floating library, whether they use vans or trucks, and whether they use a contract delivery service or an internal delivery group. All, however, do have one thing in common: the delivery process is usually hidden away from the main activities of the library and usually occurs early in the morning. As a result, most of the staff rarely sees or focuses on the issues surrounding this part of the delivery service chain. Delivery can become out of sight, out of mind.

The delivery process, including the sorting, handling, delivery, and return of customer holds, is the most important and critical service delivery chain the library has. Rarely is it given the importance it deserves until its poor performance reaches a point where the entire library is nearly shut down due to its backlog. For this reason, in every library project I work on I schedule a time to ride along with the delivery driver. If the performance of this process drives the success of the overall library, then it is important enough for me to understand fully how the process works.

Of the ten or so multibranch delivery projects I have completed, I would say seven of them were necessary because the customer reserves delivery had reached a near state of emergency. The pick lists, sorters, drivers, trucks, and branches were just not able to keep up with the increasing holds/reserves volumes. I have seen libraries fall weeks behind in their deliveries, and when this happens books become backlogged in stacks and stacks of tote boxes. Library services throughout the library are impacted.

In the other three delivery projects, the library management team asked for my assistance not because they were in an emergency backlog situation but because they felt they could do better. These libraries had deliveries of 72 to 120 hours, in some cases even 24 to 96 hours, but they felt that they could do better. In either one of these circumstances the applications of Lean remains the same: attack and eliminate non-value-added processes and activities to improve service performance and reduce cost.

Strategy Six will present the first-touch principle of a Lean library using a case example at the Public Library of Youngstown and Mahoning County (PLYMC). PLYMC was one of the libraries performing at a fairly high level but nonetheless wanted to get better. Once again we will use Lean change methodology to present the transformation of PLYMC's customer holds/reserves delivery service chain.

Establish a Common Organizational Purpose

As I stated, each library has its own reason for initiating a project to improve customer reserves delivery performance. In PLYMC's case, the library's director wanted to know how much better they could be, to establish a best practice performance benchmark and see how close they could come to reaching it. He had heard of the new delivery concepts developed at the Tulsa City–County Library.

For me, there could be no better motivation or organizational purpose. When a group wants to strive to be the best they can be, sign me up. The question was, of course, did the rest of the staff embrace this objective, and were they willing to embrace the changes required to make it happen?

The Public Library of Youngstown and Mahoning County supported the main library plus sixteen countywide branch locations. Circulation at the time was estimated at two million items per year, holds/reserves around 150,000, serving a population of approximately 250,000. The delivery system also supported the delivery of mail, supplies, equipment, and other items to the branches. The PLYMC delivery system consisted of two trucks with five support vehicles, with the farthest library being nearly 40 miles away. PLYMC had recently converted to Innovative Interface's "III" library system.

Practice a Top-Down and Bottom-Up Management Style

As indicated in Strategy Three, the customer reserves delivery service chain crosses nearly every department and function of a library, including circulation, sorting, delivery drivers, mail services, branches, and, if the hold/reserve is for a new book, even technical services. The service chain is supported by nearly every job function and person in a library. In this regard this project required a cross-functional team that had strong management support and was comprised of staff from various departments (links in the chain). This project was conducted under a very compressed timetable, and we were able to complete the design phase in less than a month. While this created some challenges in developing full ownership, we successfully engaged a number of the delivery service chain support members, albeit at times in an update-and-review framework.

Our design support team was organized along the following titles:

Steering Committee
- Library director
- Branch director
- Operations director

Team facilitator/lean design engineer/lean consultant

Cross-functional team
- Circulation manager
- Pager
- Delivery supervisor
- Driver
- Branch managers
- Branch representatives
- Systems manager
- Systems programmer

Initiate Projects to Drive Change

The leadership team committed the time and resources of the project team and planned one-and-a-half-hour meetings twice a week during the life of the project design. As the project facilitator and Lean design engineer I did much of the behind-the-scenes legwork to keep the project moving at a progressive pace.

The approach and methodology followed the same path as the TCCL project presented in Strategy Five, including the following steps:

- Assist/confirm delivery system goals and objectives for a five-year planning horizon.
- Develop a performance gap analysis between current performance and desired performance.
- Identify and prioritize the major obstacles to be overcome.
- Recommend a best practice conceptual design to overcome these obstacles, including:
  - Comparative delivery growth models
  - Process flow changes
  - Material handling equipment changes/alternatives
  - Potential branch facility issues to be overcome
  - Vehicle modification requirements
  - Staffing growth models
  - Systems enhancements
  - Facilities layout
  - Cost–benefit analysis
  - Implementation approach

Develop Gap-Driven Performance Measures

While management was committed to change, we needed to make sure the entire group was also committed, especially since we were under a compressed time frame and it was a union environment. To initiate change, the team, support groups, and the union had to understand and agree that there was a need for change. They had to understand that a gap existed between what customers expected and how they were currently meeting customer expectations.

Strategy Four discussed how to use a balloon diagram to break a complex problem down to a level you can measure. Our first step as a cross-functional team was to define what they believed their customers expected from their reserves delivery service chain. Figure 6-1 presents the results of this effort.

I really enjoyed this particular session because the group was so aggressive at looking at their competitors as the primary benchmark of their own performance. Gaining ownership for change wasn't as great a challenge as I first expected. However, while this was a great list, it did not drive the goals to a level by which they could be measured, so the group translated the balloons to reflect specific measurable service performance measures. The results of this effort are presented in Figure 6-2.

The team quickly embraced the metrics concept of Lean and set a goal that once an item was available a hold would be delivered to customers in good physical condition within twenty-four to forty-eight hours from the time customers placed the hold to the time they were notified the hold was ready for

Figure 6-1. PLYMC Customer Balloon Diagram

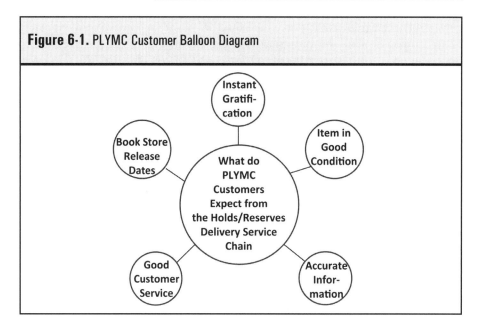

Figure 6-2. PLYMC Customer Balloon Diagram—Performance Metrics

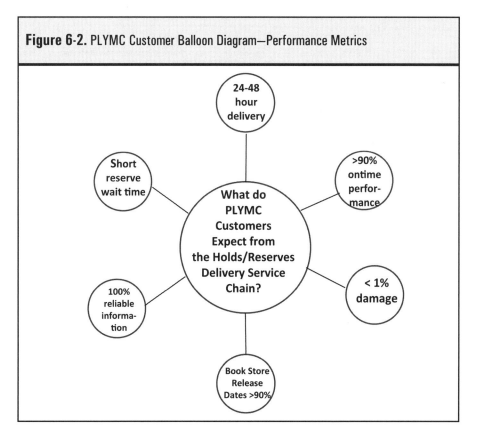

pickup. This target was to be accomplished at least 90 percent of the time. They went further to state the information available on the online reserve system should be reliable 100 percent of the time, and customers should not have to wait very long for their book to be available. Reluctantly, we did not set a goal on the time it took for a book to become available, as it was out of the scope for this project.

Following our Lean methodology, to drive home the need for change, the group took on the task to understand the gap in performance between what they felt the customer wanted and how they were performing against those expectations. We used the flowcharting/value stream mapping tool. Specifically, we documented the entire holds/reserves delivery service chain down to a step-by-step level. We used the team's experience to provide typical time stamp estimates of each step in the service chain. If we had more time we would have incorporated our time log approach to capture actual time frames. After we developed an estimated time log of the overall service chain they discovered they were not performing to the delivery lead time of forty-eight to seventy-two hours as they first thought they were. Figure 6-3 presents PLYMC's reserve delivery value map.

Figure 6-3. Customer Reserve/Hold Delivery Chain

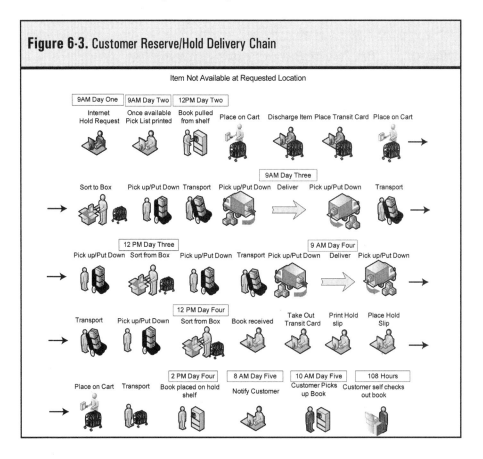

The flowchart follows one book from the time the customer places the hold until the customer is notified the book is on the hold shelf. *Note*: Delivery service chains start with the first customer event and end with the last customer event. A different chart was developed to follow the book from the time the customer returns the book until the book is returned to the owning branch shelf. In addition, the team was concerned with how much damage was being caused by the current delivery process, so we took some samples of totes to assess the number of books that appeared damaged. The results of their gap assessment are presented in Table 6-1.

Drive Change through Your Cross-Functional Team

By defining the customer expectations and comparing these metrics to our current performance, the cross-functional team became fully aware of the gap in performance and the need to change. We conducted a number of accelerated brainstorming sessions to determine what the team believed was causing this gap. Once again we used the balloon diagram to take a complex issue and drive it to a level where action items could be developed. Figure 6-4 presents the balloon diagram summarizing the obstacles that we had to overcome if we were to close the gap in performance.

Because of the compressed time frame, I combined the understanding of the current environment phase and the development of solutions phase. I was careful to present, discuss, and analyze the current-environment documents prior to our efforts to compare and contrast against other libraries' best practice models. In the end this worked well for PLYMC.

Understand the Current Environment and Develop Solutions to Drive Change

To understand the need to change, a team must have a full understanding of how their process currently works. As such, we divided the holds/reserves delivery service chain into two major areas: (1) branch receiving and processing

Table 6-1. Performance Gap Analysis

Performance Metric	Current	Desired
Delivery lead time	5 days	24 to 48 hours
Shelf paging accuracy	70%	100%
Book not damaged	95%	99%

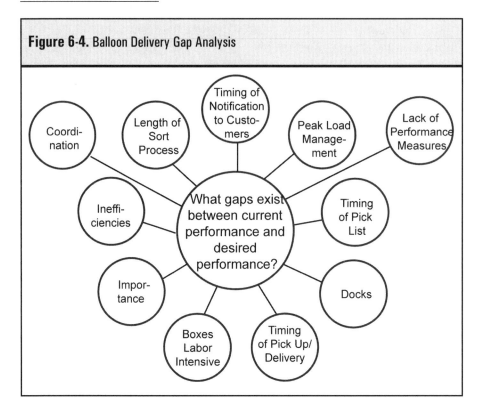

Figure 6-4. Balloon Delivery Gap Analysis

hold requests and (2) delivery physically sorting and delivering the hold requests.

Receiving and Processing Hold Requests

To better understand how the receiving and processing of hold requests worked at PLYMC we performed a series of five-dollar tours to fully document and flowchart the process. Figure 6-5 presents the flowchart of our five-dollar tours of the receiving and processing of hold requests.

PLYMC had approximately sixteen clerical steps involved in processing a hold request from a pick list. (I have found many libraries to have even more.) Ultimately the book would end up on the customer hold shelf. I have seen many presentations of hold shelves and their use of hold slips and wrappers. At PLYMC the book was presented vertically with the hold slip sticking out on top of the book. This forced the customer to flip through the series of hidden slips in the hope they would find their name. I have also seen books presented horizontally with the hold slips sticking out of the top of the book toward the customer. Libraries that do not use hold slips use hold wrappers, often taped or rubber banded around the book. Figure 6-6 presents a hold shelf at Johnson County Library in Kansas City. Libraries take extraordinary efforts to present a

Figure 6-5. Customer Reserve/Hold Delivery Service Chain

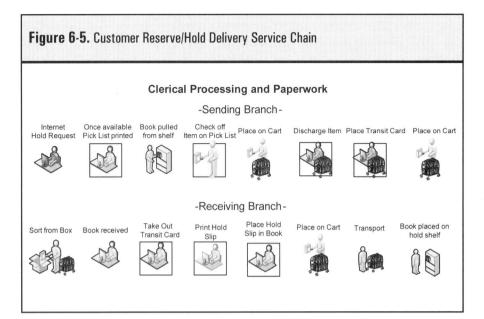

Figure 6-6. Hold Shelf—Before

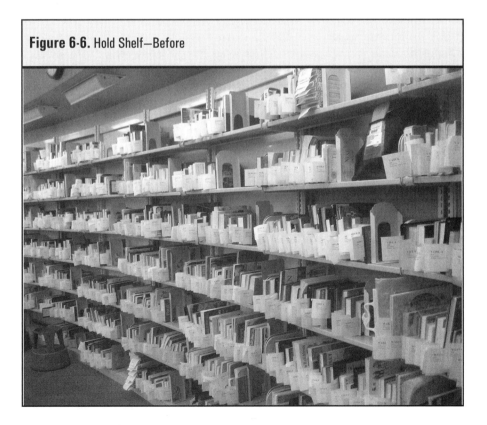

clean and professional environment to their customers; however, the one place that customers go the most—the hold shelf—is often presented in a junky fashion.

As shown in the flowchart, PLYMC used preprinted cards with branch names on them to tag and transfer a book from one branch to another. I knew there was a better way, so I introduced the team to the first-touch principle:

> *If a task can be performed the first time you touch a book, then perform that task; do not push it down the line.*

This design principle has proved to be effective in every library environment I have worked in. Staff members pick up and put down a book many times in a delivery service cycle, sometimes because a task that could have been performed earlier in the process was passed down to another link in the chain. By not passing the task down the chain and performing the task at "first touch," a library can often eliminate many non-value-added tasks down the line.

I challenged the team to make the reserved book just pulled from the shelf fully hold-shelf-ready from the start. Specifically, could they place a preprinted label on the spine of the book with all the needed information on it? Would this eliminate extra clerical steps? The answer is "yes."

Prior to the PLYMC project, I had noticed a repositionable sticky label that TCCL's interlibrary loan department was using. I challenged TCCL to develop a repositionable sticky holds label that could be printed to replace the pick list. The sticky label would have all the information needed to become hold-shelf ready, and it would be applied to the spine of the book when it was pulled off the shelf to fill a hold, thus eliminating many non-value-added steps, including the pick list, the in-transit label, and the holds wrapper.

TCCL resisted the idea at first. The common refrain I heard was: "You cannot change III Millennium; we are not allowed." With the help of an excellent programmer we customized bridge software outside III Millennium to grab the pick list print file and reformat it into the holds label design we desired. This was ten years ago. Now libraries across the country have converted or are converting to this concept. Figure 6-7 shows a picture of the holds label in its six-up format printed from a standard laser printer. It also can be provided in an eight-up format. The label contains the destination branch code, the item information and item bar code, customer name or code, and discharge date. We can custom design the label for each library's particular needs. We can even add the library's artwork to the label.

The holds label shown in Figure 6-8 is our latest generation design specially developed for Johnson County Library in Kansas City. The label can be applied to and easily removed from the book while not leaving residue. This holds label solution has been adopted by libraries all over the country and can be beneficial to both multibranch and single-location libraries. Go to http://www .jhaconsults.com to watch how the process works at Johnson County Library.

Figure 6-7. Holds Sticky Label—Six Up

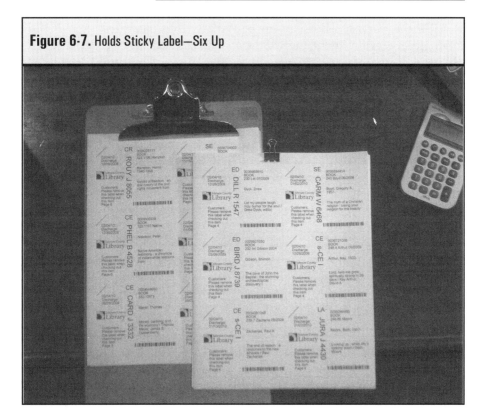

Figure 6-8. Holds Sticky Label Layout

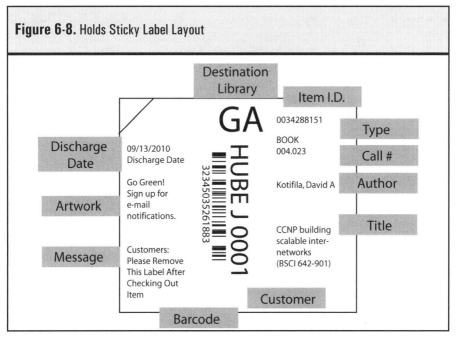

After the cross-functional team at PLYMC fully analyzed their current holds/reserves flow and identified the many wasteful activities, duplication of efforts, and excessive paperwork, I presented TCCL's best practice solution. They were very excited to adopt the holds label solution because they recognized how it could transform their performance and their hold-shelf presentation. Specifically the team realized they could eliminate the following non-value-added activities:

- Creating pick lists, transit cards, and hold slips
- Handwriting information on hold wrappers
- Handling transit cards and hold slips
- Making customers finger through hold slips

This process reduced the number of steps by about 25 percent. Considering PLYMC processed more than a 150,000 holds per year at that time, this was a significant savings in clerical time and a significant improvement in customer service. This is a perfect example of Lean improving customer service, thus resulting in a reduction of costs.

Physically Sorting and Delivering Hold Requests

Our PLYMC cross-functional team turned our attention to sorting and delivering the holds request, the second part of the customer reserves delivery service chain. I have been to more than a dozen library systems in the past ten years, and one process not only gets my attention but actually makes me a bit angry: tote boxes. Lifting a forty-pound tote box is very difficult, and possibly injurious.

At PLYMC, each driver has about forty tote boxes on his or her individual truck. They load about forty tote boxes at the beginning of their routes, unload and load on average five tote boxes at each of the sixteen locations, and then unload all forty tote boxes at the sorting location at the end of the day. Drivers picked up and put down a forty-pound tote box 560 times a day, about 140,000 pick-ups and put-downs per year. This does not include the number of times other library personnel lift or relocate a full tote box. PLYMC is a medium-sized library; these numbers are greater at a large library.

The second part of the equation is the tote box sorting process. PLYMC sorted one tote box into sixteen tote box locations. We wanted to develop a better understanding of the sorting process, so we created another flowchart representing the work flow of the current sorting process (Figure 6-9).

For a sorter to sort and empty one tote box having an average of thirty-five items per box while carrying three books at a time for eighty tote boxes, the sorter would create nearly one hundred arrows per day for this flowchart. From a Lean perspective this process is extremely inefficient, with a great deal of non-value-added activities supported. Through cross-functional team brainstorming sessions the team developed a better design that would reduce the

Figure 6-9. Sorting Flow Diagram

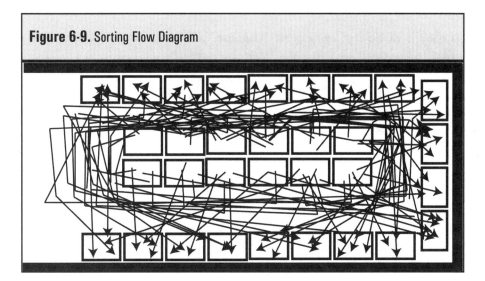

distance traveled by the sorters but not the number of sorting trips required. The sorting diagram presented in Figure 6-10 was the team's short-term solution.

Since this improved design still required nearly one hundred sorting trips from one tote box to another, there was still a great deal of non-value-added time and effort, and staff needed to bend over to get books on each trip. Since PLYMC was interested in best practice models and not half measures, I shared another practice developed at TCCL: the "no totes" solution.

During my first library project with TCCL I developed a passion to eliminate the use of tote boxes because they created a great deal of non-value-added activities in the delivery process. I had learned from my manufacturing clients that the material handling device and containers you use in a process often reflect the effectiveness of a process. I worked with the head of the maintenance and delivery at TCCL to help find a way to eliminate this inefficient and dangerous approach to moving books, and we did just that.

TCCL provided sorting and delivery services to twenty-three branches using vans, which made loading and unloading tote boxes challenging because the vans were always completely full to support the demand. As at PLYMC, the driver had to pick up and put down forty-pound boxes all day long. Finding the correct tote box in a fully loaded van required unloading and reloading many tote boxes until the right one was found. Most libraries use some kind of boxes to move books around because this is the way it has always been done. The Brooklyn Public Library used small suitcase-type boxes with holding and locking straps, which they believed they had been using since the 1920s. During my project at TCCL, having never worked in a library before, I did not have this preconceived acceptance of tote boxes. I saw them as archaic.

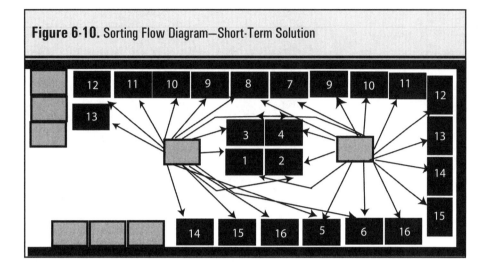

Figure 6-10. Sorting Flow Diagram—Short-Term Solution

Using a process flowchart I asked the TCCL team to show me the first time a staff member touched a book when it was destined for another branch. This was the staff member at the circulation desk processing a returned item or pulling a book from the shelf to fill a hold request from the pick list. I asked them if instead of sorting the book after it reached the central sorting location, could the book could be sorted the first time it was touched? After great consternation and weeks of discussion, we determined the answer was yes.

As I discovered later, many low- to medium-volume library systems I have worked with use this first-touch principle to their benefit. A staff member will sort the book at the circulation desk into a designated tote bin destined for a particular branch. If a library has ten branches or fewer, this works fairly well, as you can find a place around the circulation desk to fit ten sorting tote boxes. If there is not room for ten they will use a miscellaneous tote box that holds the lower-volume items and then sort these totes either inside the truck or back at a sorting location. If you have more than ten branches it is difficult for the branches to presort the items because there is not enough room around the circulation desk.

This branch presort option solution of sorting using designated tote boxes at the circulation desk was not an option for Youngstown or Tulsa due to the space required to access and store sixteen or twenty-three open tote boxes respectively at each location. This tote box approach to material handling did not support my first-touch principle of Lean, so tote boxes became public enemy number one.

The beauty of the sticky holds label design together with the first-touch sorting idea led the TCCL project team to our ultimate best practice design. Books are designed so that the spine of the book is readable as it sits on a shelf or a book cart. If TCCL planned to make the book "hold-shelf-ready," could they then sort the book directly on the cart by destination the first time they touched it? They all looked at me like I was crazy; after all, libraries had always used tote boxes. I told them that since books are designed to go on book carts, they should use book carts in delivery rather than tote bins. This sparked many questions: "How would the book carts get on the truck?" "What about when it rains?" "How do you keep the books secure on the cart when the truck hits a bump?" You get the idea. We had many design issues to overcome to meet the goal of no more tote boxes.

The idea was to have circulation staff place the hold-shelf-ready labels on the book at first touch and then place the book on a book cart in alphabetical order by branch. Then the book carts could be loaded onto a box truck and delivered to central sorting. This was apparently a really outside-of-the-box idea, because it took weeks of discussion to finally determine it was possible. We developed solutions for all the obstacles we discovered, including finding an outdoor-capable book cart, securing the books to the book cart so they did not fall during transport, securing the book cart itself inside the box truck so it did not roll around, and protecting the book cart and the books with rain covers. The results of our efforts are shown in Figure 6-11.

Figure 6-11. Book Truck in Box Truck

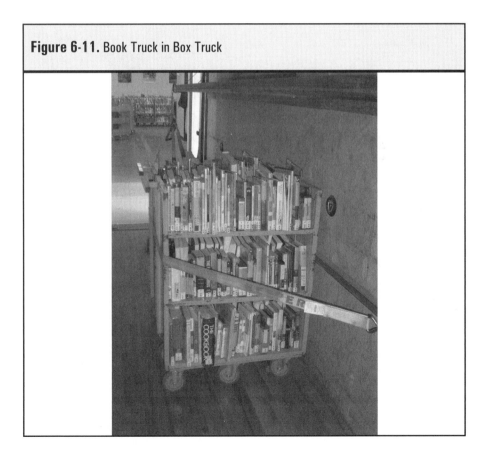

We had developed a way to eliminate all the tote boxes for every library in the world. Now I just need to convince every library in the world to follow our lead.

Even better, the "no tote box" system design makes the sorting process simple. Just like stocking grocery shelves, a sorter walks down a row of alphabetically sorted book carts and transfers alphabetically presorted books from one cart to the other. One cart can be sorted in one trip around the U-shaped design. Compare this to hundreds of sorting trips needed to sort tote boxes to other tote boxes, as seen in Figure 6-9. Not only do tote box sorters walk back and forth but they also need to bend over again and again to pick up a book before walking to the proper tote box. I have seen many sorters actually fling the book across the room to an open tote box in an attempt to eliminate all the walking. Figure 6-12 shows the original "no totes" solution shortly after being implemented at TCCL. Notice the hold-shelf-ready labels on the book and the compact and efficient U-shaped layout. Rather than the books remaining stationary in a tote box as you sort, the books move with the sorter.

Figure 6-12. TCCL Sorting Area

I believe this design is more effective than the most expensive automated sorting systems because nearly every automated sorting system is designed around the dreaded tote box. Automated sorting systems using tote boxes are a high-cost and inefficient way to sort and deliver books, even if some put tote boxes on wheels.

Train and Prepare Staff

PLYMC quickly adopted this design with a few customized changes. The new design reduced so much labor content that I recommended PLYMC combine the sorting position into the driver's responsibilities.

PLYMC is a union library, therefore changing job responsibilities created a potentially challenging environment. The library director made sure that the unions were involved in the change discussions and, as such, were able to come to an agreement about changing job functions.

The duties of staff who once handled loading and unloading of boxes were picked up by other departments. Their new process begins with technical services sorting the book carts while the delivery truck driver takes a break. The driver then reloads the truck and makes deliveries.

TCCL was able to combine the driver duties and the sorting duties into one job description, while PLYMC shifted responsibilities around to take advantage of the significant reduction of sorting and tote handling time. The key to both cases was developing ownership of the changes from the very beginning of the project and maintaining a policy of complete transparency. In the end I agreed with PLYMC's decision because they were able to gain the labor benefits without dramatically upsetting the apple cart. I had to remind myself that labor efficiency alone should not drive decision making because in the service delivery chain, service performance and safety come first.

TCCL spent many hours with staff getting them comfortable with the idea of presorting books at the branches, and over time they accepted the changes. Just like TCCL, PLYMC spent a great deal of time preparing and training the staff, branches, and drivers for the change. Now they are true believers. Visit http://www.jhaconsults.com to see a film of the original "no totes" solution at TCCL.

Develop and Share Cost–Benefit Projections and Results

The combination of the hold-shelf-ready, removable sticky label, the elimination of tote boxes, and first-touch sorting made a significant impact on delivery lead time and staff productivity for both TCCL and PLYMC. However, the changes were quite daunting for both libraries and caused great apprehension for many staff members. To eliminate their fears, many question-and-answer sessions were held. TCCL and PLYMC spent time showing the staff how their job tasks would change for the better and how the library and customer would benefit. The ideas of eliminating tote boxes and using sticky labels were eventually big hits, but change always comes with resistance. But in nearly every case these changes benefited everyone. Figure 6-13 and Table 6-2 summarize the benefits of the PLYMC project.

The initial "no tote" investment for a library varies greatly from one environment to another. It depends on the current transport vehicles you own or lease and the number of branches. I have found most branches have been able to convert from the tote boxes to book carts without any major physical changes around their circulation desks. In all cases the payback has been very attractive.

Celebrate Current and Past Accomplishments

Resistance to change crumbles in the face of success. The removable sticky labels represent a huge success for my library clients. The response to this change from all quarters has been and is still overwhelming. I have recommended to all my clients to start their Lean changes with the hold-shelf-ready label. Once

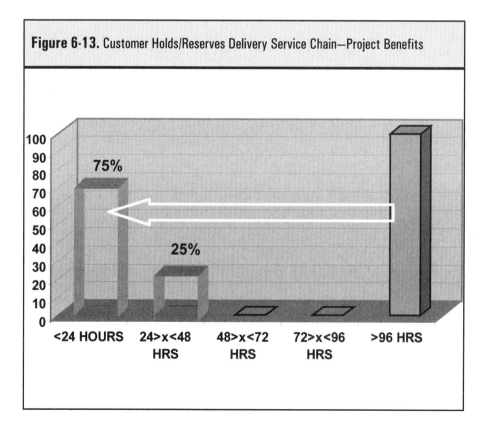

Figure 6-13. Customer Holds/Reserves Delivery Service Chain—Project Benefits

Table 6-2. Holds Service Chain Project Results

Costs	Benefits	Payback	Five-Year Benefit
$91,000	$61,000	1.5 years	$111,000

everyone sees how successful this change is, staff are motivated to move forward to eliminate the heavy and archaic tote boxes and to improve all of their delivery service chains.

Strategy Six Review

The first-touch principle of a Lean library is extremely powerful in your Lean transformation journey. By applying this principle you can dramatically improve the performance and safety of your customer holds/reserves delivery service chain. The holds-ready sticky label can transform your library, improve customer service, reduce costs, and eliminate those bulky, dirty, heavy, and injurious tote boxes. Your life just changed.

Strategy Seven

Transform Your Cost Control Philosophy to a Lean Service Improvement Philosophy

Have you ever heard anyone get excited about budgets? If you have, it is most likely the controller, but I am not even sure controllers like the budgeting process. I usually stay clear of my clients' budgeting process, but at times it is unavoidable.

Typical library budget line items include:

- Salaries and wages
- Employee benefits
- Books
- Periodicals
- Video materials
- Audio materials
- Software and databases

- Contracted services
- Staff, board, continuing education
- Public programming
- Telecommunications
- Equipment repair
- Supplies

There are three problems with using budgets to drive your cost reduction objectives: (1) Decreasing a department budget is viewed as punishment and a reflection of poor performance. (2) Departments most often will do everything they can to spend their allotted amount so that they can prove that their budget needs to be increased for the following year. (3) Cost performance at the department level does not accurately reflect the true cost of service because it does not measure the cost of the delivery service chains.

Have you ever seen a department excited that their budget has been decreased? Have you ever seen a group throw a party to celebrate a budget reduction? Of course not, because budget reduction is a bad thing. It invokes sacrifice; it states that you are in trouble. Budget cuts are a direct attack on the security and comfort of the staff personnel. A Lean library would celebrate when costs are reduced and customers are better served.

Peak Loads and Budget Spending

As we discussed in Strategy Five, the new book delivery service chain at Tulsa City–County Library (TCCL) was not performing to management's expectations. It was taking months to get a new book on the shelf of the designated branch. TCCL had up to eight weeks of unopened boxes sitting in the receiving area. Management's ultimate goal was to have all new items delivered to the designated branch within five days of dock receipt 95 percent of the time.

We applied the Lean change methodology to the new book delivery service chain by forming a cross-functional team and flowcharting the delivery service chain, analyzing it, and eliminating the delays, duplication, and errors in the process. We then simplified, automated, and integrated the process using the principles and tools of Lean. We made great progress and increased their capability and productivity by nearly 25 percent. While it did have an impact, 25 percent was not enough. It could not overcome what I call peak loads.

Peak loads are a part of every librarian's life. Library delivery personnel experience peak loads on Monday and Tuesday as they try to catch up on the weekend book returns and hold requests. Branches experience peak loads during the summer months as well as on certain days of the week and certain hours of the day. It does no good to design a process to manage and staff to average capacity; you must design and staff a process to manage the peak load capacity. If McDonald's staffed their counter for the average capacity, the lines at lunch would be out the door.

At TCCL this was a contentious issue and resulted in much debate, but our team finally recognized that the poor management of peak loads was one of the major causes of their backlog problem and subsequently their poor delivery service. As mentioned in Strategy Five, we worked with the collection development group to manage and smooth the incoming flow of books. However, we did not discuss what was driving the collection development department's buying pattern in the first place: budgets.

Year-End Spending

At the end of each fiscal year, the collection development group would make a big push to make sure they had spent all of their budgeted funds, thus creating the huge year-end surge of incoming goods at the dock. The problem became even more complicated because the technical services group, who received this surge of incoming goods, also processed the invoices. This created two competing peak loads and a choice of applying the labor resources to either receive new books to meet the budget push or process invoices to keep the vendors happy. There simply was not enough staff to handle both the year-end peak loads and processing the invoices. If a book fell into the next fiscal year because technical services could not catch up to receive it—which was the case since they were at least eight weeks behind—the collection development group would be very unhappy because those books would not fill the previous year's budget and as a result eat into the coming year's budget. The end-of-year budget push created eight weeks of unopened boxes and a surge bubble that was nearly impossible to eliminate. The result of this poor management of peak loads was a frustrated and emotional workforce on both ends. Once a surge bubble enters into the equation, lead times are pushed back, and it becomes difficult to eliminate the bubble unless you temporarily increase staff, work exorbitant overtime, or dramatically improve your capability.

There were, of course, other factors that caused the peaks and valleys in the receipt of new items, but ordering to catch up with the budget at year end was a big factor. Budgets are often not the most effective tool to support management's cost control objectives; in fact, they may have the opposite effect. In this case, budget control increased costs (overtime) and decreased service. As I've stated, what you measure drives your performance. Is budget tracking an effective tool to control cost?

As the peak load story illustrates, leaving unspent money in the budget seems a cardinal sin to most people. An increased budget proves that a department is a growing concern, and if their budget continues to grow, their jobs must be secure. If their budget is cut, then the department must be in trouble. The key points of this philosophy are: budget growth is good, spending the entire budget is good, leaving money on the table is bad, and reducing the budget is bad. Because reducing budgets is seen as a bad thing, something to be avoided, then using budgets to drive your performance is misguided. In fact, doing so will lead to less performance and more costs.

Measure Delivery Service Chain Costs, Not Department Costs

Lean drives you in a different direction. Lean does not recognize costs categorized by departments or branches—Lean does not recognize departments or branches at all. Lean does not recognize walls, or job descriptions, or hierarchies. Lean recognizes only one thing: delivery service chains. A Lean library is driven to reduce the service lead time of the entire delivery service chain, which crosses many departments. If you focus on improving the lead time of the delivery service chains, costs will naturally be reduced and service performance will improve. People will respond to improved customer service. It just happens that cost reduction will follow.

Libraries have a good idea of what their department budgets and costs are in terms of salaries, supplies, etc., but do libraries have a good idea what it costs to buy, receive, prepare, and shelve a new book? In a Lean library, the cost of the delivery service chain would be well-known, and this would drive all cost-reduction efforts. The cost to deliver a new book from ordering to shelving would be the driving performance measure, not the individual department budgets. It would be an effort that crosses the boundaries of the departments, knocks down the walls, and becomes cross-functional. Budgets are no longer the only driving factor. This also depersonalizes the department budget battles that can create larger walls between departments.

Again, I look to the Golden Arches for inspiration. McDonald's knows exactly how much it costs for their organization to order, ship, prepare, package, and deliver a product to one customer, as do most manufacturers. Can a library know how much it costs on average to delivery one book to one customer?

I have found that some libraries know parts of their delivery service chain costs, but typically only the part that is contained within the walls of their particular department. One client, the Southern Maryland Regional Library Association (SMRLA), came very close to the Lean objective. SMRLA is not a library; they are a separate group formed in part to support the new book processing and delivery services to the three counties of southern Maryland. At the end of each year, just like a vendor, they must account for their performance and propose new costs levels to the counties. Therefore they must capture and track how much it costs to receive, prepare, process, and deliver a new book and how much it costs to receive, sort, transfer, deliver, and return a customer hold.

SMRLA sees themselves as a vendor (as they should) and the three counties as their customers. The service delivery cycle has no walls or departments. This drives their performance and their improvement efforts, not departmentally driven budgets. SMRLA is driven by Lean concepts and is one of the founding members of my list of Lean libraries. In many ways this is why I like a technical services group that is outside the walls of a central library.

I predict the future for library software will be transaction cost accounting across the delivery service chains. I would encourage all of you to ask your software vendors if they can support the concept, and if they cannot, to work toward it in the future. In the meantime, if your library software is incapable of accomplishing transaction cost accounting, the following section presents a shortcut to help get started.

Transaction Cost Analysis

Capturing transaction cost estimates can be done manually without too much effort. It entails asking each of your library associates to list all the activities they accomplish during the day. Once complete each staff member provides an estimate of the percent of time in the day they spend performing that task. These tasks and percentage are applied to the various links in the delivery service chain. TCCL's technical services supervisor and I accomplished this exact task. Table 7-1 presents the results of our transaction cost analysis (TCA).

Working with TCCL management and the staff, it did not take long to establish these estimates. By having other departments—specifically the delivery group—and branches develop the same estimates for their tasks and times

Table 7-1. Technical Services Delivery Service Chain: Transactional Cost–Benefit Analysis

Staff	Staff One	Staff Two	Staff Three	Staff Four	Staff Five	Staff Six	Staff Seven	Total
Ordering								
% of Day	20	15	15	15	15	15	30	
Total Hours	8	6	6	6	6	6	12	50
% Improvement	0	0	0	0	0	0	0	0
Savings								
Rec'v Print								
% of Day	10	30	50	10	60	63	55	
Total Hours	4	12	20	4	24	25.2	22	111
% Improvement	6	6	6	6	6	6	6	
Savings	0.2	0.7	1.2	0.2	1.4	1.5	1.3	7
Rec'v Media								
% of Day	20	35	15	0	5	10	0	
Total Hours	8	14	6	0	2	4	0	34
% Improvement	41	41	41	41	41	41	41	
Savings	3.3	5.7	2.5	0.0	0.8	1.6	0.0	14
Linking								
% of Day	0	10	10	60	10	20	0	
Total Hours	0	4	4	24	4	8	0	44
% Improvement	80	80	80	80	80	80	0	
Savings	0.0	3.2	3.2	19.2	3.2	6.4	0.0	35
Admin								
% of Day	50	10	10	15	10	10	10	
Total Hours	20	4	4	6	4	4	4	46
Savings	0	0	0	0	0	0	0	0
Total Savings	4	10	7	19	5	10	1	56

(percent of day), we established a framework for our new book delivery service chain cost analysis. Once we extended each estimate by the individual staff's labor rate plus benefits, we established a cost for each process step. In addition, we also allocated an overhead rate to those labor costs that capture the utility cost, building maintenance cost, depreciation cost, etc. (We allocated the utility, maintenance costs, and depreciation cost based on square footage use. This seemed a foreign concept to my team, so for assistance in calculating overhead burden costs for your library seek help from your accounting department.) Once accomplished, we applied these estimates directly to each of the links in the chain presented in the new book delivery service flowchart. With these data we were able to drive the analysis either up or down. For example, we were able to develop the answers to the following questions:

- What is the average cost to deliver a new item to a customer? By knowing the material budget and the number of new items purchased in one year, an average materials cost was assigned. Adding in the labor estimates loaded with overhead costs from the service delivery chain flowchart, we found our answer.
- What is the cost to deliver a new media item to a customer? Once again, knowing the media budget and the number of media items purchased in one year, an average material cost was assigned plus the transaction labor and overhead costs.
- What is the cost to deliver Western books and media to our customers?

You can drive this analysis as deep or as shallow as you desire. The same process can be applied to improving the customer holds/reserves delivery service chain. What you find might surprise you; often some of the lowest volume items are costing you the most time and labor.

One of my favorite examples is a project I worked on for one of my clients in the Midwest who wanted to know if the time and effort they were spending processing, sorting, and finding a home for withdrawn and gift books was worth their investment in time and money. After defining the delivery service chains for both withdrawn books and gift books and acquiring time estimates from the staff, we applied the transaction cost analysis. We then compared the results to the income and benefits that withdrawn and gift items provided. Table 7-2 presents the transaction cost analysis of the withdrawn and gift book delivery service chain for one fiscal year.

We found it was costing them around $80,000 a year to sort and process withdrawn and gift items. We also found they were making about $50,000 in withdrawn and gift book resale, plus they were adding a value of $120,000 to their collection by retaining selected gift books. In the end it was a profitable endeavor for the library—perhaps not as profitable as they hoped, but profitable. This project also guided management to donate a large number of books throughout the year to a charity in their local city who distributed the books to the poorest in the community. It was and is a very popular program.

This transaction cost analysis can become a powerful tool to establishing your Lean transformation priorities. You can discover where most of your costs are being spent as well as what value of service you are providing for the costs. You can track these costs month to month and year to year to see if your

Table 7-2. Gifts—Transaction Cost Analysis

Transactions	Costs
Pull deselected items	$12,000
Sort gift items	$12,880
Add gift items—cataloged	$5,300
Add gift items—not cataloged	$20,270
Book sales	$12,100
Reseller	$9,300
Recycle costs	$6,700
Total	$78,550

Lean transformation efforts are having the impact you desire. This is a much more effective tool than budget cost control.

Strategy Seven Review

A Lean library does not allow "budgets" or "budget creep" to be the primary tool to reduce or control costs. A Lean library looks to the delivery service chain, which crosses departmental boundaries, captures those costs, and aggressively reduces service lead times, which will reduce those costs. Finally, delivery service improvement can create and drive cost-reduction efforts in a positive, team-driven process.

Strategy Eight

Transform Your Overall Library Service Performance Metrics

Strategy Four discussed how to define and measure your delivery service chains, and Strategy Seven discussed how to use transaction cost analysis to assign a cost to your delivery service chains. Each of these types of performance measurements can help drive and account for your Lean transformation.

For my manufacturing clients there is one additional and very powerful performance measure that rules over them all: inventory turns. Inventory turns represent how fast inventory flows through an operation. In other words, how fast the water (inventory) flows through the river. The fewer twists and turns and obstacles, the faster the river flows. In the same way, the higher an operation's inventory turns, the better they are performing. It is the ratio between costs of sales and the value of inventory required to support those sales (calculated by dividing the annual costs of sales by the average inventory level for that fiscal year). Higher inventory turns means fewer inventories in the operation's process and therefore less cash is tied up in the inventory and vice versa.

Inventory turns have a direct relationship with service lead times, costs, and quality. Lead time is defined by how long it takes to build a widget, starting from the manufacturer of the first component to the assembly of the final product. The longer the lead time the more inventories are tied up in the process. The shorter the lead time the fewer inventories are tied up in the process; therefore, short lead times result in high inventory turns, and long lead times result in low inventory turns. Inventory turns may be the most revealing and effective performance metric an operation has. This one measurement can tell you how your operation is performing in all of the most important performance metrics: lead time, cost, service, cash investment, and quality. One simple measurement can tell an operation how well they are performing as a whole.

Long rivers have more water than short rivers, and long lead times have more inventory, cash, and cost than short lead times. Lean teaches us to have a short river with fast-moving water, therefore less inventory, less cash, less lead time, and less costs and better quality. Inventory turns capture all of these measurements with one calculation.

This is all well and good, but is there a similar measurement that can be applied to the library environment? There is. I call it library service turns, and it is calculated by a second measurement I have coined for libraries, service days not available (SDNA).

Standard circulation turns are a familiar concept with libraries. Standard circulation turns divide the total number of items circulated during a defined period of time by the average number of items that can be circulated (non-reference materials) during that same period. For example, the Tulsa City–County Library in 2009 had a circulation of 4,860,570 against a collection of 1,748,751, translating into an average circulation turn per item of 2.8. Most libraries see this as a measure reflecting the popularity of the collection. However, it also is a reflection of the effectiveness of the delivery process.

What is an ideal service turn? In a perfect world, every book a library owns would always be in demand and be ready to be delivered to a waiting customer. In this perfect world the library would be able to deliver that book to the desired customer immediately, and the next customer would immediately pick up the book when the previous customer finished it. In this perfect world, how many service turns can one book support? Assumptions: Number of days an average library is open during the year = 355. Average days a customer uses to read and return a book = 10 days. In this perfect world we can turn this book every 10 days. Perfect world circulation turns for this book (355/10) = 35 turns.

Of course, there is no such thing as a perfect world. Customers do not pick up their books the same day they are available. Many books sit on the hold shelf for up to seven days, and some are never picked up. What about the rest of the time, time that the library controls? How many days are lost in the delivery cycle that might be used by a customer if the book were available and in demand? This is service days not available (SDNA). SDNA represents all the time a book or item is "in process" and not available to a customer or in the hands of a customer. In Lean terms this is defined as not adding any value to a customer either through its availability or use. Are there delays in the delivery process that keep books out of the hands of your customers?

By examining the delivery service chain flowcharts in Strategy Three (pp. 37–38) you can identify the steps and delays involved in delivering a book to a customer. These delays should be familiar to your own library; many of them were identified in our service delivery chain case examples: the book is waiting in a box to be received, waiting on a book cart to be received, being received, waiting on a book cart to be cataloged, being cataloged, waiting on a book cart to be processed, being processed, waiting in a tote box to be delivered, being delivered, waiting in a tote box to be received, being received, waiting on a book cart to be placed on a shelf, waiting in the book return bin or book cart to be checked in, discharged for transfer, waiting in a tote box to be transferred, waiting in a tote box in sorting, waiting to be sorted, or waiting in a tote box to be delivered.

Every additional minute, hour, day, or week these steps consume will add to the number of service days this book is not available to the customer. The objective of a Lean library is to increase service days available (SDA) by decreasing or eliminating the amount of time a book sits in queue and streamlining the time it takes to complete the required value-added activities. The number of books in queue or staged in the process reflects the time a book is not available. But it is just not customer service that suffers—everything suffers. The more books are backed up in the delivery cycle, the longer the service lead times, the higher the labor costs, and the higher the inventory costs, not to mention the increased space required to house all of those books.

Table 8-1 presents the perfect world service turns assuming a library is open 52 weeks less 10 holidays (365 less 10 days is 355 days open). Therefore, if you owned only one book, you would service 35 customers in one year with that book.

What happens to library service turns if you subtract from the 355 days a library is open by the number of days it takes to deliver a book? Subtract from the available days the assumed ten days it takes a customer to read the book plus four days to deliver the book (refer to Table 8-2). Therefore, every fourteen days you can turn a book, translating into an almost perfect world of service turns of $(355/14) = 25$ turns.

If you owned one book you would be able to service twenty-five sequential customers a year, about two a month. This is about a 30 percent drop in the number of customers you can serve with that one book as compared to the

Table 8-1. Perfect World Service Turns	
Number of days open	355
Average days customer keeps book	10
Perfect world service turns (350/10)	35

Table 8-2. Adjusted Perfect World Service Turns	
Number of days open	355
Average days customer keeps book	10
Transport days	4
Total unavailable days	14
New circulation turns (340/16)	25

ideal of thirty-five service turns per year [(35–25)/35 = 28.5 percent]. This drop is fully attributed to just four days of delivery time. Table 8-3 extrapolates this scenario to the entire collection of a library system.

To make up for the four days of transport time and achieve your ideal service turns, you would have to increase the materials budget by nearly 30 percent, or $1,140,000. Stated another way, if you had ten books to support the thirty-five-turn ideal, you would need to buy three additional books to make up for the four days the book is not available during transport, and this is in a near-perfect world.

SDNA at first glance appears to be a very difficult thing to measure. However, if you perceive the measurement as all the time a book is either not on the shelf or not in the hands of the customer, it becomes easier to understand. To understand SDNA you must look at your entire delivery cycle. There are three major components of your delivery cycle:

- Preparing and delivering a new book to a branch's shelf
- Delivering a reserved/hold book to a customer
- Returning a book to the owning branch's shelf

By analyzing each of these three delivery service chains you can develop a fairly good estimate of your library's overall SDA performance. The following are case examples of this process.

Preparing and Delivering a New Book to a Branch Shelf

I was hired by the public service director of Okanagan Regional Library (ORL) to help them design a new technical services and allocation layout and to improve their delivery process because they were planning to relocate to a new logistics center and administration headquarters.

The delivery system for ORL at that time supported the main library plus twenty-nine branch locations. Circulation for FY2006 represented 3,232,000 items serving a population of approximately 337,000 with 222,000 library mem-

Table 8-3. Impact on Materials Budget	
Perfect world service turns per year	35
Perfect world library materials budget	$4,000,000
% Increase required	29
Increase in material budget	$1,140,000
Value of each transport day	$114,286

bers. The ORL delivery system consisted of two drivers and a part-time driver for one truck supporting a day and night trip. Courier services were used for the four most outlying branches. The most outlying library served by the delivery truck was nearly 167 kilometers (104 miles) away from headquarters.

Similar to the Lean concepts presented in Strategies Five and Six, we flowcharted the new book and holds/reserves delivery service chains, formed a cross-functional team, and defined a service performance gap analysis between where they wanted to be versus their current performance. Table 8-4 presents our findings regarding the gap in delivery performance.

Similar to TCCL, ORL was experiencing a large backlog in the cataloging and processing areas for new books. While TCCL's backlog had appeared as the result of year-end peak loads, ORL's backlog had formed slowly over the years. They simply did not have the capacity to match the demand. This growing bubble forced them into an expediting mode, processing the highest-priority items first. Due to the backlog, bestsellers were given the highest priority, then items with hold requests next, followed by seasonable items, fiction, time-referenced nonfiction, and finally other nonfiction. In some cases some low-priority nonfiction books were falling six to eight months behind.

Strategy Eight tells us to view ORL from the prism of SDA, SDNA, and available service turns (AST). Analyzing SDA, SDNA, and AST for the "item with hold request" row in Table 8-4, the chart shows that an item was taking four to five weeks to be received, cataloged, and processed through the system, and that this was being accomplished only about 75 percent of the time, meaning 25 percent sat for more than five weeks. ORL management was not satisfied with this performance and wanted to dramatically improve this important service performance to their customers.

Assuming there are 355 service days available in a year, using a 5-week turnaround time to process new books with holds, this adds 5 weeks × 7 days,

Table 8-4. New Book Delivery Service Chain Performance against Target

Delivery Process	Current Performance	Best Practice Metrics
Best seller/quick read	1–3 days/95%	1–3 days/95%
Item with hold request	4–5 weeks/75%	3–5 days/95%
Seasonal	4–5 weeks/75%	3–5 days/95%
Fiction	1–2 weeks/75%	1 week/95%
Time dated NF / Ref.	4–5 weeks/60%	1 week/95%
NF w/ marc. (75%)	1–3 months/70%	1 week/95%
NF w/ Amicus/LC (13%)	1–3 months/70%	1 week/95%
NF Custom Catg. (12%)	1–3 months/70%	1 month/95%

or 35 service days not available that must be taken away from the 355 service days available. We also must add to the SDNA the time to sort, allocate, and deliver the new book to the hold shelf. Using our flowcharts, I estimated about six days to go through sorting, allocation, and delivery plus one day for the branch to receive and place the book on the hold shelf. Table 8-5 summarizes the results to the new book with hold—service days available.

This process supports 42 SDNA or lost days, creating 313 service days that are still available to service customers. However, the time the book rests on the hold shelf, the time the customer takes reading the book, and the time it takes to return the book to the owning branch must be considered to calculate AST. Assuming an average 5 days of hold shelf wait time, 10 days average customer read time, and 5 days to return the book to the owning library (or deliver it to the next customer), we can calculate the book can turn every 25 days. This creates an AST of 10, meaning we can service 10 customers with this book during the year. See Table 8-6.

Table 8-5. New Book with Hold—SDA

Service days available (SDA)	355
New book processing (SDNA)	35
Sorting/delivery service days not available (SDNA)	6
Receiving service days not available (SDNA)	1
Total service days not available (SDNA)	42
New service days available (SDA)	313
% Loss to service days available (SDA)	13

Table 8-6. New Book with Hold—AST

Service days available (SDA)	355
Less new book SDNA	91
SDA adjusted	264
Deliver to shelf SDNA	5
Hold shelf wait time	5
Customer read time	10
Return book to shelf (SDNA)	5
Number of days between turn events	25
Available service turns	10

By applying the Lean concepts presented in Strategies Five and Six to the ORL delivery service chains, we developed a design that could reduce the time required to receive and process a new book from five weeks to seven days. In addition, we developed a target design to reduce the sorting and delivery of a new book to the shelf from five days to two days and to return the book to the owning library (or deliver to the next customer) from five days to two days. These improvements were very similar in design to the TCCL and PLYMC projects. (Some of the ORL branches received delivery only twice a week due to their volumes or location, so they would not meet these projections, but for this analysis we will assume all the branches benefited.) Table 8-7 presents the projected new SDA and AST.

Our Lean design would help the library serve four more customers per year, or a 31 percent improvement. With these projected improvements not only would the customer receive the new book with a hold on it in a week versus more than a month, the library would now be able to service four more customers per year with the same book.

What is the impact of this improvement? If ORL can serve 31 percent more customers, does this not mean they could reduce by 31 percent the number of books bought and still service the same number of customers they did before? If the number of books bought was reduced by 31 percent, how would this affect the collections development, receiving, cataloging, and allocations departments' workloads? Would peak loads be reduced? Could ORL reach the point where they could meet their service goals while reducing the number of books required to support their goals? Could they service 15 percent more customers with 15 percent less books? What could the library do with a 15 percent reduction in their materials budget per year? In an environment of reduced funding and increased demand this is an important question.

Table 8-7. ORL SDA Benefits

Service days available (SDA)	355
Less new book processing SDNA	7
Projected SDA adjusted	348
Hold shelf wait time	5
Customer read time	10
Deliver book to next customer (SDNA)	2
Number of days between turn events	17
Available service turns	20
% Improvement to SDA	31

In a library environment, small changes are significant. Each day you add to SDA, the more customers you can serve with the same or less level of investment in materials and manpower. A 31 percent improvement can give you many choices you may not have had before.

I recently received an update from ORL, and they have made great progress toward their Lean design service performance goals. They have moved into their new building, and the cataloging and processing department has managed to reduce the backlog to a reasonable level. In the new building these departments now use book carts for storage and movement of library materials. Stated in Lean terms, they have eliminated most of the pooling and stagnant water in their Snake River, and Lean River is now starting to flow.

It will take some time to see if this new performance translates into material budget reductions, as reducing budgets, as discussed in Strategy Seven, is not an easy task. This example shows that SDA can properly reflect how well your library is performing and how much better you can perform. In this one simple measurement you can communicate to your staff what you expect out of your delivery service chains as well as drive your Lean transformation efforts.

Delivering a Reserved/Hold Book to a Customer

This book has used examples of libraries that were struggling with large backlogs and capacity issues thus impacting their service lead times and cost. But what if your library is meeting your delivery service expectations and you have been successful in avoiding the dreaded backlog? Can SDA, SDNA, and AST measurements be meaningfully applied to you? Is it worth your effort to embark on a Lean journey if you are already performing to high expectations? To answer this question, let us assume a book is in its second year and still popular. Let us assume you can deliver a book hold request from the owning library to the destination library in ninety-six hours 95 percent of the time. This translates to you being able to service nineteen customers during the year with that one book. See Table 8-8.

What happens if you embark on a Lean journey and your Lean cross-functional team sets a new target of twenty-four-hour delivery instead of ninety-six-hour delivery? Will these three days of improvement make much of a difference? See Table 8-9.

By improving AST from nineteen to twenty-two you have achieved nearly a 20 percent improvement. Let us assume the demand for the book requires the collections development department to buy ten copies of this book to meet demand based on your current nineteen service turns performance. Let us assume that these ten books totally satisfied your customer base. If you improved your AST by 20 percent, does this mean the collections department can buy two fewer books while better servicing your customers? If this 20 percent translated across your entire collection—which it could since delivery performance is universal and does not care what book or item is being deliv-

Table 8-8. Holds Service Chain Turns Available

Service days available (SDA)	355
Deliver to hold shelf SDNA	4
Hold shelf wait time	5
Customer read time	10
Number of days between turn events	19
Available service turns	19

Table 8-9. Holds Service Chain Turns Available—Lean

Service days available (SDA)	355
Deliver to shelf SDNA	1
Hold shelf wait time	5
Customer read time	10
Number of days between turn events	16
Available service turns	22
% Improvement in AST	19

ered—does this mean you can reduce your materials budget by 20 percent across the board and still have improved your service levels? What if you have a seventy-two-hour delivery and you improve to forty-eight-hour delivery, or forty-eight-hour delivery and you improve it to twenty-four-hour delivery? This is why I like working for libraries: no matter how well you are performing, small improvements can translate into huge rewards.

This is the power of Lean. The impact of reducing the delivery service chain in a library system is significant, no matter how well you are currently performing. Each time you reduce the length of the chain, the more costs you squeeze out, the less books you need on the shelves, the more customers you can serve, the more errors you eliminate, and the quicker you can serve your customer. SDNA and service turns are two powerful Lean metrics to get the message out to your staff and to show them the potential benefits of their efforts.

Your cross-functional teams should use Lean principles aggressively to attack non-value-added activities in your delivery service chain no matter how well you are currently performing. Your management team should understand the negative consequences of SDNA and the positive results of improved AST to drive your cross-functional teams in their efforts.

Strategy Eight Review

Libraries measure many things that provide performance feedback. This includes budget controls, circulation increase, number of people entering a library, and other factors; however, these measurements are a reflection only of your library's actual service performance. Service turns is one measurement that tells you how much waste you have in your library and how much better you can perform. By focusing on this measurement you can drive improvement efforts that will truly make a difference in customer service improvement and satisfaction. By focusing on eliminating the waste that reduces service turns available the costs associated with this waste can be reduced and the extra inventory supporting this waste can be reduced.

Strategy Nine

Transform Your Digital Research Delivery Service Chain

Strategy Nine will discuss the growth of "one click" digital research tools supplied by the likes of Google and how they challenge the future of your library's research service offerings. You will learn how Lean tools can help you recognize the gap between your performance and your customer's requirements and how advanced next-generation library search engines can close that gap.

A few months ago I was invited to a concert featuring the Black Eyed Peas and U2. Watching the Black Eyed Peas was an experience hard to describe; it truly felt the future had arrived. Their presentation, music, and lyrics seemed to have tapped right into the psyche of the digital generation. It was a bit of an eye opener for an old rocker; the music was imaginative with a mix of every type of music—hip hop, jazz, electronic, rock, rap, and even classic. I am now a big fan.

In one of my favorite Black Eyed Peas songs, called "Now Generation," the band's lyrics refer to Google as their professor and Wikipedia as their checker. They mention checking their accounts and Facebook and MySpace. The lyrics state repeatedly the "Now" generation's desire for immediate results; it's a generation that cannot wait. In this song I believe the Black Eyed Peas have successfully captured and described the demands of the "Now" generation, or what can be called the digital generation.

Strategies One through Eight presented numerous Lean tools to recognize and close the gap between your current performance and your desired performance. Lean can be applied to any business process, including the delivery of digital research content. The service cycle of digital content consists of a series of customer and business process steps that form a delivery chain of service. For example, processing an electronic document has many steps in common with processing a physical item. Both digital content and physical content must be selected, purchased, received, and cataloged. The tools presented in Strategies One through Eight can streamline your digital delivery back-office processes just as well as the delivery of physical materials. The major difference in the service chain between physical or digital delivery of materials is the part the customer plays in the process. In particular, the tasks required to request and receive a digital research document have been moved to the online experience of the customer. The non-value-added steps, delays, and wasteful activities the online customer experiences creates an even larger service gap between you and your customer than those non-value-added processes the customer never sees. This places even greater importance on how you digitally interact with the customer and therefore is the primary focus of Strategy Nine.

In his book *What Would Google Do?*, Jeff Jarvis, faculty member of New York Graduate School of Journalism, discusses Google's organizational purpose:

> One of Google's own principles—the "10 things Google has found to be true"—is: "Faster is better than slow." "Every millisecond counts. . . . Speed is a boon to users. It is also a competitive advantage."[1]

Using Mr. Jarvis's guidance, one might interpret Google's organizational purpose for delivery of digital content is: *Any question answered, instantly.*

Should libraries be concerned with Google? Is Google really a competitor of public and academic libraries? When I asked the associate dean of collection and technology services at Oklahoma State University this question, she did not hesitate to say, "Yes." She sees her university students using Google more and more: "Students will find the path of least resistance to accomplish their research. If our tools are too difficult to use they will turn to other resources, such as Google, to get their answers" (A. Prestamo, personal communication).

The Project Information Literacy Progress Group study titled *Lessons Learned: How College Students Seek Information in the Digital Age*[2] provides support for the dean's assessment. The study surveyed 2,318 college students across six campuses distributed across the United States in the spring of 2009. The report presented a summary of college information seekers' research behavior as follows:

- 97 percent use course readings
- 96 percent use Google
- 94 percent use scholarly research databases (e.g., EBSCO, JSTOR, ProQuest)
- 92 percent use OPAC
- 88 percent use instructors
- 85 percent use Wikipedia

- 72 percent use classmates
- 70 percent use library shelves
- 58 percent use friends
- 54 percent use other search engines than Google (Ask, Yahoo, etc.)
- 47 percent use librarians
- 25 percent use blogs

From this study it appears that Google, scholarly research databases, and OPAC are on the top of the list for finding course-related research material. Based on the results of the report we can assume that the "Now" generation of college students is fully aware of the strengths and weaknesses of both service tools. (The low percentage of students who seek out a librarian for help highlights an important gap in performance between a library's desired organizational purpose and its current performance.) Lean teaches you to create a desire to change by recognizing the gap in performance between where you want to be and where you are now. Therefore, your library staff must project their desired "after" performance metrics for the digital research delivery service chain.

In my research efforts with Oklahoma State University, I asked the dean of collection and technology services to help me define what she expected from her library's research tools. Figure 9-1 presents the results of our efforts.

I translated these results to the following performance metrics for the digital research delivery service chain:

- Online research tools will be available 24/7 both on and off campus 100 percent of the time.
- By using common language and terms, peer-reviewed articles and research documents will be made instantaneously available to our customer using a one-click search box 98 percent of the time.
- If the information our customer seeks is not available, with one click the customer will be directed to other information sources that will provide the customer the information he or she seeks 85 percent of the time.

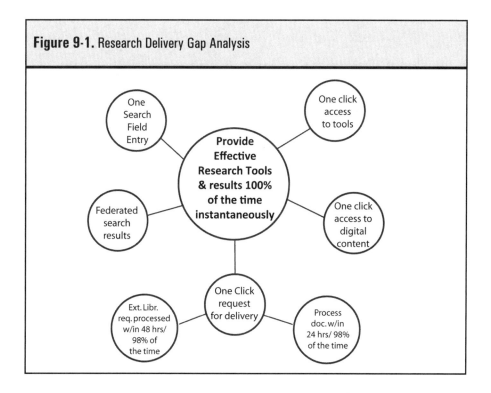

Figure 9-1. Research Delivery Gap Analysis

How does your library match up to these performance metrics?

I solicited the help of an actual university student to help me better understand the gap in performance between his university's research tools' capability and the previously stated objectives. Figure 9-2 presents the results of the Lean value map flowchart.

In this case the student actually knows which database and subdatabase he is seeking; however, without guidance from instructors or librarians, most students do not have a real clue which database they should choose. In this example the student must go through twenty-three steps to acquire the document he is seeking. If the student did not know which of the three hundred databases offered he should use he would have spent a significant amount of time repeating these steps and floating from one database to another. If a student is guided to one particular database his or her research experience is being limited. In a

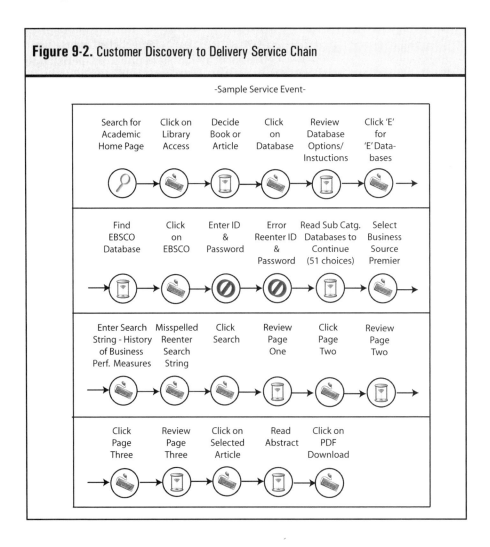

Figure 9-2. Customer Discovery to Delivery Service Chain

-Sample Service Event-

Search for Academic Home Page → Click on Library Access → Decide Book or Article → Click on Database → Review Database Options/Instuctions → Click 'E' for 'E' Databases

Find EBSCO Database → Click on EBSCO → Enter ID & Password → Error Reenter ID & Password → Read Sub Catg. Databases to Continue (51 choices) → Select Business Source Premier

Enter Search String - History of Business Perf. Measures → Misspelled Reenter Search String → Click Search → Review Page One → Click Page Two → Review Page Two

Click Page Three → Review Page Three → Click on Selected Article → Read Abstract → Click on PDF Download typical Google search a person is exposed to alternative information such as images, videos, books, articles, and even products being sold that relate to the subject. Instructing students to limit their search to one database limits the learning experience.

Do you know what your customer experiences while navigating your research tools? Do you know how effective the results are for your customer search requests? The dean of collection and technology services at Oklahoma State University asked this exact question. She spent a year analyzing the gap between her student and faculty expectations and the performance results of the university's proprietary research tools. She explained her findings as follows: "incredibly informative and downright frightening."

Figure 9-3 presents the results of the dean's study. The data show that title and keyword searches represented 73 percent of all searches, and 34 percent to 36 percent of these searches resulted in zero hits. Note that subject browse searches represented less than 6 percent of the searches. In some title searches zero was the "correct" answer because the library does not own the book. In the vast majority of cases, however, zero hits were the result of the user not

Figure 9-3. Traditional OPAC Search Results

Searches	% of Total Search/Browse	% w/ 0 hits
Builder	17.27%	12.69%
Call number	0.18%	0.00%
Command	49.61%	40.33%
Keyword Relevance	3.37%	3.52%
Keyword Search	30.97%	34.02%
Simple Search	6.99%	30.32%
Title	42.37%	36.58%
Blank	0.26%	3.93%
Browses		
Author Browse	7.88%	
Call Number Browse	1.44%	
Name Title Browse	0.15%	
Subject Browse	0.55%	

knowing or following the OPAC search rules. If you extrapolate the data, 28 percent of all the searches resulted in zero hits.

The dean explained that students don't necessarily search for material in the way the library has categorized it. She was not just focused on the quality of her search engine results but the customer experience itself. On the wall of her office are her daily customer service reminders:

- The customer is not broken.
- Your system is broken until proven otherwise.
- Information flows down the path of least resistance. If you block a tool the users want, users will go elsewhere to find it.
- You cannot change the user, but you can transform the user experience to meet the user.[3]

When customers enter an institution, either physically or virtually, they have a certain perception of the service they expect to receive. For example, customers entering McDonald's might expect a hamburger to be delivered within a five-minute window. They may not actually measure the time by looking at their watches, but they have an intuitive understanding of what they expect and know when it is not met. Anything beyond their expectation is a poor service event and therefore should be a poor service event to McDonald's. When customers enter an expensive restaurant they expect to receive their food over a course of time; it is the experience and quality of the food provided that they are paying premium prices for.

In the "Now" generation's digital world of service, customers want quick and easy service and a high-quality product served in an enjoyable and easy-to-use service environment. They expect to find easy-to-use tools and immediate delivery of high-quality results. Google seems to meet the McDonald's model of fast and quick service, and they have established a very high bar for customer service expectations for most if not all of today's search engine users. But do they provide the steak?

There is an ongoing debate within academic library circles on the value of libraries' sophisticated research tools and the quality results they provide versus Google's instantaneous but not necessarily high-quality, peer-reviewed results. The debate is centered on the differences between what is called the "deep web" and the "surface web." Mike Bergman, CEO of Zitglist LLC, a provider of quality linked data products and services states,

> Searching on the Internet today can be compared to dragging a net across the surface of the ocean; a great deal may be caught in the net, but there is a wealth of information that is deep and therefore missed. Most of the Web's information is buried far down on dynamically generated sites, and standard search engines do not find it. Traditional search engines cannot "see" or retrieve content in the deep Web—those pages do not exist until they are

created dynamically as the result of a specific search. The deep Web is several orders of magnitude larger than the surface Web."[4]

Are libraries presenting results from the deep web that Google might miss? Can libraries rest on their laurels and assume that since they provide higher quality results than Google it does not matter how quickly and easily these results can be achieved or how enjoyable the user experience is? Should libraries consider Google's one-click search box approach to delivering instant answers to research questions a threat to their own more sophisticated and higher quality research service?

As I mentioned, this debate is a hot topic in academic libraries and in the research arm of public libraries. The University of Rochester felt this debate was so important they embarked on a research project to find answers. Their research project titled *Studying Students: The Undergraduate Research Project at the University of Rochester* states:

> One staff member reflected on how staff used to debate, again and again, whether we should have a simple search interface or a more complex interface. Being involved with the study helped us all realize that as far as our students were concerned, we did not really know what was best. . . . As we learned more about our students, it became clear that we needed both simple and complex interfaces; we can now focus our energies on the interactions of both.[5]

While libraries continue to have this debate, Google is working aggressively to close their service performance gap of providing scholarly answers to scholarly questions. Google Scholar speaks volumes in this regard. Google's model of providing free services through targeted advertisement placement has proven highly successful for the surface web. Will it prove just as successful for the deep web and scholarly materials? Will scholars determine that it is more worth their while to publish their content to the surface web rather than burying it into the deep web? Will they determine that they can reach more users and make more money on the surface web? While some librarians continue the debate, some are moving forcefully to meet Google's challenge.

The dean of collection and technology services at Oklahoma State University recognized this service performance gap. She embarked on a project to transform how Oklahoma State students will search for research materials in the future.

> She was the first to sign on to a beta site service which allows libraries to align their broad array of collections and resources behind a simple, obvious starting place—a search box. It provides a view of the library that is consistent with what the user experiences when using Amazon or Wikipedia. The library search box will seamlessly bring to the surface for the user the expanse of library materials relevant to the search—books, videos, e-content, local digital collections at the article level, whatever the format.[6]

The dean explained that the key to linking the old technology with new technology is the use of link resolvers. These link resolvers are driven by unique identifiers at the article level. This advancement along with a federated search approach and next-generation catalogs (taking a simple query and broadcasting to a number of databases or other web-based resources) creates a user experience much like Google provides.

Marshall Breeding, director for innovative technology and research at the Vanderbilt University Libraries and an authority on library technology, supports this urgent need for change. He agrees that libraries must offer access to their resources in ways that compete with popular Web destinations such as Amazon and Google:

> Library users find these competing interfaces much easier to use and more compelling than that of their library. . . . One of the great challenges that libraries face today involves finding ways to provide access to their content and services to today's Web-savvy users. A new genre of technology products have emerged that will allow library customers to use methods more consistent with what they are experiencing elsewhere on the Web. . . . As these products evolve, it's becoming feasible to think of a single consolidated search that addresses all the resources managed by the library, spanning print collections; electronic resources that include vast numbers of journal, newspaper, or magazine articles; and collections of digital materials such as images, video, or digital sound recordings.[7]

Libraries must examine the complex steps their online users must follow to access information. Separate interfaces for different media does not contend well with for-profit competitors that offer simple search options of a great amount of content. Simpler interfaces providing authoritative results from various sources will help libraries be more relevant to "Now" generation users.

Breeding explained that libraries can choose from a variety of both commercially provided and open-source products in this genre of discovery interfaces. You can find more information on these products in Breeding's book *Next-Gen Library Catalogs*.[8]

The future of search tools lies in these next-generation search interfaces, and your library and your users will benefit greatly from this conversion. With forward-thinking librarians joining forces with forward-thinking service providers, significant changes and advancements in meeting your customers' service expectations are quickly becoming available.

To be a Lean library, your library must eliminate the non-value-added activities you force by design onto your customers. In this case, the answer does not lie in just streamlining flows or eliminating a task here or there; it requires embracing new technology. Libraries have proven over and over again that they are fully capable of meeting this challenge and fully capable of staying viable. To close the gap between your current performance and your competitors', libraries must embrace these next-generation tools and this one-click approach to service. To move in this direction your library should form a Lean project team to analyze your current performance, discover the gap between you and your competitor, and research how these next-generation tools can close that gap. Managing and implementing this change is beyond the scope of this book, but recognizing the need to change certainly is not.

Strategy Nine Review

With digital content growing every day, academic and public libraries must streamline the delivery of digital research materials just as aggressively as streamlining the delivering of physical materials. The gap analysis tools of Lean presented in this book apply to the digital service delivery chain in the same way they apply to the more familiar physical service delivery chain. Your library must define the service delivery chain for all of these processes, including and most importantly how your customers use and interact with your virtual service window. Your management team must ask, "Will our current delivery service chain carry us into the future?" If the answer is no, you must research and pursue technological advancements now being developed and tested. This will allow your library to close the gap between your current performance and your most aggressive competitors as well as better secure your future.

Notes

1. Jarvis, Jeff. 2009. *What Would Google Do?* New York: HarperCollins.
2. Eisenberg, Michael. 2009. *Project Information Literacy Progress Report*. Seattle: The Information School, University of Washington.
3. Schneider, Karen. 2010. "The User Is Not Broken: A Meme Masquerading as a Manifesto." *Free Range Librarian* (blog). Accessed November 12. http://freerangelibrarian.com/2006/06/03/the-user-is-not-broken-a-meme-masquerading-as-a-manifesto.
4. "Deep Web." 2010. Wikipedia. Accessed November 12. http://en.wikipedia.org/wiki/Deep_Web.
5. Foster, Nancy Fried, and Gibbons, Susan, eds. 2007. *Studying Students: The Undergraduate Research Project at the University of Rochester*. University of Rochester River Campus Libraries. http://docushare.lib.rochester.edu/docushare/dsweb/View/Collection-4436.
6. Serials Solutions. 2010. "Transforming the Library to Embrace the User." Serials Solutions. Accessed November 12. http://www.serialssolutions.com/assets/publications/Oklahoma_State_Summon_Case_Study.pdf.
7. Breeding, Marshall. 2010. *Next-Gen Library Catalogs*. New York: Neal-Schuman.
8. Ibid.

Strategy Ten

Transform Your Delivery Service Chain from a "Push" to a "Pull" Philosophy

Previous strategies have examined the transformational power of Lean. Strategy Ten will explore the most forward-looking philosophy Lean has to offer: the power of "pull" versus "push" demand management. If you have embraced the concepts of Lean you have learned that you can reduce the delivery lead-time gap between you and your customer. In particular, you can reduce the gap between when customers decide what book or media item they want and your ability to acquire and deliver that item to them. By reducing this lead-time gap you have introduced a new competitive element and a new kind of flexibility into your acquisitions decision-making model. As the gap is reduced or eliminated, your library can shift from "pushing" your forecasts of demand onto the customer to having the customer "pull" their demand requirements from you. This is a game-changing proposition.

Henry Ford has been commonly quoted as saying, "The customer can have any color of Model T they want, as long as it is black." While the reasons he purportedly said this can be debated, from a production point of view, he has a point. There is no simpler production model than to build the same product over and over again. There is no guesswork required to know what the customer wants, because you know what they want: you told them what they want and gave them no other choice.

Imagine a library that provides just one book title and every customer is satisfied with that one offering. Imagine how simple running a library would be. Or, on the other side, imagine a library that makes all the decisions on what a customer may read. Over time Ford's competition offered automobiles in different colors, and Ford had to respond in kind. As Ford added different colors, models, and features, the complexity of the production process increased leaps and bounds. The concept of large component batches was introduced along with longer lead times, hidden quality problems, and huge facilities to store in-process and finished goods inventory. The longer lead times required the manufacturer to "guess" what model, color, and feature the customer wanted and to "push" these guesses onto the customer. The larger the distance (delivery lead time) between the purchase and production of the component parts to the time of delivery to the customer the more the manufacturers had to guess what the customer actually wanted and in what quantities. This, of course, led to a great deal of at risk inventory to support this forecast delivery model.

The Toyota Production System (TPS), or what we now call Lean, ushered in an entirely new era of manufacturing and a totally new production model concept called "demand-side pull." As they attacked the waste in their production process, created focused work cells, and reduced their delivery lead time by up to 95 percent, they discovered they had dramatically reduced the time from when customers discovered what they wanted and the time they could start to manufacture it. This created a huge opportunity and a paradigm shift on how manufacturers viewed their forecasted demand relationship with their customers. No longer did they have to guess what customers wanted years ahead of time; they simply could wait for customers to pull demand from their showrooms. This purchase from customers became a "pull" signal to Toyota to replace the car that was pulled from the retail lot. Actual demand as opposed to forecasted demand drives Toyota's production decisions. This also created a dramatic shift in the relationship of the manufacturer and their suppliers. To further reduce the lead-time response window, Toyota went so far as to have their suppliers build plants next to their final assembly plant. When Toyota consumed the vendor components required to replenish the customer pull, this would create another "pull" signal to the suppliers to replenish the component parts consumed, and the vendors of the vendors would then be "pulled" as well. All of this started with the customers' decision to buy a particular car. Therefore, purchasing decisions are driven by real-time customer decisions. This TPS/Lean "pull sided" approach transformed the manufacturing industry.

As the Internet progressed and enterprise-wide software systems became more sophisticated, the concept of a "demand-side pull" system advanced even further. Dell took this concept to its next pinnacle. On Dell's website customers can build their own custom computer by selecting from a menu of options. This became, up to that time, the ultimate demand-side pull production model; that is, until Amazon.com came along.

Jeffery P. Bezos, founder and CEO of Amazon.com, wrote to his shareholders, "Kindle is a good example of our fundamental approach. More than four years ago, we began with a long-term vision: every book, ever printed, in any language, all available in less than 60 seconds."[1]

As mentioned in Strategy One, the concept of Lean has been fully embraced by Amazon.com, and they see it as an effective competitive tool. They are well advised to continue their focus on streamlining their processes and improving their customer service, as the competition is hot on their trail. Apple's iPad and uncanny ability to tap into what the "Now" generation wants is a direct challenge to Amazon.com's desired domination of digital entertainment.

Amazon.com maintains warehouses across the country, allowing them to support a twenty-four-hour delivery model of physical materials to their customers. To do so they must adhere to a supply-side push model by predicting what the customer might want and stocking that physical inventory in their warehouses. With digital content, they are replacing this model of a physical warehousing with a digital warehouse. (In fact, in 2009, they announced the closing of three of their twenty-one warehouses.) Their digital library now allows Amazon.com to shift from a supply-side push model to a demand-side pull model. As the amount of content shifts from physical to digital, the more and more Amazon's costs will go down and the more low-cost content they will be able to offer to their customers. The stakes (and benefits) are huge, and it is obvious Amazon.com is dedicated to this path.

In July 2010 a key milestone event occurred. The headline in Techcrunch read, "Kindle Books Outselling Hardcover Books. 'Tipping Point' Reached, Amazon Says." The article states, "In the past three months, for every 100 hardcover books sold, Amazon.com has sold 143 Kindle books."[2] In the next few years it will be more than a tipping point; critical mass will be reached, and once critical mass is reached, a new norm has been established.

Libraries face the same transition from a physical world to a digital world. As discussed in Strategy Nine, the concepts of Lean presented in this book apply to both physical and digital delivery models. The service delivery chain begins when customers realize their desire for your product or service ends when that product or service has been delivered. Whether this requires physical movement of materials or digital movement of information, process steps exist, non-value-added activities exist, and there is always an opportunity to make it faster and make it better.

As you pursue a Lean transformation and begin to experience the dramatic reductions in lead-time delivery, you should look for opportunities to shift from a supply-side push model to a demand-side pull model.

For example, the dean of learning resources at Tulsa Community College has fully embraced this push-versus-pull transformation. He eliminated the position of selectors and empowered his entire staff to be selectors. Each staff member is encouraged to work directly with their students to determine what research materials they need and, if necessary, to order that material for them. Any staff member at any time can access their vendor's online site to order books, and if the book needs to be delivered in twenty-four to forty-eight hours, he has empowered his staff to order directly from Amazon.com. This does not mean they do not work with the academic staff to determine what course materials need to be ordered before the class work begins, but the dean has recognized that empowering his staff allows customers to "pull" their actual requirements as opposed to having materials pushed on them. "Pulling" customer demand seems a natural fit for smaller and single-location libraries. However, does it apply to larger university and public library environments?

The associate dean for collection and technology services at Oklahoma State University Library provides us an answer. In their approach to purchasing research journal subscriptions, she explains their shift from a supply-side push model to a demand-side pull model:

> In the past, we subscribed to about 370 journals. Our research showed customers only used about 100 of them. Now we subscribe to a large package deal, allowing us to offer over 1,700 journals and the customer decides which ones they want to access. These digital journal packages allow us to offer a much larger amount of information to our customers at the same or at lesser costs, and, more importantly, we now have a feedback cycle to what the customer actually wants. This allows us to make more informed decisions on what we subscribe to. (A. Prestamo, personal communication)

This pull-versus-push transition also exists in the public library environment. The manager of the collection development department at TCCL explains how they have shifted from a push-demand model to a customer pull-demand model using a combination of purchasing and leasing books:

> In the past we would decide the number of books we wanted to purchase based on our experience and the history of similar books for this author, category, or genre. We therefore were forecasting and committing to buying the total number of books we needed three, six, even nine months in advance. A few years ago, we arranged to lease additional copies based on demand. Now we do not have to make a total purchase commitment so far in advance. We will choose to purchase a certain number of copies, but it will be based on how many copies we want the library to own in the long run, not based on the initial peak load demand of the initial release. Three to four weeks before the book is released we check to see how many holds are on the book, and using our three customers for every one book service target, we lease the remaining number of books required to close the gap. Once the initial surge is gone we return the leased copies and, of course, keep the books we purchased. We allow this "pull" lease option to close the gap between what we want to own in the long run and what we need to acquire temporarily to satisfy the initial customer demand. We save a lot of money this way, and we are better able to service our customers' requirements. (R. Moran, personal communication)

By reducing the lead time between the purchasing (leasing) decisions and the understanding and recognition of actual customer demand, TCCL and other libraries are shifting to this purchase/lease pull-demand model.

For public libraries this purchase/lease combination option of acquiring print materials is a great example of closing the time gap between your customers' desires and your purchasing decisions; however, as stated, the world is shifting to a digital world, and e-books will soon hit a "tipping point" within libraries as well.

If e-books can be purchased in seconds and delivered in seconds, there is no time gap between when the customer decides they want a particular e-book and when you make your purchasing decision. Theoretically, Amazon.com could actually wait to purchase a particular e-book from the publisher until the customer actually orders that e-book title. They could even receive payment from the customer before they pay the publisher. This is the ultimate pull-demand model of Lean. Customers pull their demand request, the company immediately purchases requested materials, customers immediately pay for them, and they are delivered immediately at very little if any cost to the customer. Amazon.com may even have a positive cash flow between buying the materials and paying for the materials.

Where will libraries fit into this new e-book delivery model? This is a difficult customer service issue that every library faces, so I'll discuss the options currently available to libraries today and predict what options might (or should) exist in the near future.

Let us assume an English teacher has given a reading assignment to her thirty students. The book is not a book the school provides to students, so she asks the students to acquire the book on their own. The teacher has not contacted library staff to warn them of this upcoming assignment. A few of the smarter students act immediately and check out the six copies the library owns. The other students go to the library's online site to request the book and find that the wait time to receive the print book is outside their assignment window. They notice that there is not an e-book option available. They approach their local branch librarian and request help. The branch librarians subsequently call the acquisitions group with the students' request. A few branch librarians are able to find some books through interlibrary loan, but in the end, the library cannot even come close to providing the total number of books needed. What options are available to a typical library in this situation? How would Lean guide us in these situations?

> **Option 1:** The library tells the students they are a tax-funded, nonprofit organization and they are not able to compete to the same standards as a bookstore or an Amazon.com. The branch librarians tell the students to go to their local bookstore or Amazon.com to acquire their book.

This book began by discussing how important it is to recognize that libraries are complex businesses with tough competitors. Lean tells us to recognize the gap in performance between your delivery model and the competitor's and to aggressively close that gap. Therefore, if we allow Lean to guide our way, we should reject this option. It is not a valid competitive choice, and to make it worse we are sending our customers to our competitors.

> **Option 2:** The library establishes a partnership with Amazon.com and embeds a link to Amazon.com on the library's website. The branch librarian guides the student to the link, and they help the students order the book from Amazon.com directly.

It is my understanding that this is an option available to public libraries and is already in place in some libraries today. The bottom line is a library customer who has to wait longer than he or she wants for a book can "pull" the book more quickly by simply and easily clicking on the Amazon.com link made available by the library. I would assume libraries share in the profit of the book sale. While the library is providing a service solution to the customer, Lean would force the library to recognize that this is no better than option 1. The library has simply given up. The risks of such a partnership should be evaluated.

Amazon.com CEO Jeff Bezos once said, "Whenever something is done inefficiently, that creates opportunity."[3] In other words, when a library is doing something inefficiently, it is a huge opportunity for Amazon.com to step in. Amazon.com wants to improve their sales and exposure to library customers by using the library website as a storefront. Do you think Amazon.com would allow a link to public libraries on their website showing where they can get the book they want to buy for free? It seems to me that Amazon.com has shown by their actions they want your customers. If your library has long delivery times or the online experience for your customers is cumbersome, then your customers are a prime target for Amazon.com. Allowing Amazon.com to provide a link on a library website to supplement a weakness in the library's service model is an admission that the library cannot meet their customers' service window of expectations. Option 2 is a great threat to libraries. If libraries simply give up and ask someone else to provide for their customers, or even willingly direct their customers to their competition, what future do libraries have?

> **Option 3**: The library prepares for this situation by allocating a certain part of their budget for emergency service situations like this. In this case, the selectors see that they have enough funds in their emergency services bank to purchase (or lease) these books from a twenty-four- to forty-eight-hour delivery provider, and they order enough books to service the students' requirements.

This appears to be the only competitively valid option the library can choose. If a library has been aggressively pursuing Lean concepts, then they will have dramatically improved their delivery lead time, increased their service days available, and, more importantly, reduced the number of books (and materials budget) required to fulfill customer demand. Therefore, shifting newly available material budget funds to this emergency delivery fund would allow the library to service unexpected peak loads as well as remain within the budget (if not well within the budget).

Therefore, in this environment, your best option is to streamline your services and reduce your delivery service chain's lead time, thus reducing your required materials budget and allowing more funds for emergency "pull" services. Do not send your customers to your competitors—provide the service and do it within your cost and budget framework.

This discussion was based on the assumption that the library did not offer e-books to students. The following options assume e-books are available.

> **Option 1**: The library owns five e-books of this title. This plus the five print books do not service all the students needing the book. The library branches are not able to fulfill this service requirement and they send the students to Amazon.com to download or order the books themselves.

> **Option 2**: The library partners with Amazon.com and has an embedded link on their website. The branch librarian guides the student to the link and helps them order and download the e-book from Amazon.com directly.

As you can see, there is no real difference between the print material delivery option and the e-book delivery option in these two options. From a Lean perspective, whether it is an e-book or a print book, the end result is the same. The library did not fulfill customers' requirements and it failed to meet their service objective.

This is an important discovery. Many libraries are quite nervous about the impact digital media will have on the future of libraries. Libraries should recognize that from a service point of view, there is no difference between delivering an e-book or a print book. The only difference is the delivery service chain required to fulfill that service, and within this delivery service chain great opportunities exist for libraries.

> **Option 3**: The library implements the concepts of Lean and frees up 25 percent of their materials budget to add a large selection of e-books as well as emergency funds for peak load events. The branch librarians help each student download the e-book from the library's website.

Once again, there is no real difference between the print and e-book service models, except the books can be downloaded immediately at no delivery cost, versus a delivery charge for twenty-four- to forty-eight-hour delivery of physical print material.

Keep in mind that not all students have a computer or e-book ready. However, as of December 2009, 91 percent of the U.S. population had a cell phone subscription,[4] and almost all public libraries have made personal computers and Internet access available to their customers. Not all cell phones have the capability to download and display an e-book, but this is changing. In the not-too-distant future most if not all cell phones will offer the ability to download and display digital media.

You may initially react negatively to my proposal that cell phones will become the primary e-book reader for library customers, and I would understand this reaction. After all, cell phones are expensive, and the primary organizational purpose of a library is to make information available to everyone, regardless of class or income. However, cell phones may be the perfect vehicle for libraries to accomplish this mission. Edward Nawotka, founder and editor in chief of *Publishing Perspectives*, believes so:

> In highly populated growth markets, such as China, India, Indonesia, Brazil, and much of Africa, a dedicated e-reader will remain a very pricey luxury for the foreseeable future; in the meantime, the cheap cell phone and the low-cost, high-speed Internet access that comes with it will become nearly universal. If a publisher want(s) to reach readers—especially a new generation of readers—they will have to start there. The cell phone will be the gateway device, something many may very well own long before they even have a modest collection of "books," whether real or digital.[5]

Libraries must recognize that whether it is digital media or print media, a service chain is required to support the delivery of a customer request. The more you reduce the delivery gap, the more capable you are of meeting the actual demand requirements of your customer. By doing so you eliminate the non-value-added costs associated with poorly managed delivery models. As you eliminate these wastes you create opportunities to reduce operating costs as well as the amount of material investment required to match your customer demand. As you free up costs and material budgets you create more flexibility in your service and collection development strategies. Purchasing print materials and e-books for your collection development remains a core value of every library; however, predicting what peak load demand will be months ahead of time wastes funds and eats away at your available funds. By allowing your customer to "pull" peak load demand and being capable of immediately responding to this peak load demand does not increase materials budgets but actually introduces a new kind of flexibility into your material allocations, allowing you to reduce budgets and be more responsive. I truly believe libraries have a great future, and as the digital world comes down the track like a runaway freight train, libraries must respond with their own e-book solution, and they must respond quickly.

Strategy Ten Review

As the delivery cycle shifts from weeks to days and hours to minutes and seconds, the old demand forecast approach of pushing your purchasing decisions onto the customer has shifted. Libraries must aggressively reduce their delivery lead times, which causes them to guess what customers want instead of knowing what they actually want. As this happens libraries can shift from a push-side demand approach to a demand-side pull approach and better service their customers. Libraries should not fear the future; the transition to digital content enables libraries to fully close the gap between prediction and actual need.

Notes

1. Bezos, Jeff. 2009. "Letter to Shareholders." In *2008 Amazon.com Annual Report*. Scribd. http://www.scribd.com/doc/14670406/Amazon-Annual-Report-2008.
2. Siegler, M. C. 2010. "Kindle Books Outselling Hardcover Books. 'Tipping Point' Reached, Amazon Says." TechCrunch, July 19. http://techcrunch.com/2010/07/19/kindle-sales/.
3. Dignan, Larry. 2010. "Amazon CEO Jeff Bezos: Cloud Services Can Be as Big as Retail Business." ZDNet, May 27. http://www.zdnet.com/blog/btl/amazon-ceo-jeff-bezos-cloud-services-can-be-as-big-as-retail-business/35111.
4. CTIA. 2010. "Wireless Quick Facts." CTIA. Accessed November 12. http://www.ctia.org/media/industry_info/index.cfm/AID/10323.
5. Nawotka, Edward. 2010. "Are Phones More Important than E-readers to the Future of Publishing?" *Publishing Perspectives*, February 18. http://publishingperspectives.com/?p=11895.

Strategy Eleven

Think Lean Before the Concrete Is Poured

If the delivery process is the heart and soul of a library system, the circulation service desk is the heart and soul of each branch library and each librarian. The previous strategies focused on the flow of materials as it navigates through the back-office processes of technical services, circulation, and delivery. Many of these flow design issues directly impact how quickly and effectively these materials are delivered to the customer. Strategy Eleven will shift our focus to the service areas of the branch, including the service flow of your customer; after all, the lasting service impression a customer will have is ultimately their service experience with their local branch.

As I mentioned previously, I often join delivery drivers on their delivery routes. I visit a large number of library branches on the way. During my visit I try to focus on the circulation service desk and the hold shelf layouts. I enjoy comparing and contrasting the various approaches library management and their architects have had for each individual library. I allow myself a brief time to enjoy the character and ambiance of the libraries, but I soon turn my attention to the functionality of the library, as this is my primary focus. I have found many curious designs and at times I have felt in many cases the architects were more concerned with the ambiance and visual presentation than functionality. A library's performance is defined the moment an architect puts pen to paper, and in many cases the results are unexpected.

I was asked by the director of one library to help them "fix" the problems that had surfaced at their newest library. This request came less than a year after the library had been built and dedicated. Upon arrival at the library I was struck by how wonderful the design was. The choice of colors, woodwork, and lighting was most impressive. The visual beauty and ambiance of the library were getting rave reviews. However, it did not take long to see why the library management group was concerned. There were some major issues with how the customer interacted with the library services and staff.

As in all cases I relied on our previously presented Lean change methodology to organize and drive the project. However, in this case the project team was limited to the branch staff of about eight people. Following our methodology we began the project by using a balloon diagram to define how the branch defined customer service. Many of these metrics are similar to the metrics presented in Strategy Four. We then focused on measuring the gap in performance between their current environment and their desired performance. Table 11-1 presents the results of our time studies and sample logs.

We determined that the library's gap in performance between where they wanted to be and their current performance was not very large. In fact, from my observations I could see this was a hardworking, highly motivated, and service-oriented staff. But the staff shared some issues that went beyond how productive or hardworking they were. Specifically it centered on the library design itself, issues that were out of their control. They brought to my attention issues I had not considered before. Customers were bumping into one another as they tried to drop a book off or access the hold shelf and public computers. We set out to develop solutions to eliminate this serious service issue.

Using a balloon diagram technique we evaluated the library from a customer's viewpoint and determined what we believed the customer and staff should expect from the library design. The following were the team results:

• No congestion in high-traffic areas
• Clear entrance and exit areas
• Easy access to the book drop area
• Customers waiting in line do not block natural flow of library
• No easy access to work areas by public

Unfortunately because this was a brand-new library, any solution our team developed would not start with a blank piece of paper. While the management team stated that they would commit funds for minor reconstruction, it was quite apparent this was not a preferred option. So we focused on low-cost, low-impact solutions for these two priority issues.

Table 11-1. Branch Performance Gap Analysis

Search Category	Time Objective	Service Performance	Sampling Result
Customer search/find at hold shelf	60 seconds	95% of the time	88% of the time
Customer checkout at circulation desk	60 seconds	95% of the time	91% of the time
Customer checkout at self-checkout	60 seconds	95% of the time	84% of the time
Customer questions at circulation desk handled correctly	3 minutes	95% of the time	92% of the time
Pay fine	60 seconds	95% of the time	83% of the time

Circulation Service Desk Congestion

The team developed visual diagrams and flowcharts of the issue. In this case we focused on how the customers interacted with the circulation desk. Figure 11-1 presents a snapshot of customers entering and exiting the library and interacting with the circulation service desk.

As Figure 11-1 presents, we found congestion all around the circulation desk, in particular at the security gate entrance. Specifically, customers attempting to enter the security gate found themselves blocked by people standing in line to check out books at the nearest station to the entrance. On top of this the book drop-off slot was located in the same spot; therefore customers attempting to drop off their books would have to maneuver their way through other customers to access the drop slot. I observed an elderly woman carrying about eight books enter through the security gate entrance and elbow her way through three people so she could drop her books in the slot. You could see that she had done this many times before and that she was not happy about it. Her only alternative was to wait in line to gain access to the book drop, or wait in line to drop the book off to a staff member at another station. There was an outdoor book drop, but it was not convenient for customers who planned to actually enter the library. While the original designers might have seen this as a positive (that customers who wanted to drop off their books at the book drop

Figure 11-1. Circulation Desk Performance Issues

A3 - Book drop may be blocked by someone checking out at the stand up station.
B7 - Customers leaving the service desk may run into traffic entering library.
B9 - Customers entering library have to divert if people are at the book drop or stand up station. (The security gate guides people entering library toward the book drop/service area.)

could do so immediately upon entering the library), the reality of the design was that the area quickly became congested, preventing quick access and smooth flow. The book drop area, entry gate, and checkout station were all sharing an area of about five feet by five feet. From a Lean perspective, this was not a smooth-flowing river; the customers were being forced to navigate Snake River.

To improve the flow our first idea came from the director herself, as she recommended the team look at using stanchions to guide the incoming and outgoing traffic. We moved the stanchions around until we found the right location. Locating the stanchions as presented in Figure 11-2 guided the customers entering the library to quickly move to their left, away from the service desk and the book drop. This also encouraged customers exiting the library to flow away from the service desk and toward the security gate naturally designated as an exit. Not surprisingly, customers entering the library quickly learned to use the exit side of the security gate as the entrance (as long as no other customers where exiting at the time).

Although this helped reduce the traffic congestion for customers entering and exiting the library, it did not alleviate the congestion around the book drop and checkout station. Our best recommendation involved extending the service desk, adding a second book drop, and moving the first checkout station away from the original book drop location. Figure 11-3 presents the concept. The second book drop added the additional benefit of sharing the processing load between two stations as opposed to one. Unfortunately, this required

Figure 11-2. Incoming/Outgoing Traffic Flow

Figure 11-3. Second Book Drop

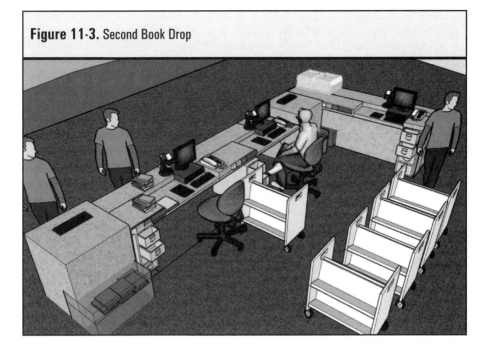

some reconstruction of the service desk and was not an immediate option to the library leadership team. However, the leadership team is keeping the design in their files for future consideration.

Since we could not pursue this solution, the team looked for ideas to work within the current service desk design. There were not many available. One solution was to move the first checkout station to the lower level with the others. Figure 11-4 presents this concept.

We accomplished this by relocating the printers from the right side of the service desk to the book drop area and shifting the stations to the right, but for customers and staff this was not an ideal location for the printers. It also required us to compress the amount of space for each checkout station, and this was not a popular option for the staff. The circulation desk itself had built-in file cabinets that designated where the stations would be located. Once again this would require some remodeling and was not a preferred choice, so this option was ultimately rejected.

In the end I recommended they move the checkout station's terminal directly over the book drop slot so that customers checking out books would stand to the left of the book drop rather then being forced to stand right in front of it. While the staff member who worked at that station preferred to check out books from right to left as opposed to left to right, he was willing to adapt for the common good. This solution is presented in Figure 11-5. The original design of the architects limited our flexibility, and therefore our solutions were not ideal, but we accomplished what we could.

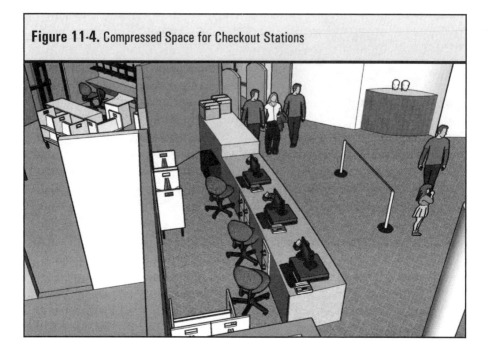

Figure 11-4. Compressed Space for Checkout Stations

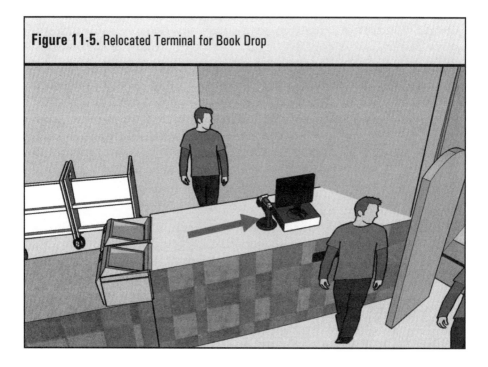

Figure 11-5. Relocated Terminal for Book Drop

Hold Shelf Access

We then turned our attention to the congestion around the hold shelf and the public access computer terminals. We once again created a visual representation of the issue, shown in Figure 11-6.

Every library knows that besides the circulation desk the two highest-traffic areas are the hold shelf and the public access terminals. In this case these two functions were forced to share a very small aisle together. Customers attempting to find their holds had to be careful of the chairs being pushed back into the shared aisle, and customers using the terminals were uncomfortable with other customers nearly breathing down their necks as they walked behind them. In addition, the new books were located on the back wall, and they would have been better displayed in a more prominent area.

We examined many reorganization alternatives, including relocating the hold shelf entirely, but due to space constraints we were once again limited in our options. Ultimately the team decided to split up the public access com-

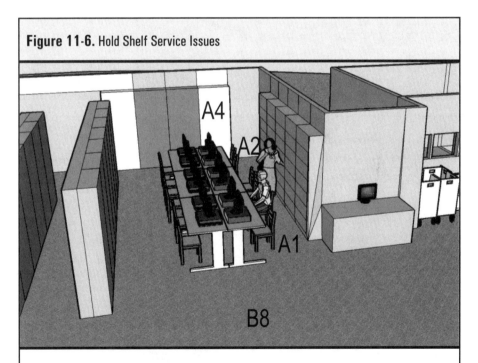

Figure 11-6. Hold Shelf Service Issues

A1 - Customers wanting computer access have difficulty navigating aisle.
A2 - Customers pulling holds have difficulty navigating aisle.
A4 - New books on back wall are hidden from view.
A4 - New books on back wall are difficult to access.
B8 - There is no sitting or waiting area for customers waiting for a terminal.

puter area into two locations, thus freeing up space around the hold shelf. The solution is presented in Figures 11-7 and 11-8. Turning the remaining computer stations ninety degrees eliminated most of the competition for the hold shelf aisle. Notice the U-shaped flow for customers searching the hold shelves

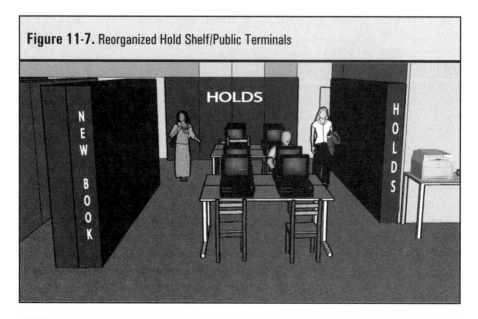

Figure 11-7. Reorganized Hold Shelf/Public Terminals

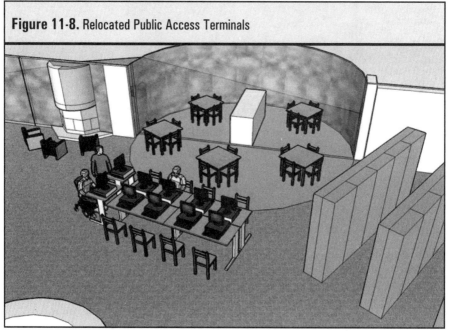

Figure 11-8. Relocated Public Access Terminals

leading to the "new books" shelves. The staff liked the solution, even if they did not like that the customers using computers at the back of the library had to walk to the front to ask questions, requiring staff to walk back with them to their station to answer their question. Once again, this was not an ideal solution, but it was a step.

I cannot say that this project was a huge success. Because of the project constraints, we had to compromise our best Lean flow solutions. If a Lean perspective had been introduced in the design phase, all of these issues would have been resolved before the drawings where approved. Unfortunately, I have seen many similar situations. I have seen new technical services and delivery buildings and library branches developed without Lean concepts considered, and the libraries and their customers have been forced to compromise as a result.

Strategy Eleven Review

It is critical that your library incorporate the concepts of Lean into your new designs before the design is approved and the concrete is committed. Every library design should include a presentation on how material flows, how customers flow, and how staff members flow before the designs are approved. Any potential bottlenecks, encumbrances, or just poor designs must be exposed. In addition, flexibility of the design should also be incorporated. Questions should be asked on how easy it is to relocate book shelves, computer stations, cable, power, and the circulation desk itself. Your needs will change over time, and if flexibility is built into your design, then you are much better prepared to adapt to these changes.

Afterword

Lean Continuous Improvement

Lean has its roots in total quality management, the Toyota Production System, and just-in-time manufacturing. Common to all of these movements is a term called *continuous improvement*. Continuous improvement teaches that when improving a delivery service chain, reducing non-value-added activities, and streamlining value-added activities, it is a nonstop effort; there is always room for improvement. Your delivery service chains will continue to advance and change, and new efforts to improve them will be constantly required and discovered.

By applying the Lean concepts your library will achieve great success. You may, for example, reduce your delivery service chain of holds/reserves from a seventy-two-hour delivery to a forty-eight-hour delivery. If you do so, you should celebrate. But are you done? Of course not. Why not achieve twenty-four-hour delivery? Twelve-hour delivery? Or why not sixty-second delivery? In every delivery service chain, no matter how much you have improved, there is always room for more improvement. In Strategy Eight we discussed how reducing your SDNA by one day can have a ripple effect on service lead times, material budgets, and processing cost. Many companies I've worked with have been on the continuous improvement journey for nearly thirty years, and they see no reason to stop, because Lean is a never-ending story, a matter of survival.

This book has explained the reasons libraries and all organizations resist change, and it has reviewed techniques to overcome this resistance. The Lean tools and methodologies provided are designed to initiate and foster change throughout your organization. This is not enough; management must be diligent in nurturing and fostering this change until you reach a critical mass of change within your organization. This critical mass is the tipping point of progress. When you have more people who desire change than people resisting change you have reached this critical mass. To keep your Lean transformation going I would recommend the following:

- Establish a strategic Lean transformation plan that will guide your efforts for the next five years.
- Start the Lean transformation plan with a small cross-functional team made up of the best in your organization. The hold-shelf-ready label solution is a great place to start.
- Engage and transform the most negative person in your library system into a productive team member. Converting the most negative person has a huge impact on the rest of the staff.
- Publish updates on the progress of the Lean transformation in your library newsletter. If you do not have a newsletter, create one.
- Have the cross-functional team present their findings to senior staff members. Nothing will get a team more motivated than knowing they have to get in front of the top members of the library and present their findings. Make this a standard operating procedure.
- Celebrate the accomplishments of the team. Bake desserts, hold parties, invite important people on your staff. Show the library organization how important change is to your future.
- Repeat this process until you have reached critical mass. When you have more people who have been on a team than not, you have reached critical mass.
- After the teams have had success, raise the bar. Ask them to take the library to new levels of service performance.
- If you do form a team within one department as opposed to a cross-functional team, you should make sure you include someone from another department. This will encourage other departments to make their own improvements.
- Do not let a cross-functional team exist for more than three months. They should be able to develop their conceptual design in this time frame. If the team goes on longer than this the team will become stagnant and the meetings will become useless. Once this team is finished, form a new one with a different mix of members.
- Do not treat the Lean transformation as a program—it is not; it is a way of life.
- Encourage trips to organizations outside the library environment. Benchmark service performance and technological trends in manufacturing, distribution, and retail organizations.
- Send your star performers to a Public Library Association or American Library Association conference to present their accomplishments. For some of my clients' cross-functional team members, the highlight of their career was presenting in front of an audience of more than 300 people.
- Remember, change is a process, not an attitude. A process must be organized, managed, reviewed, and measured.

I have referred to TCCL many times in this book because they have worked on many Lean projects, touching every department and process they support. They have made great progress in transitioning from a top-driven organization to both a top-down and bottom-up-driven organization. New improvement initiatives are cropping up all over the library, supported by both the leadership team and the staff. They are well positioned to handle the challenges the future will bring, including tougher competition, growing digital content, and higher customer demands.

In the end, it is up to you. If for whatever reason your organization or management team does not embrace the Lean transformational journey, this does not mean you cannot embark on your own Lean journey. The change process starts with you. Learn the tools and philosophies of Lean. Learn the key success factors to a Lean transformation. Look for large batches, long lead times, and non-value-added activities in your work environment. If you are a supervisor, initiate team meetings, invite staff from other departments, teach others the tools and concepts of Lean, and become the spark that creates change. As long as you stay committed to the Lean transformation, the process has a bright future. It must be planned, nurtured, measured, celebrated, and, once the cake has been eaten, you must do it all again in a continuous cycle of improvement.

Appendix

More Lean Tools

This book presented a number of Lean tools to help you facilitate your Lean transformational efforts. These tools were embedded within a number of case examples. Here are the Lean tools you have already discovered:

- Change methodology
- Organizational purpose
- Ownership development
- Cross-functional teams
- Delivery service chain mapping
- Performance gap analysis
- Streamlining and simplifying flow paths
- Eliminating staging areas
- Eliminating large batches
- Smoothing peak loads
- Balloon diagramming
- Service performance drivers
- Cost performance drivers
- Work cells
- U-shaped process flow
- Eliminating imbalances
- First-touch principle
- Performance metrics measurement devices
  - Time studies
  - Service chain time logs
  - Process performance logs
  - Mystery shopper feedback

But these are not all the Lean tools available to you to help you in your Lean transformational journey. In addition to the Lean tools you have already learned about, the following are a number of additional tools you can add to your Lean tool kit:

- Value stream mapping
- Video recording and analysis
- Group problem solving
- Communication skills
- Pareto analysis
- Bottleneck management
- Stop, observe, and correct philosophy
- *Poke-Yoke*
- Work simplification and improvement
- Automation is a tool, not a solution

Value Stream Mapping

Value stream mapping creates a visual picture of where people, materials, information, and machines work together. It presents and analyzes how all the parts work together to provide a service or product to a customer. I have already presented to you a few high-level value stream maps for a typical library's primary delivery service chains. Mapping a value stream drives the analysis down even further, examining every individual link and task in the chain. Each movement, each pick-up or put-down, each delay, each piece of paper used, is added to the map for everyone to see and examine its value. When I develop a value stream map I use figures and images to represent each step. I then identify each step as a value-added step or a non-value-added step. I also identify the steps as either a delay, a pick-up or put-down, a transport move, a computer input, or a computer output.

Once the value stream map is understood the team has a wonderful visual to challenge aggressively every step in the map. The team should take each link in the chain and ask, "Is this step necessary?" For each step, the team should try to eliminate it, streamline it, automate it, or change it in such a way that it reduces lead time or costs. Once you have analyzed your value stream map, indicating which tasks should be improved, you have the means to develop a best practice model. You can now look at your map and say, "If we eliminated or improved all of these non-value-added tasks and streamlined and improved the value-added tasks, how good can we be?"

This value stream map or flowchart represents a vision for the delivery service chain that has no waste or delays, only streamlined and productive value-added activities. This is the ultimate target, a delivery service chain with only productive value-added steps. This represents the best you can be, and it becomes your team's goal to come as close to the best practice model as possible. By using the value stream mapping tool, your team will understand the service delivery chain and its process steps, volumes, performance objective, and current performance as well as the gap that exists between where you want to be and where you are now. Figure A-1 represents an actual case study from one of my clients' projects. The process we mapped included the steps to receive and check in a box of CDs.

After creating the value stream map we analyzed the steps, looking for ways to eliminate, resequence, reorder, and streamline tasks with the objective of eliminating as many non-value-added tasks as possible. Figure A-2 presents our new value stream map. Instead of moving all the CDs to the desk and back onto the cart, we came up with

Figure A-1. Acquisitions CD Receipt Process—Before

Task	Move Cart to Desk	Move CD's to Desk	Alpha Sort CD's	Enter / Receive CD's	Check Off CD from Invoice List	Move CD's to Cart
Visual						
Value Symbol		Repeat 125 times	Repeat 125 times	Repeat 125 times	Repeat 125 times	Repeat 125 times
Cycle Time	120 sec	5 sec	10 sec	30 sec	5 sec	5 sec
Ext Time	120 sec	625 sec	1250 sec	3,750 sec	625 sec	625 sec
Total Time						116.5 min
Lean Process Improvement	Move Off Line To M/H	First Touch Principle/ Sort on Cart/ Eliminate	Sort on Cart		Combine w/ Enter/ Receive CD	Eliminate/ First Touch Principle/ Sort on Cart

the idea of leaving them on the cart, making sure all the titles were sorted together, and then using the invoice list to drive the check-in process. Rather than sequencing the CDs by invoice title, we simply used the invoice to find the CDs on the cart, saving 34 percent of the time it took to alphabetically sort CDs to drive the receipt process, a significant savings.

You do not need to use fancy drawing tools to develop these maps. You can use your own stick figure drawings and make up your own symbols to represent moves, delays, and computer entry tasks. What is important is that you break the process down to each small step and visually represent it, categorize it, and assign a time to it. This not only becomes a great tool for your team but the developer of the map acquires a great deal of knowledge of how the process is performed.

Video Recording and Analysis

In addition to value stream maps, I often film the processes to study how a value stream map can be improved. I have filmed many of my clients, and I would recommend it to everyone—but be prepared; you may not like what you see.

Video playback is a powerful tool. I use videos on every library project I have worked on. I record the processes of the delivery driver, circulation department, processing department, branch circulation desk, and even the bookmobile. I would recommend you use it for every process you are trying to improve; after all, "seeing is believing." Videos force you to see what is really happening and therefore there is no

Figure A-2. Acquisitions CD Receipt Process—After

Task	M/H Stages Cart to Desk	Group Sort CD's On Cart	Use Invoice Sequence Enter / Receive CD's Check mark Invoice	Total
Visual				
Value Symbol		Repeat 125 times	Repeat 125 times	
Cycle Time	0 sec	5 sec	32 sec	
Total Time After	0 sec	625 sec	4000 sec	77 min
Total Time Before				116.5 min
Total Time Savings				39.5 min 34 %

better way to create a desire for change than to have a mirror reflect back to you a process screaming for improvement.

Each time I show clients a video of their delivery service chain I always get the following response: "I didn't know we were doing that." The videos can also be used to develop time studies; just make sure you video the process enough times to reflect an accurate time estimate. There is no tool more valuable to analyze a process than reviewing the video of the process. Your team should use this tool as frequently as possible. These videos can also help you develop the value steam map, as you can pause and rewind as many times as you like. It also provides you a simple means to develop time estimates for each task.

Communication Skills

Communications skills, and more important team communication skills, are the bedrock of a good Lean transformation. Management consultants spend a great deal of time communicating. The objective of any communication should be to gather as much important information from others in the least amount of time in a professional and friendly manner. I was once videotaped during a group communication exercise, and while watching the video I was surprised by how poorly I communicated with the others. I learned from the video that I needed better communication skills to become a better consultant, businessman, and person. The following is my own communication technique that I have learned and honed over the years. There are six key items to remember:

1.   Show respect.
2.   Choose open-ended questions.
3.   U should never telegraph what you want the answer to be.
4.   Learn by repeating what is said.
5.   Listen and people will share more.
6.   Silence is a communication tool.

I use these techniques when I am at a restaurant ordering food, discussing which movie to see with my wife, talking with my kids, and participating in team meetings. This is the basic foundation toward developing better communication skills.

Did you notice the acronym, **SCULLS**? It is my hope that you will carry this acronym with you at all times, that you will remember the most effective teams in a sculls race are those who are working and communicating together best as a team.

Show Respect

It seems this would be obvious, but it is often the most frequent reason I see teams falter. Recognizing the value of the other people in the room is how you show respect. You can show this respect (or disrespect) by your actions:

- Show others that you respect the value of their time as much as you value your own time by showing up at the appointed time; arriving late sends the opposite signal.
- Leave your title at the door. If those in the room do not rank as high as you or are not as educated as you, get over yourself. Everyone in the meeting is there for a reason. They are experts in the job they perform every day, and they deserve the respect any expert in a field deserves.
- Do not talk down to people.
- Do not embarrass or insult those you work with.
- Use people's names as often as you can.
- Do not interrupt another person in midsentence when they are trying to make a point.

Create Information through Open-Ended Questions

An example of a closed-ended question is: Do you like vanilla ice cream? The person you asked this question to can answer only with a short one-word answer: yes or no. You have acquired very little information by asking this question. The open-ended question would be: What kinds of food do you like? The person answering this question cannot answer this question with a yes or no. He or she has the entire world of foods to answer from. You could learn much about this person from this open-ended question.

You should always begin your questions with *what, why, when,* and *how* to avoid closed-ended discussions.

In a meeting, remember, you already know what you think; to become an effective member of the team you must learn what others think as well. This way you become more informed and improve the quality of your own opinion. When you finally do voice your opinion, you are much better prepared to communicate and defend your position with others.

U Should Never Telegraph What You Want the Answer to Be

This is one of the hardest things for people to overcome. Many of us are driven by one goal: winning an argument. These arguments often have nothing to do with learning more about the issue but are about the act of arguing. Growing up in a family that loved to debate, I got pretty good at learning how to dominate and win an argument. I learned many years later that I had developed very poor communication skills as a result, mostly the use of closed-ended questions to control and dominate the conversation. So avoid leading statements and leading questions; it leads to you being the only one listening to yourself.

Listen

Listening is a skill. It requires discipline. Have you ever left a conversation unable to remember anything the other person said to you? This is likely because you spent the entire time talking at the person and not listening to him or her. And there's a chance the other person did the same thing, leaving both of you knowing no more than what you did before the conversation. You must become active listeners to fully understand and solve a problem.

Learn More by Repeating What Is Said

This may be the most powerful communication technique there is. It encapsulates all four of the communication techniques I have discussed thus far. When communicating with others, you should always repeat back to the person what the person said to you originally. This shows respect. By repeating what the other person said you are showing the other person that what he or she said is important, important enough to repeat. Repeating what is said provides you a chance to verify that you fully understood what the other person was saying to you, and it improves the quality of the conversation. By using your own words to state the same point you are adding a different flavor and value and understanding of the information being discussed. It provides an opportunity for the other person to clarify a point or expand on a point, thus improving your understanding of the point. And repeating shows that you listened, and by doing so you have encouraged the person to share even more information.

Silence Is a Communication Tool

Knowing when and how to be silent is perhaps the hardest communication technique to learn. It is, however, very powerful. Learning when to talk and when to not talk is a unique skill, one many of us have not mastered. Everyone communicates at a different pace. Some people will voice every random thought that comes to their head. Others like to filter their thoughts before speaking. Put these two types of people in a room and the person who voices every random thought will dominate.

To fully communicate with others, you must learn to blend your own communication style with the others you work with. To allow the other person to fully voice their thoughts you have to learn to be silent at the right times. Silence can also be a powerful tool to bring someone out of his or her shell. In nearly every team I have facilitated there is often one person who just does not want to speak or voice his or her opinion. Either the person is timid, not confident, or afraid to talk in front of others. But people by nature do not like things to be quiet, especially in an environment where noise is expected. The awkward moment of silence is at times unbearable for some. In a team meeting, noise is expected.

I experienced this in one of my brainstorming sessions. We had five people in our cross-functional team meeting. Four of the members were very vocal, but one (we'll call her Julie) did not seem comfortable expressing her thoughts. However, what Julie knows is very important to the rest of the team. I showed a video to the team that primarily showed tasks that Julie performs. When I asked Julie if she saw any issues that she wanted to discuss, she replied, "No, whatever you guys think." This was followed by a long period of silence. Julie broke the silence by offering a suggestion.

In this exchange, most likely someone else in the room would have jumped in to fill in the uncomfortable silence before Julie finally spoke. In that event we would not have heard Julie's suggestion (which was a good one). I encouraged the talkative team members before the session to practice silence to encourage Julie to speak. If you can learn to be patient, and at times this requires coordinated patience, silence will bring out the thoughts of others who might otherwise not engage in the information-sharing process.

The better communication skills your cross-functional team has the better they will perform. The better your library staff's communication skills the better your library will perform. Grab an oar, climb into your sculls boat, and learn to row together with better communication skills.

Group Problem-Solving Skills

Solving a problem as an individual is much easier than solving a problem as a group. When solving a problem as an individual, you understand your own thoughts, language, and problem-solving approach. When solving problems as a group, everyone sees the problem in a slightly different way. They bring different experiences to the problem and different terminology and approaches to solve it. An engineer might approach a problem different than an artist would.

Therefore, there need to be rules for a group to work together. The group problem-solving rules I teach my cross-functional teams are the following: There are two steps to solving a problem: discovering the problem and then solving the problem. When discovering the problem, as a group refrain from trying to solve the problem until the group fully understands it. When solving a problem, remember:

- There are no bad ideas. Every idea is worth listening to.
- Crazy ideas are encouraged. The farther outside the box you go, the easier it is to discover what kind of box you are in.
- Do not judge or disparage others' ideas; in fact, try to piggyback on other ideas, allowing the ideas to constantly move forward.

- Write down the ideas. The bubble diagram is a great tool to facilitate this process.
- Use facts, diagrams, flowcharts, value stream maps, and edited videos to illustrate the problem. Putting it into a visual forces you and the group to fully understand the problem and see it from the same viewpoint.
- Use project work plans and status reports to coordinate and communicate team responsibilities and progress.
- Always use SCULLS when communicating with others.

Pareto's 80/20 Principle

An Italian economist named Vilfredo Pareto observed that 80 percent of his nation's property was owned by 20 percent of the population. This 80/20 rule observed in 1893 is a fundamental tool for the Lean practitioner. For example, if you learned that 80 percent of the errors are caused by 20 percent of your workforce, would this change how you approached solving the problem? If 80 percent of your circulation is drawn from 20 percent of your population, would this change your marketing approach? The actual numbers will vary, but in nearly every case the majority/minority rule of Pareto holds true.

The beauty of Pareto is that it helps you and your cross-functional team quickly prioritize what is really important to the project and process. Pareto will help your team focus on the 20 percent of change that will affect 80 percent of the results, thus getting the most "bang for your buck." For example, when streamlining a process, you may find 80 percent of the products are staged between two stations while the remaining 20 percent are spread throughout the rest of the department. The priority should be to focus on the 80 percent to have the most immediate impact. Another example is gift books. If you perform an 80/20 analysis on your gift books you may discover that the majority of what is being gifted are paperbacks. You also may find that 80 percent of the paperbacks are romance novels. Using the 80/20 rule to better understand what is being gifted might lead you to a different approach in accepting, processing, and storing these items. I performed a Lean transformation on gifted books and learned more cost goes into the gifted book delivery service chain per book than any other delivery service chain in the library. Using the Pareto analysis to better understand what these costly books are was well worth the effort to make better decisions on how to handle these items.

I also used the Pareto principle on a project to evaluate the circulation performance for one of my library clients. We found 20 percent of the categories of books provided 80 percent of the circulation. We also found which 20 percent of the titles provided 80 percent of the circulation in each category. This information became invaluable feedback to the acquisitions group. One selector eliminated a whole category of books as a result. Further 80/20 analysis of what categories are being used by what branches is also extremely valuable to the branch managers.

Look for the following types of business issues when using the Pareto principle:

- 20 percent of the customers provide 80 percent of the volume.
- 80 percent of fines come from 20 percent of the customers.
- 80 percent of the books not picked up come from 20 percent of the customers.
- 80 percent of labor costs come from 20 percent of the activities.

- 80 percent of delays come from 20 percent of the activities.
- 80 percent of errors come from 20 percent of staff.
- 80 percent of the complaints come from 20 percent of the customers.
- 80 percent of the complaints are caused from 20 percent of the staff.
- 80 percent of carpal tunnel injuries come from 20 percent of the activities.

Once again, the numbers might not stick directly to the 80/20 rule—it might be 70/30 or even at times 60/40. However, I have found time and time again that the majority of problems are created by a minority of issues, and these should take priority. Your management team should use the 80/20 rule to drive their strategic planning initiative and to analyze the data that drives the value stream map. In other words, work smarter, not harder.

Bottlenecks

A bottleneck is like two funnels with one turned upside down and connected to the other. You can pour as much water into the top of the funnel as you want, but the amount of water that is going to come out is limited by the size of the narrowest part of the funnel.

In your delivery service chain, you have pinch points that limit the amount of product or service you are capable of providing your customer. You can throw as many book carts full of books into the top of the funnel, but the amount that is going to come out is determined by the smallest bottleneck. You cannot see the bottlenecks because they are hidden behind large batch sizes and staging areas. By reducing batch sizes and eliminating staging areas these bottlenecks will become apparent. Just as water backs up above the bottleneck in the mouth of the funnel, so will your book carts and customers back up and pool together in the delivery service chain.

Lean teaches us to not hide bottlenecks but expose them. Without knowing where they are, you cannot break them. Once identified you can improve the process, shift some tasks away from the process or, if necessary, shift some resources to this bottleneck to expand capacity. Once this bottleneck is broken, you move on to the next one and repeat until River Lean appears.

Stop, Observe, Correct

Murphy's Law: "If anything can go wrong, it will." Assuming Murphy is correct, we must assume something will go wrong when we are traveling the path of the delivery service chain. What is important is not that something will go wrong but what we are going to do about it.

There is a reason why something went wrong. If you understand the cause and what impact it had, you can prevent it from happening again. Lean says that when a problem occurs, stop everything, gather everyone around, and figure out what went wrong. The balloon diagram is a great tool to perform this cause-and-effect analysis. Once the team figures out the relationship they can develop a means to prevent it from ever happening again.

Many U.S. manufacturers have followed Toyota's example by installing red lights at every stage of their assembly operation. They have empowered their workers to turn on their red light whenever a quality or assembly problem is uncovered. When that red light goes on, the entire assembly line shuts down. A team immediately gathers around the red light to discuss the problem and develop a solution. Over time as problems are dealt with at the source, fewer problems occur. The Japanese call this concept *Jidoka*. Combine Murphy's Law with *Jidoka* and you can see its power. Stopping when something goes wrong to force problem solving is a valuable lesson for any business entity, including libraries.

Poke-Yoke

Poke-Yoke is a Japanese term that means "mistake proofing." It is a Lean philosophy that states: If we can find a way to prevent a problem from happening in the first place, then let's do it. For example, a library team might discover that the spine labels are not being applied consistently from one staff member to another. It turns out that one staff member's view of how much one inch from the bottom is is a little different from another staff member's. One possible solution is to eliminate the variable of how much is an inch by clearly defining it with a holding fixture and a measuring device. *Poke-Yoke* looks for jigs and fixtures that will eliminate all variables from a process and force the process to be consistent while also enhancing the productivity of the process.

The library environment has many opportunities to apply the concept of *Poke-Yoke*. Here are a few examples:

- When cataloging a book, catalogers often must enter the dimensions of a book into the book's item record. A cataloger usually uses a ruler to measure the book. A *Poke-Yoke* session might suggest a ninety-degree ruler painted on the top of the desk. This improves the accuracy as well as the productivity of the process.
- A great deal of inconsistency occurs around the hold slip process, as discussed in the book. Most library staff will handwrite a customer's name on a slip of paper and rubber band it to a book for the hold shelf. Different people and different branches often have different writing styles and approaches to writing the names. Other libraries and customers at times have trouble deciphering the information. This can create errors and inefficiencies. By applying the *Poke-Yoke* philosophy of Lean we developed a means for our clients to have the hold slip printed on a removable/repositionable label in place of the pick list. The printed hold slip is placed on the spine of the book at the time the book is pulled from the shelf to fulfill the hold request. The removable label remains with the book throughout the delivery service chain, ending at the hold shelf. This creates a common means to present the customer's name as well as eliminate many labor steps, paper supplies, and rubber bands along the way. I call this the "holds label solution."

Poke-Yoke is a valuable companion to the stop, observe, and correct concept. Many times when a problem surfaces, ideas to foolproof the process can lead to preventing the problem from ever happening again.

Work Simplification and Improvement

Productivity improvement is defined as improving the amount of product or service delivered for the amount of time invested. Reducing cost through productivity improvement is fundamental to a Lean transformation process. When you consider that in a library environment a task will be repeated thousands of times you realize the power of small productivity improvements. If you can improve just one task it has a ripple effect across your entire library system. By filming and breaking down a process into its elements, you will discover many opportunities to simplify a process and thus improve the productivity of the process. The following is a list of work simplification techniques you should pursue to improve your library's productivity:

- Process redesign: The value stream analysis we discussed at the beginning of this appendix will uncover inefficiencies and opportunities for work simplification and improvement. Once the value stream map is complete, each step can be evaluated and identified as either a value-added step or a non-value-added step. Your team should aggressively try to eliminate the non-value-added activities and improve the value-added activities.

- Motion study: As an industrial engineer I have been trained to view an operation in terms of movement, such as bending, reaching, walking, and turning. The goal of any repetitive process is to eliminate as much movement as possible. Every step in the delivery service chain is supported by some kind of workstation or work area layout. This includes the delivery area, sorting room, the interior of the delivery truck, book drop check-in, the circulation desk, the new book receiving area, the cataloger's desk, the processing workstations, and even management offices and desks. All of these have a repetitive work flow with pick-ups, put-downs, reaching, walking, and turning. A motion study using videos will identify excessive movements so solutions to eliminate, combine, rearrange, or simplify these movements can be designed.

- Workstation design: The following diagram illustrates the parameters I use to design a workstation (see Figure A-3).

Every item a worker needs to complete his or her task should be within easy reach. The worker should not have to walk, bend, or reach beyond arm's length. Working with my library clients, we have successfully redesigned circulation desks, book drops, receiving workstations, technical service workstations, and cataloger's workstations to meet these objectives.

Lean teaches you to eliminate all the waste in a process. These steps are called non-value-added activities. Each and every day libraries across the country excessively walk, reach, bend, and turn to support their daily repetitive tasks. Not only does this add extra wear and tear on your employees, it contributes to longer delivery lead times and operating costs. Lean is a win-win solution: if you eliminate the wasteful activities, you will lower costs, improve customer service, and have a healthier and happier workforce.

Note: To provide full disclosure, not all of my clients' staff has been happy with the newly efficient process designs. In one project we eliminated the need for workers to get up from their desk and leave their work area to retrieve their own book carts. The next book cart they needed to process was staged ahead of time at their station. The staff was very unhappy with this idea because it eliminated the opportunity for them to get

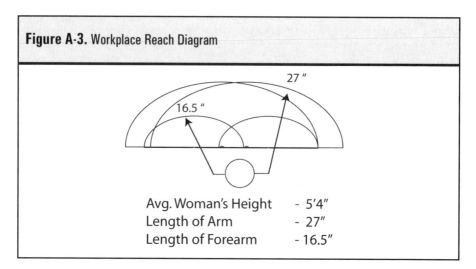

Figure A-3. Workplace Reach Diagram

Avg. Woman's Height   - 5'4"
Length of Arm   - 27"
Length of Forearm   - 16.5"

some exercise and visit with other staff members. These are all good points; however, the workstation and process itself should be designed to be as productive as possible. Breaks for exercise and camaraderie should be scheduled for the group as a whole; otherwise the overall flow of the process will be disrupted and lead time, customer service, and productivity will suffer (not to mention the return of batches and staging areas).

Flexible Job Descriptions and Titles

This book has discussed how important flexible job descriptions are in creating a change-resistant culture. If job descriptions are inflexible and cannot be changed then the best Lean designs and customer service improvements can be stopped in their tracks. Use the Lean change methodology discussed as your guide to changing job descriptions:

* Understand and embrace your organizational purpose.
* Practice a top-down and bottom-up management style.
* Practice process change ownership.
* Initiate projects to drive change.
* Develop gap-driven performance metrics.
* Drive change through your cross-functional teams.
* Develop and share cost–benefit projections and results.
* Celebrate current and past accomplishments.

Define Common Organizational Purpose between Management, Staff, and Union

The primary purpose of a union is to maintain and advance the wage rates and working conditions of its members and to defend and promote a fair and safe working environment. The primary purpose of library management is to provide high-value services to the community in an effective and productive manner as well as encourage the funding to support these continuing services. Looking between the lines you can see that the union or employee group and management might be at cross-purposes. The history of labor and management in the United States certainly proves this point.

However, if you look for one common purpose that binds management and employee groups together you'll find that both desire a healthy, thriving library. An unhealthy business concerns both management and labor; just ask General Motors and the United Auto Workers. So how do we define a healthy thriving library? A thriving library:

- provides high value services to the community and individual customers;
- provides highly valued services at a low cost;
- is highly adaptable to changing business conditions such as economic downturns, increasing competition, and increasing customer service expectations;
- protects the safety and well-being of its employees;
- provides a means for staff to pursue a common purpose; and
- is recognized by the community as providing value, and the community is willing to generously fund it.

These characteristics also define a Lean organization:

- The organization has eliminated all non-value-added tasks and delays needed to service its customers; therefore, it provides the highest quality service in the least amount of time.
- The ratio of value to cost is high, thus promoting community support and funding.
- The ratio of cost to value is low, allowing the company to better handle economic downturns.
- The ratio of output to cost is high, allowing the organization to be less vulnerable to large peaks and valleys in demand.
- The organizational staff is flexible, cross-trained, highly adaptable, and has a team attitude to changing job conditions and demands.
- Dangerous tasks or tasks that injure employees are considered non-value-added activities and are aggressively eliminated to improve employee health and well-being.
- Lean provides a cross-functional vehicle for the staff to pursue their common purpose of community service.
- The organization is not satisfied with the status quo and is constantly pursuing ways to eliminate non-value-added activities to improve customer service.
- The effectiveness of each employee is enhanced, making individual contributions more valuable to the organization.

Management and employee groups must join forces to pursue a healthy Lean organization. This is the best chance to achieve protection of jobs, wage rates, working conditions, happy customers, and a supportive community.

There will be times that jobs will be reduced, wages will be stagnant, and funding will drop. Many libraries are experiencing this as I write this book. However, a Lean library is better prepared to respond and adapt to a drop in funding and still provide high-value services to its customers and community. Lean will allow the library to provide high customer service even when times are tough. As economic conditions decline, library use increases. Therefore, there might be no type of organization in the world that needs to be Leaner than libraries.

A healthy, thriving library is a common purpose of both management and the staff. Lean and flexible job descriptions can help fulfill this purpose for both groups. Before moving forward with creating more flexible job descriptions, management, key staff, and union representatives must recognize one another's primary purpose and find common ground on how changing job descriptions can support this common purpose.

Practice a Top-Down and Bottom-Up Management Style

The changing of job titles is an important factor to both management and staff. In fact, there may not be any topic that creates more emotion or opinions. For this reason it is critical that the solution be developed together by management, union, and the staff. If management dictates job description changes without the involvement of employee groups, it could cause great fear and consternation with the employees. If the staff develops job descriptions without management leadership, the larger objective of the customer service may not take priority. This effort must be pursued by both a top-down and bottom-up approach. Therefore, a project with management leadership, union, and staff membership should be created to organize and gain ownership of all interested parties.

Initiate Projects to Drive Change

This book has discussed the benefits of a project-driven approach to making change. A project is the best means to redefine job titles. It should have a steering committee, a project leader, and a cross-functional team of employees, management, human resources, and, if applicable, union representation. The project should have a budget, goals, and objectives and a start and end date with progress milestone dates defined.

Develop Gap-Driven Performance Metrics

The cross-functional team should develop a full understanding of how job description, titles, and pay grades are currently defined. They should identify how well these definitions support a flexible and adaptable process flow environment. The team should research and benchmark other libraries' policies and procedures as well as organizations outside the library world. The ultimate goal is to create job descriptions that recognize the value, experience, and skills of the staff member while allowing that staff member to be flexible enough to support a flexible and adaptable process flow.

Specific examples of how job descriptions have prevented customer service improvement in the past may be useful. The team should flowchart the library's customer service delivery chain and analyze how the current job descriptions match up with how they actually deliver services. A spreadsheet should be developed listing all the links in the service delivery chain as compared to the job titles that support it. A flexibility yardstick could be developed showing a ratio between the number of job titles and current staff that can support each link in the service delivery chain. Gaps between flexibility and inflexibility should be identified. Priorities to improve the service through improved flexibility should be established. These priorities could be based on peak-and-valley demand patterns, ergonomic issues, and job experience growth paths. Ultimately they should be driven to improve customer service.

Develop Flexible Job Policies

The cross-functional team should look to redefine their job descriptions to be more flexible in supporting the service delivery chain. For example, the definition of the customer reserves service chain begins when a customer requests a book and ends when the book is delivered to the customer hold shelf. A Lean service delivery chain job description might be written as follows:

* Provides support to the overall service delivery chain as best fits the staff members' skills, training, and experience
* Follows the standards established for the staff members' assigned portion of the service delivery chain process
* Participates in improving the assigned link in the service delivery chain
* Participates in improving the performance of the overall service delivery chain

Jobs are not assigned to support one function but are defined to support a service, a service that might cross various areas, departments, and even locations.

Does this mean a clerical staff person processing customer hold requests in the morning could be reassigned to driving the delivery truck and picking up and moving hundreds of tote boxes? You might initially say no. However, if the person pulling pages that day has had prior training and experience driving a truck, has the physical capability, meets the certification standards, and you need a backup for an unavailable driver, then yes, that person could fill that position for that day and ensure there is no drop in customer service. In fact, this type of person would be a highly valued member in the library. This might be an extreme and perhaps unlikely scenario, but the point is still valid. A library staff member has the responsibility to support the performance of the overall service chain. The better the staff member is cross-trained, the better their skills are and the more flexible and capable the organization is to successfully service their customer. By having your staff cross-trained across the service chain and by having job descriptions and pay grades flexible enough to support this cross-training, department walls, job titles, and pay grades are no limitations to your organization's service flexibility.

Some manufacturing organizations have actually established progressive pay grades based on how many links of the service chain a person can support. The organization recognizes that an employee who is adaptable and capable of supporting any part of the supply chain is more valuable than an employee who can do only one thing. Therefore, they reward those employees with the most experience, flexibility, cross-training, and willingness to support the overall service of the customer. I believe a person's job is more fulfilling if he or she is able to perform various tasks rather than just one repeated task. There are exceptions, of course, but I would rather reward those who want to expand their skills rather than those who limit themselves to just one skill. Length of service does not reflect value to an organization alone—capability and flexibility is just as important, if not more important. Combine length of service with one who can do any job in the library and you have an extremely valuable employee.

In a perfect world everyone within an organization would realize that they are all in the same boat. They would understand that the organization's success depends on community funding. The common purpose of both the management and employee groups is to improve value of services the library provides to the community. Protecting inflexible job descriptions does not add any value to anything except protecting stagnation, and this only prevents the library from improving its value proposition.

Develop and Share Cost–Benefit Projections and Results

Changing job titles and descriptions as well as pay grades is a scary proposition to most staff members. The greatest fear staff members have of realigning job descriptions is that they do not know what their new responsibilities might entail. What will they be required to do? Will they have to work with people they do not know? How will they gain a promotion? What if they do not want to work in another area?

Once again, knowing what the change will entail eliminates the fear. A plan to retrain the staff to prepare for changes and new responsibilities will eliminate fear. Having the staff be a part of developing the change will not only eliminate the fear but will also gain ownership from those who were once concerned. The staff must understand why the change is being pursued, what benefits the customer will gain, what benefits the organization will gain, and what benefits they will gain. Every organization will be different when answering these questions; however, the following can provide you a foundation as you move forward.

Benefits to the Customer
- With more flexible job descriptions, your organization will be prepared to adjust your resources to better fit the changing demand patterns. The more flexible it is the quicker the library can respond to customer needs.

Benefits to the Organization
- Your organization is committed to aligning your resources with the delivery chain of services to your customer. Your ability to adapt and change with the customer's needs will make you a more viable and healthy organization.
- An organization incapable of change will not improve. Static and inflexible organizational charts, department walls, and job grades can create barriers to change. Creating flexible job descriptions will allow you to change as your customer requirements change.

Benefits to the Staff
- Staff members will have the opportunity to expand their job skills.
- Staff will be rewarded based on the more job skills and experience they acquire.
- The more flexible the staff is, the more opportunity you have to rotate staff members in and out of repetitive and ergonomically difficult tasks.

While it is difficult to place a dollar value on flexible job skills in and of themselves, these dollar benefits will be captured on different projects as you realign your staff with your service chain.

Celebrate Results

There are people within your organization who can do just about any job the library has. Prior to making any job description changes and to gain momentum for change, you should celebrate these people. Develop an award ceremony not based on years of service but on the number of service links a staff member can support. Perhaps a necklace representing the number of links in the service chain they can perform would be appropriate and appreciated. The longer the necklace a person wears, the more value he or she offers the library's customers and the organization. If you celebrate and acknowledge those who have the most to offer the organization, you establish a foundation for moving the organization in a new direction.

Inflexible Staff Reduction

One final note on the reduction of non-value-added labor activities and changing job descriptions: When job descriptions are based on the overall service chain, tasks and responsibilities can be shifted more easily, therefore allowing labor savings to be absorbed as the savings occur. These savings are achieved incrementally over time. Natural attrition will take care of the reduction in overall labor costs. On the other hand, in a specifically defined job description environment, labor savings can be achieved only if a specific staff position is targeted and eliminated. If parts of job tasks cannot be reassigned or combined, the only option management has is to eliminate a staff position. This can create a great hole in a department. Therefore, flexible job descriptions actually can help prevent wholesale cuts in staffing, allowing natural attrition to absorb the savings. While perhaps counterintuitive, flexible job descriptions can actually protect people's jobs better than inflexible job descriptions.

Automation Is a Tool, Not a Solution

Let us revisit our rafting trip competition. Soon after the River Lean team won the race, the Snake River team called for a rematch. They argued that it was not fair that they had to navigate Snake River with all its challenges and difficulties while the River Lean team was able to raft an easily navigated river. The Snake River team proposed another race. Proud as they were, rather than requesting they should switch rivers, they requested Snake River once again. This time they wanted to use a powerboat instead of the rubber raft. They also demanded that the River Lean team continue to use a rubber raft on their river. The River Lean team agreed, and the teams prepared for the new race. The Snake River team felt that automation would make up for the fact they had a more difficult river to navigate.

Both teams launched their crafts at the sound of the starting gun. The River Lean team in their rubber raft paddled their oars in perfect sync. With a roar, the Snake River team powered their boat up and quickly moved far out in the lead. But the River Lean team closed the gap on the second leg as the Snake River team found trouble navigating through the white-water rapids. They hit rock after hidden rock, nearly punching a hole in the bottom of their powerboat. The Snake River powerboat team regained the lead on the third leg as they powered through the slow-moving water once again. At the last leg the Snake River team ran into shallow water, and their large, heavy-engine boat lodged into the muddy river bottom. They could not finish the race. The River Lean team won again.

I have frequently referenced Toyota as they pursued and developed the Toyota Production System. But what of General Motors? General Motors during this same time period was so focused on labor efficiency that they seemed to have lost sight of the customer delivery service chain. Their strategy at this time was to invest heavily in automated assembly lines. They did this to try to eliminate as much of the labor component in the process as possible, viewing labor efficiency as the primary cost driver. They did all of this before they analyzed and simplified the entire delivery service chain. Toyota, on the other hand, first *simplified* their entire delivery service chain, attacking all the waste and pursuing small batches, and then and only then did they apply automation where it would best fit and support the overall delivery service chain.

I see libraries in the same place that U.S. manufacturers were in the late 1970s. Libraries are taking a hard look at automating their sorting systems to reduce labor costs, and some have already done so. I would caution these libraries to make sure that the overall delivery service chain is first simplified before investing in expensive sorting automation that may or may not reduce the lead time and cost of delivering a book to a customer. If you automate an ineffective process you will only be more ineffective more quickly and more frequently.

Automation is very cool and very seductive; it appears as a solution to all our problems. If we have a very difficult process, then the answer is simple: automate it. The foundation of the Toyota Production System and Lean disagrees. Lean says that you must improve and simplify a process before you ever look to automate it.

Our rafting teams learned that a powerboat is totally ineffective on Snake River, but if Snake River is turned into River Lean, just imagine what the powerboat could do.

Lean Tools Review

A Lean transformation will require top management commitment and leadership as well as the full ownership of your staff. The competition is coming on strong, and it is time for libraries, specifically your library, to respond. Lean can represent many things to you and your staff; it can be a philosophy, a strategy, and a tool. This appendix illustrates that beyond the tools you have already learned there is a wealth of additional Lean tools available to you and your staff to attack the waste that exists in your delivery service chains. After reading this book you should be well prepared and motivated to transform your library. Good luck in your Lean transformation!

Index

Page numbers followed by the letter "f" indicate figures; those followed by the letter "t" indicate tables.

A

Accenture, xiii–xiv, 2–3
Acquisitions CD receipt process, 176f
Aging report/study, 58–59
Amazon.com, xiii, xiv, 3, 7–10, 145–146, 151, 153–155
Apple, xxii, xxiv, 117, 150
Audit results, 61f
Automation, 189–190
Available service turns, 134–137

B

Balloon delivery gap analysis, 108f
Balloon diagram
 academic library service performance measures, 52
 audits, 60
 circulation desk performance measures, 160
 holds delivery service performance, 48–49
 PYLMC delivery performance, 104–107
 sample diagram, 49f
 technical service performance measures, 72
 workstation design issues, 95
Baltimore County Public Library (BCPL)
 acknowledgments, xviii
 introductions, xxi–xxii
 service chain time logs, 55–57

Bergman, Mike, 144
Bezos, Jeffery P., 3, 4, 150, 154. *See also* Amazon.com
Book drop
 batching, 83
 circulation desk design issues, 151–163, 163f, 164f
 motion study, 183
Book Now Program, 44–47
Book trucks, vi, xx, 84, 90, 115f
Bottlenecks, x–xi, 78, 167, 174, 181
Bottom-up management
 change management, 22
 customer hold delivery service chain, 103
 delivery service chain, 70
 flexible job descriptions, 184
Box truck, xx, 115, 115f
Branch performance gap analysis, 160t
Breeding, Marshall, 146
Budgets
 continuous improvement, 169
 as cost control, 121–127
 crisis, ix–xi, xiii–xv
 Lean library, 36
 peak load management, 97
 performance measure, 41, 136

C

Cart backlog analysis, 74t
Cause-and-effect analysis, 181
Cell phones, 64, 155

Change methodology
circulation desk design, 159
definition, 17
delivery service chain, 39
flexible job descriptions, 184
holds/reserves delivery, 100
new book delivery, 73
peak loads, 122
Change resistance
continuous improvement, 169
digital services, 140, 144
flexible job descriptions, 35
methodology to overcome, 13–20
new book delivery, 78, 98
no totes solution, 118
Circulation
book now, 44–46
as business risk, 8–9
Okanogan Regional Library, 132
as performance measure, 41
Pareto principle, 180
service turns, 130
Tulsa City–County Library, xx, 102
Circulation desk
checkout time study, 63f
checkout stations, compressed space
for, 164f
comparison to retail, xiv–xx
no totes solution, 114, 118
performance issues, 161f
redesign, 160–167
3:1 standard, 51
time chart, 65f
time studies, 62
Collection development
peak load management, 70–71, 88,
122–123, 156
push vs. pull demand, 152
Communication skills, 25, 175–179
Congestion, in flow path, 76, 160–165
Continuous improvement, ix, 25, 169–171
Cost–benefit analysis
change methodology, 17
flexible job descriptions, 184, 188
functional support, 26
gap performance measures, 28–29, 71
holds/reserve delivery, 104, 117
new book delivery, 97
transactional cost analysis, 125
Critical mass, 23, 151, 169–170

Cross-training, x, 8, 92, 185, 187
Cross-functional teams
change management, 17, 22, 26, 28
flexible job descriptions, 184
group problem solving, 179
performance measurements, 48, 137
Customer delivery service balloon
diagram, 50f
Customer discovery to delivery service
chain, 142f
Customer holds/reserves
reserve/hold delivery chain, 38f, 106f,
109f
service delivery chain, project benefits,
118f

D
Deep web, 144–145. *See also* Surface web
Delivery service balloon diagram, 49f
Digital research tools, 139

E
80/20 rule, 180–181
Expediting, 76, 92, 133

F
Federated search, 146
First in/first out
expediting, 92–93
peak loads, 99
principle of Lean, 79–80
processing, 75
small batches, 84–85, 89
First-touch principle, 101–102, 110, 114,
119
Five-dollar tour
delivery service chain, 33–35
holds service chain, 108
new book delivery, 73, 76, 90
performance measures, 41
Flexible job descriptions, 17, 30–31, 80, 92,
117, 184–189
Flinders University Library, 51
Ford, Henry, 149
Forecast delivery model, 150

G

Gap analysis
  circulation desk design, 160
  digital services, 141
  holds/reserves delivery, 104, 107–108
  new book delivery, 73
  performance measures, 133
Gift books, 126, 180
Gifts, transaction cost analysis, 127t
Google, xiii, 3, 139–140, 143–146
Group problem solving, 179

H

Holds service chain
  available service turns, 137t, 137t
  delivery flowchart, 448f
  project results, 119t
Hold shelf
  access, 159–160, 165–166
  examples, 109f, 166f
  holds delivery, 101, 107–110, 114–118
  labels for, xx, 56, 78, 110–119, 111f, 170
  performance measures, 47, 51, 56–57, 66, 131, 134
  service issues, 165f
  service turns, 130, 134–137

I

ILS, 57–60, 88, 93
Imbalances, 76, 79–80, 90–92, 101
Incoming/outgoing traffic flow, 162f
In-transit aging report, 59f
In-transit aging study, 58–59
Inventory turns, 129–130
Invoice processing, 70, 93–95, 99, 122, 175

J

Jarvis, Jeff, 140
Jidoka, 182
Just-in-time manufacturing, 169

K

Kaizen, ix
Kindle, xiii, 150–151

L

Labels, hold shelf, xx, 56, 78, 110–119, 111f, 170
Large batch impact diagram, 82f
Large batches, 76–90, 101, 171, 181
Lead time reduction
  continuous improvement, 169–171
  cost control, 123
  history, 2–3
  holds delivery chain, 101
  inventory turns, 129–131, 136
  large batches, 81–90
  push vs. pull, 149
  work simplification, 183
LibQUAL+program, 46
Link resolvers, 146

M

Master scheduling, 88
Materials budget, impact on, 132t
McDonald's, 43–47, 53, 122–124, 144
Motion study, 183
Murphy's Law, 181–182
Mystery shopper, 67

N

Nawotka, Edward, 156
New book service
  with hold, SDA, 134t
  with hold, AST, 134t
  delivery chain, 37f
  delivery chain performance against target, 133t
New York Public Library (NYPL), xviii, 19, 48, 50, 58, 193
Next-generation catalogs, 139, 146, 147
Nickel tour, 33–34. *See also* Five-dollar tour

O

Okanagan Regional Library (ORL), xviii, 32
Oklahoma State University, xviii, 10, 140–145, 151, 193
Organization chart, Lean project, 24f

Organizational purpose
 change resistance, 17–22
 flexible job descriptions, 184
 holds/reserves delivery, 101–102
 new book delivery, 70, 98
 push vs. pull, 155
 search engine, 140–141
Ownership
 change resistance, 17–26, 31
 flexible job descriptions, 186–188
 holds/reserves delivery, 103–104, 117
 new book delivery, 71, 75, 98
 performance measurement, 50

P
Pareto analysis, 180
Pay grades
 change resistance, 16, 28–31
 delivery service chain, 33
 flexible job descriptions, 187
 gap performance measures, 186, 188
 performance measurement, 50
Peak loads
 budgets, 122–123
 change resistance, 16, 28–31
 impact diagrams, 87f
 Lean design principles, 71, 76, 85–90,
  98
 performance measurement, 66, 133,
  135
 push vs. pull demand management,
  152, 154–156
Peaks and valleys. See Peak loads
Perfect world service turns, 131t
Performance audits/logs, 54, 60
Performance gap analysis, 107t
Pick list. See Hold shelf: labels for
PLYMC customer balloon diagrams, 105f
Poke-Yoke, 182
Prestamo, Ann, 140, 152
Process redesign, 73, 78, 93, 183
Preprocessed technical services flow, 77f
Price, Pamela, 18
Productivity improvement, 73, 78, 93, 183
Project Information Literacy Progress
  Group, 140
Project management, 25, 31
Public access terminals, 165, 166f

Q
QuikTrip, 22, 52–54, 66–67

R
Rapid Receive, 93, 95, 98
Receiving stations, 96f, 97f
Research delivery gap analysis, 141f
River Lean
 automation, 189–190
 bottlenecks, 181
 comparison, 69
 design principles, 76–80, 88–93, 99
 introduction, 1–2

S
SCULLS, 39, 177–180
Search engines, 139–140, 144
Service days available (SDA), 4, 131–137,
  135t, 154
Service days not available (SDNA),
  130–137, 169
Service gap, 140
Service log label, 56f
Service performance chart, 58f
Service time logs, 54–55
Service tolerance, 53
Shelf accuracy, 60–61
Small batch impact diagram, 83f
Snake River
 automation, 189–190
 circulation desk, 160
 comparison, 69
 design principles, 76–101
 introduction, 1–2
 performance measures, 136
Sorting
 automation, 190
 CDs, 99
 five-dollar tour, 34–35
 flow diagrams, 113f, 114f
 holds/reserves delivery, 102–103
 Lean design principles, 89
 no tote solution, 108–117
 service turns, 131, 134–135
 TCCL, xx
 work simplification, 183

Staging areas
 bottlenecks, 181
 carts in process, 74f
 Lean design principles, 74, 76–81
 technical services, 88, 93, 98–99
 work simplification, 184
Sticky holds label. *See* Hold shelf: labels
  for
Supply chain management, 33
Surface web, 144–145

T
TCCL sorting area, 116f
Technical services
 acknowledgments, xvii
 all flows, 77f
 change resistance, 13, 25–27
 circulation desk, 159, 167
 delivery balloon diagram, 72f
 delivery chain, transactional
   cost–benefit analysis, 125t
 holds/reserves service delivery, 48,
   103, 117, 122–125
 new book delivery, 76, 80–99
 performance measures, 57
 service turns, 134
 staging areas, 80f
 U flow layout, 94f
3:1 Standard, 52–54
Time studies, 54, 60–64, 160, 176
Top-down management, 21
Total quality management, 169
Tote boxes
 delivery service chain, 34–35
 flexible job descriptions, 187
 introduction, xx
 no tote solution, 102, 112–119
Toyota/Toyota Production System
 automation, 189–190
 continuous improvement, 169
 delivery service chain, 33
 pull demand, 150
Traditional OPAC search results, 143f
Traffic flow, 42, 160, 161f, 162–163, 162f,
   165

Transaction cost analysis, 124–127
Tulsa City–County Library (TCCL)
 acknowledgments, xvii
 audits, 60
 continuous improvement, 171
 foreword, x
 hold/reserve delivery chain, 104,
   110–119
 introduction, xix–xxi, 9
 new book delivery chain, 122, 124, 133
 peak loads, 122–123
 pull demand, 152
 technical services, 69–99
 time studies, 62
 service turns, 130, 133–135
Tulsa Community College, xviii, 16, 151

U
U flow, 78–79, 79f, 90, 93–94
Unions, 16, 117
University of Rochester, 145, 147
Unpacked boxes, 75t

V
Value stream map, 91, 106, 174–175,
   180–183
Vanderbilt University, 146
Video recording and analysis
 change resistance, 13
 Book Now, 44
 Lean tools, 174–176, 179
Virtual service window, 147

W
Withdrawn books, 126
Work cells, 76, 89–90, 150
Work simplification, 183
Workplace reach diagram, 184f
Workstation design, 95–96, 183
www.jhaconsults.com, 138, 145

About the Author

John Huber formed the management consulting firm of J. Huber and Associates in 1986. Focused on the tools, principles, and concepts of Lean, Mr. Huber has dedicated his career to helping organizations dramatically improve their customer service through improved process performance. As a pioneer in the TPS/Lean revolution, Mr. Huber has traveled the country assisting more than 100 manufacturing, distribution, retail, and library organizations transform their operations. For the library world, Mr. Huber has developed breakthrough ideas including the holds-label solution and the no-totes delivery solution. Sample library clients include the New York Public Library, Carnegie Library of Pittsburgh, Tulsa City–County Library, and Youngstown Mahoney County Public Library. Sample manufacturing clients include Midas, American Airlines, Safelite Glass, Rheem/Ruud, Zebco, Home International Products, and B. E. Aerospace. Mr. Huber has a bachelor's degree in industrial engineering and management from Oklahoma State University and holds three U.S. patents. He can be reached at jhaconsults.library@gmail.com.